The political economy of Marx

D0681318

Modern economics
Series editor: David W Pearce

The political economy of Marx

M C Howard & J E King

Longman

iv

Longman Group Limited

Burnt Mill, Harlow, Essex CM20 2JE

Distributed in the United States of America by Longman Inc., New York

Associated companies, branches and representatives throughout the world

© Longman Group Limited 1975

First published 1975
Reprinted 1977

ISBN 0582 44610 4 cased
         44611 2 paper

Printed in Great Britain by
Lowe & Brydone Printers Limited, Thetford

3-1303-00046-7259

Contents

Acknowledgements

We are grateful to the following for permission to reproduce copyright material:
American Economic Review for an extract from 'Papers and Proceedings' by M. Bronfenbrenner from *American Economic Review* May 1967; Cambridge University Press for extracts from *The Production of Commodities by Commodities* by P. Sraffa; Doubleday & Company, Inc. for extracts from *Karl Marx on Colonialism and Modernization* edited and with an introduction by Shlomo Avineri. Copyright © 1968 by Shlomo Avineri, reprinted by permission of Doubleday & Company, Inc; the authors and The Econometric Society for an extract from 'Aggregation in Leontief Matrices and the Labour Theory of Value' by M. Morishima and F. Seton from *Econometrica* Vol. 29, No. 2 April 1961; The German Economic Review for an extract from 'Marx as a growth theorist' by W. Krelle from *The German Economic Review*, 9 (2), 1971; The National Academy of Sciences for an extract from 'Transformation from Marxian values to competitive prices a process of rejection and replacement' by P. Samuelson from *Proceedings of the National Academy of Sciences*, 67 (1); The Quarterly Journal of Economics for an extract from an article by Paul Samuelson from *The Quarterly Journal of Economics*, 73 (1) and (2), 1959; the author and The Review of Economic Studies for an extract from an article by F. Seton from *The Review of Economic Studies*, 24 (3), 1957; and Science and Society for an extract from *Science and Society*, 31 (4), 1967.

Introduction

The last ten or fifteen years have seen the beginnings of a crisis in orthodox economic theory. Rigorous, technically sophisticated and sometimes elegant, modern theory is increasingly seen by both academic economists and students to be trivial, arid, irrelevant, methodologically unsound, and suspect in its political assumptions and implications. This growth of dissatisfaction with orthodox theory has been largely responsible for the recent revival of interest in Marxian economics, which confronts neoclassical theory with a radically different perspective and a contrasting analytical structure. One example of this growth in interest is to be seen in the rapid expansion of the academic literature on Marxian economics.

There seems to us to be a need for a book assessing the current status of Marx's political economy from a standpoint of critical sympathy; which shares Marx's hostility to capitalism and his view of economics as an historical, *social* science, but which treats his economics as Marx himself would have wished: as a piece of scientific analysis which, therefore, is capable of refinement and susceptible to error. We do not intend to prove Marx's infallibility, nor wish to apologize for his mistakes. At the same time, we are convinced that in many important respects his analysis is superior to that of orthodox economics; that the latter suffers from major defects; and that many of the neoclassical attacks launched against Marx's political economy cannot be sustained.

Our aim is thus twofold: to outline the structure and content of Marx's economic theory, and to assess its coherence and relevance in the light of modern criticism. It must be stressed that this is a book about *Marx*, and—if only for reasons of length—we have very little to say about those subsequent developments in "Marxist" economics which are not directly relevant to an appraisal of Marx's own work. The great bulk of Marx's own analysis, for example, is conducted on the assumption that the relationship between capitalists is one of free competition; attempts to develop "Marxian" theories of *monopoly* capitalism, though of considerable interest and immense practical significance, are thus tangential to our purpose.

We are not, however, primarily interested in Marx from the viewpoint of historians of economic thought. Both the problems which Marx posed and the theoretical solutions which he provided to them have a *contemporary* relevance to issues which remain open questions in orthodox economic theory. Thus we appraise the coherence and validity of Marx's political economy, not merely as a historical problem in its own right, but to investigate the possibility that Marxian economics might supplant modern orthodoxy itself.

Before it is possible to judge Marx's economics as a whole, the core of his own analysis must be outlined. To do this it is necessary to understand how Marx developed his political economy, and Chapters 1 to 4 are devoted to this task. Chapter 1 examines the reasons why Marx studied economics, which we see as an extension of his interest in the historical and sociological analysis of capitalism. Marx's intellectual background was a richer and more complex one than is commonly the case among economists, and this richness and complexity are reflected in the methodological foundations of his political economy, which form the subject of Chapter 2.

Having developed an interest in economics, Marx turned to a massive study of the work of the classical economists, in the course of which (and in reaction to whom) his own analysis emerged. Chapter 3 provides a thumbnail sketch of classical political economy, seen through Marx's eyes. It is impossible to understand Marx's own thought without a comprehension of his criticism of classical economics, which was both detailed and fundamental. An account of this critique is given in Chapter 4, in which the outlines of Marx's own substantive economic analysis emerge.

We then turn to an assessment of the strengths and weakness of Marx's theoretical structure. In Chapter 5 we deal at some length with the labour theory of value, which is seen to be less defective, and rather less important, than is often believed. (Rejection of the labour theory of value, that is, would not entail rejection of an exploitation theory of class shares, nor rejection of Marx's theory of capitalist development.) In the course of this chapter we look too at the recent emergence of "neo-Ricardian" economics. Chapter 6 discusses Marx's macroeconomics: his theory of growth, of unemployment and the falling rate of profit, and his account of economic crises. We argue here that Marx's analysis of these issues is suggestive rather than definitive, and is not sufficiently well developed or coherent to form the basis for predictions about the economic decay of capitalism. Chapter 7 is a brief account of Marx's theory of imperialism.

In Chapter 8 we draw together our conclusions about Marx's political economy. We are in no doubt that Marx's economic *methodology* is wholly superior to that of the orthodox economists. His substantive economic theory is less satisfactory: a theory of value which cannot deal with monopoly, and a theory of economic crisis without the state, are of doubtful relevance to twentieth-century capitalism. Even these short-comings, however, can be seen as a vindication of Marx's fundamental claim that economic theory must be historically specific, and that analysis applicable to one epoch in social development may be inappropriate in later stages. It remains our belief that the central problems facing economics today are those posed by Marx, and that it is only by Marxian methods that they can be solved. We hope that this book, by exposing the achievements and limitations of the political economy of Marx, may contribute a little to this task.

Our deepest debt is to the published work of Maurice Dobb, Ronald Meek and Paul Sweezy, whose names appear frequently in the text, and to whose influence we owe whatever understanding of Marxian economics we have. Mr Dobb and Professor Meek read and commented on the manuscript, and we are extremely grateful for their painstaking and helpful criticism. Thanks are also due to Ian Bradley, Al Cohan, Martin Hoskins, Leo Katzen, Russell Keat, Professor M. Morishima, Nick Oulton, David Pearce, Dr F. Seton, Ian Steedman, John Urry and Rod Whittaker. Needless to say, the full responsibility for errors and opinions rests with the authors.

M.C.H.
J.E.K.

1

The purpose of Marx's political economy

1.1 Introduction

Here we deal with the purpose Marx assigned to his political economy. However, since Marx came to economics from philosophy, via sociology, and indeed as a direct result of his theoretical developments in these areas, it is impossible to consider the question without dealing with his overall social theory. Therefore, this chapter also attempts to give a brief sketch of this theory. We stress that the chapter is only expository: critical analysis of certain aspects raised here will be developed in later chapters. Also our exposition abstracts from Marx's intellectual development, although it obviously underwent certain changes and shifts of emphasis in a period of some forty years of study.

We begin with the most abstract aspects of Marx's theory and move successively to the more concrete. Section 1.2 outlines Marx's conception of human freedom and the relationship it has to his economic theory. The points thrown up here are developed in more detail in the following sections. Section 1.3 deals with the main ideas of the "materialist conception of history" and shows how Marx's views on freedom are built upon it; this leads directly on to 1.4, which considers the class nature of social production, the positive and negative role it has in history, and relates it to conditions Marx regarded as necessary for freedom to be realized.

The argument then naturally goes on from this to consider Marx's theory of alienation in 1.5. This shows precisely why Marx was so critical of bourgeois society. Section 1.6 then takes up the class struggle aspects of Marx's materialist conception of history. This parallels parts of 1.3 by showing class conflict as the main motive force of historical change. However, the analysis is now at a much lower level of abstraction. It provides a background to 1.7 which takes up these ideas and relates them to the liberating potentialities inherent in capitalism. The position is now reached where we can relate Marx's political economy to proletarian revolution in 1.8.

The aim of all this is to show how Marx conceived the relation of political economy to freedom; how this freedom was constrained by historical social structures; why Marx believed scientific analysis showed the proletariat to be the historical agency capable of realizing a free society through revolutionary action, and how this same scientific analysis could itself be used as an aid in bringing this about.

1.2 Marx's conception of freedom

Stated at the most abstract level, the purpose of political economy for Marx was to aid the realization of human freedom. Human freedom can be considered synonymous with a state of affairs where men live in conformity with their nature (their needs, abilities and consciousness). The reader is probably accustomed to think of this in terms of freedom as defined in bourgeois society. Here it refers to the absence of constraints on individual action. It is recognized that this can never be complete when men live in society; some limitations are necessary, because the exercise of some freedoms by some citizens requires restraint by others. But, whatever the particular qualifications, the essence of freedom is still seen as the ability to follow one's individual interest without interference by others.

Marx is sharply critical of such a view of freedom. This stems from his specific theory of human nature and of the potentialities for its development. Essentially, the distinctive character of man's humanity, for Marx, lies in his ability to engage in consciously planned action directed towards the realization of his ends. Of all the animal species man alone has this ability, or at least is able continually to develop this ability. Thus men do not simply *use* nature, they progressively *master* it in a process of historical development. Further, Marx argues, in this process men become capable of consciously creating their social conditions of life, of organizing their societies and making their own history consciously. These form the twin components of Marx's conception of freedom. Men are free to the extent that they consciously master and control both nature and their social conditions of existence in line with their developed and developing needs and abilities.

Marx argues that this is a condition in which each individual is able to develop his personal capabilities in both material and intellectual activity. Or, to put the point in another way, freedom is a situation which exists in so far as men have the power consciously to create what they are and what they will become. As we shall see, Marx argues that this condition is far from being identical with the social context in which the liberal conception of freedom is historically manifest. In fact, in Marx's theory of historical development, bourgeois society is at the apex of a certain type of unfreedom.

Marx is, therefore, faced with a contradiction. Contemporary social reality does not conform to the standards of the ideal. This does not arise because the ideal is utopian (see below, p. 20). Marx argues that scientific analysis shows that men potentially can and actually will attain freedom. This complex set of ideas is outlined in more detail below.

1.3 Labour and historical development

Marx's social theory was built on a unique and profound conception of the role of labour in history and, as will be shown later, this view had immense importance for the theoretical structure of his political economy. Marx sees the activity of labour not only as the basic condition for all human existence, but also as that activity which creates man himself.

"Labour is, in the first place, a process in which both man and nature participate, and in which man of his own accord starts, regulates and controls the material reactions between himself and nature. . . . By thus acting on the external world and changing it, he at the same time changes his own nature. He develops his slumbering powers and compels them to act in obedience to his sway" (Capital I, 177).

Marx emphasizes that labour is always carried out socially. As he puts it "Whenever we speak of production, then, what is meant is always production at a definite stage of social development — production by social individuals" (*Grundrisse*, p. 85). Labour is social because man is for Marx a social animal, an animal which can develop his human faculties only in a society. Marx draws from this the methodological rule that man must be analysed as a social being. He therefore rejects any analysis of economic actors abstracted from the historical societies in which they act. (A leading example of this is the neoclassical conception of economic agents as "utility maximizers"). Marx believed that theoretical analysis on such a basis led to distortions in logic and empirical validity.

History, as Marx conceives it, is a process of the continuous creation and satisfaction of men's needs through labour. Marx in fact sees the labour process as characterized by a *dialectic of development*[1]. From a certain stage in the development of social production there arises in men's consciousness the perception of new needs and through the same faculty of consciousness men recognize the possibilities of their satisfaction. This leads to a course of activity designed to realize these possibilities, and through this process there arises a new organization of social labour with increased productive power. These new abilities allow the perception of new needs, which in turn generate a qualitatively new phase of development. This abstract representation of the dialectic of social change is the basis for Marx's explanation of how men, although products of their social relationships, can through consciousness and activity effect social change which will result in changing themselves, their own natures. Therefore men do not have a fixed and unchanging nature. Nor are they simply passive products of their social circumstances. Social circumstances make men what they are, but what they are involves a certain form of consciousness and purposive action, which leads to social change. This change to a new social form changes men themselves. Consequently men and their nature are historical products and history is a process of men's self-creation.

Although this process of historical development is continuous, it can, according to Marx, be separated into definite stages. It is not the case that the development of men's needs, their satisfaction and regeneration is random and unstructured. It is not only true that men's needs, abilities and knowledge—in short their nature—changes, but also that human nature develops in particular ways. However, Marx also conceives the historical pattern not as one of continuous, linear quantitative social development, but as dialectical. While there is continuous quantitative change, this takes place through a series of *stages*, each of which forms a qualitative whole. Each stage emerges from the forces of opposition and disharmony in the structure of the previous stage and, through its own laws of development, in turn generates the emergence of a new stage. Thus each stage marks off a qualitatively different mode of social production, a historically specific system of economic relationships. Each stage arises from the dialectical development of its predecessor and dialectically develops into a higher stage: "In broad outline, the Asiatic, ancient, feudal and modern bourgeois modes of production may be designated as epochs marking progress in the economic development of society" (*Critique*, p. 21).

Each stage of material production has its own characteristic internal dialectic of change. This specific logic of development leads to its dialectical abolition and transcendence. Through the operation of its own structure, it generates new and specific human needs and actions to satisfy them, which result in the emergence of a qualitatively new and specific structure of economic relations or organization of social labour. These historically specific laws of development can, according to Marx, be discovered only through empirical analysis, not *a priori* or speculatively. On this basis Marx, in *Capital*, attempts to delineate the "laws of motion" of the bourgeois mode of production.

Each qualitative stage of development of social labour is made up of an historically specific set of economic relations which constitute the economic structure of society. This economic structure, Marx maintains, is "the real foundation, on which arises a legal and political superstructure and to which correspond definite forms of social consciousness. The mode of production of material life conditions the general process of social, political and intellectual life" (*Critique*, p. 20).

In the previous section we saw that Marx conceives human freedom in a dual sense. Man is free to the extent that he consciously controls *both* nature *and* his social conditions of life. What relevance does the above analysis have to this conception of freedom and its realization?

Marx argues that through the development of social labour men become capable of increasingly developed production, and hence have a growing ability to achieve the satisfaction of higher and higher needs. Through successive stages of social production social labour is progressively reorganized, and the means of production develop so that nature is increasingly subjected to man's ends. Nowhere is this more true than in capitalism, which has created "more massive and more colossal productive forces than have all preceding generations together. Subjection of Nature's forces to man . . . what earlier century had even a presentiment that such productive forces slumbered in the lap of social labour?" (*SW* I, 113).

However, Marx perceived no parallel development in man's control over the structure and history of his own society in accordance with his own developing needs. Society and history are the product of man's own actions and interactions, but they have escaped his conscious control. "In the social production of their existence, men inevitably enter into definite relations, which are independent of their will" (*Critique*, p. 20). Social relations, therefore, impose themselves on individuals irrespective of their preferences and needs. Thus, if human history is defined as the conscious development of social relationships appropriate to historically developed human abilities, needs and potentialities, then, according to Marx, there has not yet been "human" history. Man has made history but not as a human. History to date is "prehistory" (*Critique*, p. 22).

In what sense then have men made history? Marx's theory of history making is briefly stated by Engels as follows:

"Each person follows his own consciously desired end, and it is precisely the resultant of these many wills operating in different directions, of their manifold effects on the outer world, that constitutes history . . . the many individual wills active in history for the most part produce results quite other than those intended—quite often the opposite" (*SW* III, 336).

Thus history as it has so far existed is activity undertaken in the pursuit of ends. But the historical effects cannot be explained in terms of these ends alone because social interaction takes place in a structure which is not consciously constructed and governed by men. However, the result is not chaos. Marx considers history as *law-determined*. The effects of social interaction conform to dialectical laws of development. But, to repeat an important point, the specific laws of development of any particular society are empirical questions for Marx, and cannot be determined *a priori*.

The question which now arises is why
"man, the history making animal has been so little successful in the performance of his distinguishing function . . . why man, though he has been able to subdue the forces of nature . . . has himself remained a slave to the forces of society, forces which give history a form so inappropriate to his consciousness?" (Venable, 1966, p. 79.)

Only an adequate theoretical answer to this question, in Marx's view, can lead to an effective position in changing the world.

Marx considers the answer to lie in further analysis of the economic structure, which he considers the key determinant of the social structure in general. In terms of this theoretical position the crucial factor is that, except in the most primitive societies, social production is always production on the basis of a class structure.

1.4 Class and social production

Marx, in fact, defines the character of social labour in terms of its historically specific class structure when such a structure exists. Although Marx uses the concept of class in various ways[2], in this context he defines classes as social strata that are "grouped" as a result of the relationship they have to the possession of the means of production as private property. Possession or non-possession of the means of production, however, is not merely a legal relation, but also an economic relationship between men. Class relationships allow the *surplus product*[3] to be appropriated by the possessing class, which thus stands in an exploitive relationship to the producers. In terms of their class structures societies differ primarily in the economic method that extracts the surplus social product from the labour of the producers (*Capital* I, 217). And this method provides the key to understanding the dialectical possibilities of development.

Classes then, for Marx, constitute the crucial relations of production. Relations of production are above all class relations. Since production is social production, which in turn is class production, this means that the developing needs of men proceed through the mediating factor of the interests of the possessing classes; this becomes the crucial factor in the operation of the mode of production and its historical development.

Furthermore, in Marx's theory it is the class structure which determines the form of political domination and social consciousness. It is the ownership of property in the means of production which is the crucial social power that allows the possessing classes to gain control of the state. Their economic and political domination is supported by the ascendancy of their class conception of the whole social structure in social consciousness.

"The ideas of the ruling class are in every epoch the ruling ideas, i.e. the class, which is the ruling material force of society, is at the same time its ruling intellectual force. The class which has the means of material production at its disposal, has control at the same time over the means of mental production, so that thereby, generally speaking, the ideas of those who lack the means of mental production are subject to it. The ruling ideas are nothing more than the ideal expression of the dominant material relationships, the dominant material relationships grasped as ideas" (GI, p. 64)[4].

Given this framework Marx's answer to the question of human freedom can be stated. Although he states that class relations involve dominance and exploitation, he does not see social production within class societies as entirely negative. Class production is, for Marx, part of the logic of history in developing man's humanity. Class production is the mechanism by which history creates and expands man's powers over nature. This is so not because class production in historically specific forms of society progress-ively aligns nature *directly* to man's needs, but precisely because it does so via the mediation of class interests. These favour the development of the forces of production in spite of, and at the expense of, the needs of the dispossessed class at any particular time. Nowhere is this more true than in capitalism, where the bourgeoisie constantly accumulates capital despite the fact, indeed as a result of the fact, that even the most immediate needs of the proletariat are not fully met (*Capital* I, 149 and 621).

The positive side of the process, therefore, lies in the progressive conquest of nature. In Marx's view this is not only progressive in itself, it is also a necessary condition for an emancipated society. This is so for four closely interrelated reasons. Firstly, it is only when there is material abundance that men will cease actively to compete, and thus come into conflict with each other, for control over scarce resources. Marx argues that such social conflict is not compatible with conscious communal control over society, because it means social division; particular interest vying with particular interest, particular interest vying with common interests. Secondly, a high degree of development in the means of production is required in order to abolish the specialization inherent in the division of labour, which is also a source of particular interests and social conflict. But division of labour also needs to be abolished in order to allow each individual to develop his many-sided capabilities from dormant potentialities. Marx argues that it is only in a society that creates such individuals that men can consciously and collectively control their social conditions. Individuals cannot dominate the social relations of their society until they understand them in relation to their needs, and they cannot fully understand them unless they universally participate in them.

Thirdly, if the universal development of individuals is necessary for control over society, it is equally true that such control is necessary in order to allow men to be *individually free* and fulfil themselves as individuals. Marx argues that at this stage of development men will consciously desire to develop themselves individually, and that this will be conceived as progressively changing themselves into universal individuals: to develop their capabilities for many-sided activity and experience. The individual ceases to "reproduce himself in one specificity, but produces his totality. Strives not to remain something he has become, but is in the absolute movement of becoming ... [Here there is the] ... complete working out of the human content" (*Grundrisse*, p. 488). Fourthly, because such activities go well beyond material production, the development of the productive forces is required to allow *all* sufficient free time to engage, for example, in art, music and science. Such activities, so far in historical development, have been the specialized province of minorities.

Thus class production is necessary in the development of man's control over nature. Above all, capitalism is a necessary stage because of its historically unique power of developing the means of production[5]. However it is precisely this factor that explains man's inability to make conscious history. The important point here is that the class relations of production which drive social labour into channels of increasing dominance over nature also, *and through the same process*, create a social order which is not subject to the conscious control of the individuals who make it up. This is Marx's theory of alienation.

1.5 Marx's theory of alienation

Alienation may be defined as a social condition in which men's own powers become independent forces which control their actions[6]. Men create a social world in which they are strangers: a world dominated by their own powers which exist independently of their conscious control, and instead control them.

Alienation is, therefore, dehumanization. For Marx it reaches its apex in capitalism (see Meek, 1973, and p. 40 below); the specific causes of its extension and intensification in capitalism Marx sees in the bourgeois relations of production, which have three aspects. Firstly, the complete expropriation of the mass of the population from ownership and control of the means of production, so that they form a class of formally free workers selling their labour power[7]. Secondly, the monopolization of the means of production as the private property of the capitalist class. Thirdly, the fragmentation of this private property into autonomous competing capitals[8].

Social production structured in terms of these economic relationships results in a situation where all economic ties are reduced to a cash nexus, to the ties of the market. Furthermore, the specific property relations of capitalism *compel* each individual capitalist to maximize the expansion of exchange value through the exploitation of labour[9]. The economy becomes a compulsive mechanism, in terms of which men fulfil their purely private ends. Social reality becomes determined by the sum total of the interactions and conflicts of these various aims, and as a result is controlled by no communal consciousness, not even that of the capitalist class.

Thus, on "the one hand the system itself is a resultant of the myriad of individual acts, but on the other, it creates for each acting individual a specific situation which compels him to act in certain ways" (Parsons, 1968, p. 492). Thus while Marx considered that the bourgeoisie was rapidly developing man's productive powers over nature and had abolished personal dependence of one man on another as, for instance, in slavery or feudalism, nevertheless the economic relations of bourgeois society had greatly increased and universalized man's dependence on material objects or things through the extension of commodity production, that is, production for the market (see p. 47). Each economic actor in bourgeois society exercises his economic power over others through his property in commodities. Likewise the economic control which others have over him is exercised through material things, that is, commodities, their prices and quantities, to which each economic actor responds. *Social interaction, therefore, takes place through material objects*, and in this sense economic domination is not "personal" but "material". Economic alienation is, therefore, material domination.

For Marx, all men are alienated in bourgeois society. However, since the cause of alienation in capitalism is the specific relations of production which determine the manner in which social labour is organized, the alienating consequences of these relations translate themselves with greatest force into the situation of the proletariat. Marx thus concentrates on the alienating condition of the proletariat, because it is in the condition of this class that it is most intensified and most clearly exposed.

The crucial factor is that, as a result of the specific property relations of capitalism, the worker is subordinated to the material objects he produces. There is thus a complete devaluation of his humanity. Not only is the product produced by his labour a commodity expropriated by the capitalist and realized into exchange value on an autonomous market, but his labour power itself becomes a commodity and the conditions in which he works are determined by the technical considerations of producing material objects within capitalism. The rationality inherent in the bourgeois mode of production progressively reduces his work task to the most simple of operations, through the division of labour, in order to increase the production of material objects. It therefore brutally separates the intellectual from the physical activities of labour, and the physical activities themselves are progressively narrowed with the development of the division of labour in capitalism. The worker is reduced to an appendage of the machine. Capital dominates labour and stands opposed to the worker as an autonomous alien power. Capitalism therefore brings about a complete inversion of a *human* subject—object or *human* ends—means relationship.

As a consequence, work becomes not an expression of man's humanity, not a means of developing his potentialities for conscious creativity, but a simple, degrading activity undertaken purely to earn a physical subsistence. The property relations of capitalism thus separate the worker from his "species being", from those qualities which make his activity human, as distinct from animalistic. Marx expresses this as follows,

"The worker, therefore, feels himself at home only during his leisure time whereas at work he feels homeless. His work is not a satisfaction of a need, but only a means for satisfying other needs. Its alien character is clearly shown by the fact that as soon as there is no physical or other compulsion it is avoided like the plague . . . the worker feels himself to be freely active only in his animal functions—eating, drinking and procreating, and at most also in his dwelling and in personal adornment—while in his human functions he is reduced to an animal. The animal becomes human and the human animal" (Early Writings, p. 125).

Both classical and neoclassical economic theory see such "disutility" as a necessary aspect of labour. Marx is sharply critical of such an ahistorical view. Thus he writes that labour, for Smith, is a curse.

" 'Tranquillity' appears as the adequate state, as identical with 'freedom' and 'happiness'. It seems quite far from Smith's mind that the individual,

*'in his normal state of health, strength, activity, skill, facility', also needs a
normal portion of work, and of the suspension of tranquillity. Certainly,
labour obtains its measure from the outside, through the aim to be attained
and the obstacles to be overcome in attaining it. But Smith has no inkling
whatever that this overcoming of obstacles is in itself a liberating
activity—and that, further, the external aims become stripped of the
semblance of merely external natural urgencies, and become posited as
aims which the individual himself posits—hence as self-realization,
objectification of the subject, hence real freedom, whose action is,
precisely labour. He is right, of course, that in its historic forms as slave
labour, serf-labour, and wage labour, labour always appears as repulsive,
always as external forced labour; and not—labour, by contrast, as
'freedom, and happiness' "* (Grundrisse, pp. 611—12).

It can achieve the latter form, however, in certain social conditions (see
above, pp. 7—8).

The alienation which characterizes capitalist society is reflected, Marx
argues, in the consciousness of that society. As we have shown, society and
history are for Marx the products of man's own activity, his actions and
interactions within specific systems of social relationships. The laws
governing society are not, therefore, independent of men's actions, but are
expressions of the structure of social relationships. However, in the
alienated social conditions of bourgeois society, social relationships
become reified into relations between things. Men tend to see their social
relations as relations of their products, which are independent of their
control. In the consciousness of men, the social order therefore takes the
form of a "second nature" — an autonomous world existing outside and
opposed to man. "Men are degraded to the status of mere objects and the
objects receive human attributes. Society ceases to be the texture of inter-
human relations and appears to be a system dependent upon objects and
objective laws" (Avineri, 1968, p. 118). Subjective consciousness is, therefore, appropriate to the objective state of alienation. Marx sees a clear
example of this in the theoretical work of political economy, which
emphasizes natural laws and universal concepts, and devalues conscious
social action (see chapter 3).

Thus a false consciousness pervades the structure of social thought,
bearing only a perverted relation to the actual social relations that underlie
it. This condition Marx also describes as ideological in the sense that it is
society's distorted selfconsciousness. And this is above all class consciousness: the consciousness of the bourgeois ruling class, and therefore the
ruling ideas of the epoch. False consciousness is not simply false; it is also
a rationalization in universalist terms of the class's particular interest—a

statement of a particular interest which is thus projected as a universal interest.

Marx's criticism of the view that the freedom of bourgeois society was the absolute form of individual liberty is based on the above analysis. Here

"the ties of personal dependence ... are in fact exploded ... and some individuals seem independent ... but they appear thus only for someone who abstracts from the conditions, the conditions of existence within which these individuals enter into contact. ... [The conditions of existence] are independent of the individuals and, although created by society, appear as if they were natural conditions. ... [Personal ties of dependence are] personal restriction of the individual by another ... [but in bourgeois society the restriction is one of] objective restriction of the individual by relations independent of him. ... Since the single individual cannot strip away his personal definition, but may very well overcome and master external relations, his freedom seems to be greater in case 2. A closer examination of these external relations, these conditions, shows, however, that it is impossible for the individuals of a class etc. to overcome them en masse without destroying them. ... These external relations are very far from being an abolition of 'relations of dependence'; they are rather the dissolution of these relations into a general form; they are merely the elaboration and emergence of the general foundation of the relations of personal dependence" (Grundrisse, pp. 163–4).

Marx therefore took the social conditions of bourgeois freedom to be conditions of man's alienation; that is, conditions where man existed contrary to his human potential of being in conscious control of his own activities and history. For Marx, freedom consists precisely in realizing this potential; in "bringing back man's world and relationships to man himself" (*Early texts*, p. 108).

On the basis of this analysis, Marx sees the abolition of bourgeois society as the necessary condition for the overcoming of alienation. Since it is the bourgeois property relations which engender alienation in capitalism, the question of the abolition of alienation is a political one. Only conscious revolutionary action by an appropriate social agency can realize the full potentialities of man, the ideal of human freedom. *And it is precisely in the conditions that engender alienation in capitalism that Marx sees the development of such an agency.*

Alienation is the breaking up of the community of men. Man is alienated because the communal relations between men are broken. Thus the proletarian is alienated from the product and the labour process because the capitalist exploits him. The power that controls his life is the power of capital, the private property of the capitalist. The power of capital therefore finds personification in the capitalist. The condition which brings about alienation in capitalism thus also brings about conflict between classes. This conflict is accentuated because it is also precisely those conditions which cause alienation in capitalism which also cause contradictions in the production process. These considerations lead us into Marx's analysis of the contradictory character of history and the role of class conflict.

1.6 Contradiction, class struggle and historical change

Since production is social production structured by class relations, this means that the developing needs of men as mediated through the interests of the possessing classes play the crucial role in the historical development of social production. Marx summarizes his theory of historical change, which illuminates the role of contradiction and class struggle, in the following manner. Men's needs lead to the development of the productive forces which at

"a certain stage of development ... come into conflict with the existing relations of production or—this merely expresses the same thing in legal terms—with the property relations within the framework of which they have operated hitherto. From forms of development of the productive forces these relations turn into their fetters. Then begins an era of social revolution. The changes in the economic foundation lead sooner or later to the transformation of the whole immense superstructure. In studying such transformations it is always necessary to distinguish between the material transformation of the economic conditions of production, which can be determined with the precision of a natural science, and the legal, political, religious, artistic or philosophic—in short, ideological forms in which men become conscious of this conflict and fight it out. Just as one does not judge an individual by what he thinks about himself, so one cannot judge such a period of transformation by its consciousness but, on the contrary, this consciousness must be explained from the contradictions of material life, from the conflict existing between the social forces of production and the relations of production" (Critique, p. 21).

Although in this passage there is no explicit mention of class conflict it is implicit, for Marx believes that the contradictions give rise to class struggles in most forms of historical social structures, and that this is especially the case with capitalism.

The mechanism of historical change is the contradiction at certain periods between the forces and relations of production. The concept of contradiction does not mean economic breakdown or logical incompatibility; it refers *to internal conflicting factors which through their opposition transform the whole of which they are parts.* The forces of production which are an outgrowth of social needs are no longer compatible with the class relations in which they operate. To attain their potential for development a reorganization of social labour is required. Class relations must be changed. Thus the dominant class, whose position and power rests on these relations of production, becomes an obstacle to progress and is replaced in a process of conflict by another system of class relations which will allow the further development of social production. The class which achieves dominance on the basis of these relations thus has as its interest a particular interest which coincides *at this period* with the general social interest of increasing material production. However, with the progressive development of the forces of production a new contradiction between the forces and the relations of production manifests itself again in a new class struggle. In short, in *prehistory* men engaged in social production unknowingly create and recreate through their own activity structures in which their activity develops but which simultaneously conflicts with the potentialities which that activity creates. Contradictions arise, because the structure of society in which social labour takes place creates needs that cannot be satisfied through that structure. Thus it is precisely because human needs are conceived, not generally and directly, but as mediated by class interest, that contradictions arise and become manifest in class conflict.

The contradictions and resultant class conflicts are manifested consciously as ideological struggles. The classes do not see their struggles as they really are, but as a clash of "principles". And the classes engaged in the struggle do so by presenting their own class interest in an ideological framework which asserts them to be "the only rational, universally valid ones" (*GI*, p. 66). Thus men make their own history, and history is the process of their self development, but they do not make history as *humans*. They do not make history in unison, but through the class struggle; and they do not make it consciously, but through the development of "false conscious" ideologies. Marx's analysis of historical development in terms of the dialectic of the forces and relations of production thus implies a theory of class struggle and social revolution. The question which now must arise concerns the significance of this theory for the realization of human freedom.

With the development of capitalism Marx believes that the crucial breakthrough in man's struggle to dominate nature has occurred. This is a necessary condition, as we have seen, for the realization of *human* history. The key problem now is to find an agency to carry out the necessary social changes. To find this one must, in Marx's view, look deeper into the mode of production—to the historically specific forms of contradiction, class struggle and consciousness in capitalism.

1.7 The dialectics of capitalist development

The key to the nature and functioning of capitalism lies for Marx in the specific property relations of the system. What is crucial here is the historically specific form that private property takes: the fragmentation of the property of the dominant bourgeois class into autonomous competing units which employ the proletariat as formally free wage labour in the market. In determining the historical development of the system, the competitive relation of bourgeois to bourgeois is pivotal. This relation determines the historically specific form of compulsion in the system, the essence of which Marx takes to be the accumulation of capital.

Through the mechanism of competition between autonomous private capitals which are independent of any *conscious social control*, Marx elevated

"the whole structure of the economic order into a great control mechanism, a compulsive system. . . . Thus for Marx exploitation was to be blamed on neither the unreasonableness nor the plain selfishness of the individual employer, but the employer was placed in a situation where he must act as he did, or be eliminated in the competitive struggle" (Parsons, 1968, p. 492).

Capitalism therefore is not, as classical and neoclassical economists envisage it, some direct and free expression of a universal economic impulse, but in Marx's eyes it constitutes a definite, historically specific form taken by the general need for material production (see pp. 27–32).

As such, capitalism exhibits a particular form of rationality, a rational orientation in the service of unlimited acquisition and accumulation. This is not to say that Marx saw action in societies before capitalism as non-rational, but he did maintain that in capitalism the area of rational action had vastly expanded and had taken a historically specific form in the service of unlimited accumulation. This aspect of rationality is clearly expressed in the *Communist Manifesto*, where Marx states that through the alienating structure of its own internal relations the bourgeoisie is incapable of not revolutionizing the means of production. Capitalism has thus brought out the most in man's material creative abilities (*SW* I, 108–19).

The efficiency of the bourgeois mode of production allows the bourgeoisie to absorb all earlier possessing classes, and all private property in the means of production into capital. Simultaneously there takes place the process of the centralization of capital as the competitive process reduces the number of independent capitals[10]. This expansion of capitalism is only made possible by the creation of an increasingly large proletariat. Bourgeois society therefore progressively universalizes the position of the worker; class relationships become simplified. Marx held that his dichotomous model of the class structure was increasingly realized with the development of capitalist production.

The contradictions of capitalism derive directly from its organization and development as a system of production based on capital accumulation rather than on production directly and consciously for developing human needs. There is an incompatibility between *social production* and *private appropriation* in capitalism. Production is increasingly socialized through the progressive extension of the division of labour. The property relations of production, however, are such that appropriation is private and individual. The development of the forces of production is thus inhibited, not by the technical possibilities of production, but by the property relations of private appropriation. The most evident manifestation of this contradiction Marx takes to be the periodic crisis of overproduction. Here production and employment are reduced despite that fact that "too little is produced to decently and humanely satisfy the wants of the great mass" (*Capital* III, 257).

Furthermore, Marx argues, "in the bargaining process between capital and labour the dice are in the long run very heavily loaded against the workers" (Meek, 1967, p. 117) so that the "social gulf which divides him from the capitalist ... [is] ... widened" (*SW* I, 167), as capitalism develops. This expanding gap between the conditions of the ever expanding numbers of the proletariat and the increasingly centralized and diminishing capitalist class is not a mere quantitative factor. It relates not only to the workers' ability to consume relative to the capitalist, but also to a qualitative factor, the increasing domination of labour by capital, of human activity by things; in short, the increasingly alienating conditions of the proletariat. Thus the organization of social labour in capitalism which progressively conquers nature, and as such creates the preconditions for other freedoms, is at the same time necessarily an organization of social labour producing inhumanity, domination and servitude. Although Marx believes this to be historically necessary, it is an increasingly disappearing necessity as the productive power of society grows. And with this disappearing necessity there grows a social demand for its transcendence with the formation of the proletariat into a revolutionary class.

Since Marx, as we have seen, argued that our "desires and pleasures spring from society; we measure them, therefore, by society and not by the objects which serve for their satisfaction" (*SW* I, 163), every fresh development of the productive powers of labour must tend to deepen social contrasts and sharpen social antagonisms. Thus with the development of capitalism the perceived needs of the proletariat must necessarily extend beyond their actual satisfaction within capitalism, and lead to the demand for *social* change. Precisely because it is the capitalist organization of social labour that separates the potential from the actual, the interests of bourgeoisie and proletariat must thereby become irreconcilable within capitalism. In this process the proletariat not only increases in strength but also recognizes its true interest and organizes its strength. It forms into a revolutionary class, a class not only *in itself* but *for itself*.

The revolutionary overthrow of the capitalist social order by a class-conscious and hence revolutionary proletariat is consistent with Marx's general conception of the dialectic of historical change as outlined in the previous section of this chapter. Marx himself makes the parallel at many points in his work, but it is clear that the proletarian class struggle is also qualitatively unique for Marx. As he sees it, it is the agency for the realization of man's humanity. Here then we must analyse Marx's idea that the path to humanity is through the inhumanity of the proletariat.

The proletariat's dehumanized condition in capitalist society is only the concentrated suffering of all men within that society. A revolution which emancipates the proletariat, therefore emancipates humanity:

"From the relation of alienated labour to private property it also follows that the emancipation of society from private property, from servitude, takes the political form of the emancipation of the workers ... because this emancipation includes the emancipation of humanity as a whole. For all human servitude is involved in the relation of the worker to production, and all types of servitude are only modifications or consequences of this relation" (*Early Writings*, pp. 132—3).

And again,

"The possessing class and the class of the proletariat represent the same human self-estrangement. But the former is comfortable in this self-estrangement and finds therein its own confirmation, knows that this self-estrangement is its own power, and possesses in it the semblance of human existence. The latter feels itself annihilated in this self-estrangement, sees in it its impotence and the reality of an inhuman existence" (*YM*, p. 367).

The proletariat's interest, therefore, although a particular class interest, expresses the interest of man's humanity conceived universally.

This for Marx is not utopian but is increasingly an empirically developing sociological inevitability (see pp. 52–5). Not only does capitalism develop man's control over nature, which is a necessary prerequisite for man's conscious control over society, but it also helps form the proletariat into the social agency which can realize the *human* potentialities of this development. It is such an agency, not only because of its opposition to the capitalist class, but also because its internal social relations of rational and conscious cooperation are a development of socialist relations of production within capitalism itself. These will be universalized to society as a whole in socialism, as a result of the realization of its class interest.

Therein lies the historical uniqueness of the proletariat as a revolutionary class. Furthermore, since the proletariat is in the structural position where the inhumanity of contemporary society is concentrated, the proletariat (and the theoretician who views reality from that position) can perceive historical reality for what it really is, without the ideological distortions of previous revolutionary classes. Marx sees in the proletariat's revolutionary activity a new form of social consciousness. This form of consciousness is an outgrowth of the structural position of the proletariat and is a necessary prerequisite for "human" society. For Marx the end cannot be separated from the means of its historical realization; such a consciousness is in his view another way of expressing the historical uniqueness of the proletariat.

The relation between capitalism and socialism is always considered by Marx, therefore, as dialectical. Socialism is not seen as a complete break with capitalism. On the contrary capitalism increasingly produces, through the operation of its own laws of motion, social structures, consciousness and productive power that will only be fully realized in socialism[11]. Marx considers capitalism always through a dialectical method which concentrates on its possibilities of development. His concept of capitalism is thus, strictly speaking, not one of a certain unchanging structure (see pp. 45f). Its structure is always in a process of development, transforming itself through its own operation into a structure requiring a different total social organization. Capitalism, for Marx, always points beyond itself.

Capitalist production is based on the private appropriation of a system of competing capitals. The resultant progressive socialization of production is the basic contradiction of capitalist society. And it is precisely in this socialization of production that Marx sees the key to the development of socialism. The contradiction of capitalist production can only be resolved in socialism, because production in capitalism is increasingly a distorted and alienated form of production within socialism. The structures of socialism are developed within the womb of capitalism. It therefore necessarily points beyond itself to socialism.

"No social order is ever destroyed before all the productive forces for which it is sufficient have been developed, and new superior relations of production never replace older ones before the material conditions for their existence have matured within the framework of the old society" (*Critique*, p. 21).

As concrete examples of these developments, Marx points in *Capital* to the decline in laissez-faire within British capitalism through the enactment of various social legislation. Thus Marx says of the Factory Acts that they represent "the first conscious and methodical reaction of society against the spontaneously developed form of the process of production" (I, 480). And of the development of joint stock companies and the resultant separation of ownership and control in capitalism he says:

"This result of the ultimate development of capitalist production is a necessary transitional phase towards the reconversion of capital into the property of producers, although no longer as the private property of the individual producers, but rather as the property of the associated producers, as outright social property. ... This is the abolition of the capitalist mode of production within the capitalist mode of production itself" (III, 437—8).

Another example of this important idea can be seen when he writes:

"However terrible and disgusting the dissolution, under the capitalist system, of the old family ties may appear, nevertheless modern industry, by assigning as it does an important part in the process of production, outside the domestic sphere, to women, to young persons and to children of both sexes, creates a new economic foundation for a higher form of the family and of the relations between the sexes ... a source of human development" (III, 489—90; see also I, 487—7; III, 606—7).

The most significant development of all for Marx is the changing organization of the proletariat within capitalism. It is in the proletariat's formation into a revolutionary class that Marx discerns a crucial characteristic of socialism. Their class unity creates a social solidarity within a cooperative social process. Unity, at first a means, becomes an end, and as such is a projection of future society. It is exactly this process of class organization within capitalism that is so conducive to the formation in the proletariat of a true consciousness of itself, its social position, historical role and what may be achieved through *conscious action*. "The end-results of the revolution are thus historically formed and determined during and by its occurrence" (Avineri, 1968, p. 143).

1.8 Conclusion

We are now in a position to answer the question implied in the heading of this chapter concerning the purpose of Marx's political economy. As we have seen, Marx's life work was orientated on the problem of how to realize the ideal of human freedom in social reality. Thus he saw the purpose of his own theoretical work to expose *scientifically*, not only what man in society potentially could become and what he actually is, but also how that contradiction can be resolved through conscious action.

It should be made clear that the nature of the ideal as Marx conceives it is *not* utilitarian, and no utilitarian basis can be imputed to his political economy (as it can to classical and neoclassical economics). This is not only because Marx rejected as false the belief in a quantitative expression of utility, but more significantly because his theoretical framework did not concentrate on "effects" independent of social structures[12]. Man is, for Marx, whatever he happens to be at any time because of the nature of his social relationships at that time. The key to the realization of the ideal of human freedom must therefore lie in changing society. Given Marx's conception of man, emancipated society must involve the emancipation of the men who compose it.

Marx does not promise "utility maximization" or "happiness" as such in future society, and he does not fight for it as such in the present. Capitalism is condemned not because it is "suboptimal" or makes people "unhappy" but because it *dehumanizes* them and, therefore, devalues and degrades them whatever their subjective state of happiness or unhappiness may be. Marx is not indifferent to happiness but the question is secondary to his main concern, and it is clear that utilitarianism was not a basis for either his ethics or his social science. *In short Marx's political economy is not "welfare economics" however radically conceived.*

Marx's view of history proves to him that ideals, no matter how desirable, can only be historically effective when linked to a class interest. It is, therefore, also invalid to regard him as a utopian. It was exactly his practical criticism of the utopians that they failed to specify a historically effective and therefore relevant means for realizing socialism. Instead they propose that historical action is "to yield to their personal invective action, historically created conditions of emancipation to fantastic ones" (*SW* I, 134), in which they appeal to the reason of the ruling class. Marx therefore remains in the world of empirical social science, and it is in relation to the class struggle that one must see the purpose of his theoretical work. It is crucial that the revolutionary proletariat have an adequate empirical interpretation of reality before they can carry through the socialist revolution. Theory itself, therefore, becomes part of the force changing reality, a part of *praxis* — the conscious determinate shaping of history.

Thus Marx argues that the ideal can be realized only by a union of theory and practice; through "integrating the study of the emergent transformations potential in history with a programme of practical action which can actualize these changes" (Giddens, 1971, p. 20). Since Marx sees class struggle as the realm of the appropriate agency, the function of his political economy is to inform and guide the revolutionary activity of the proletariat. As such his "theory was to give vision and articulate an explicit definition to political and moral stances forced upon individuals in consequence of the positions they occupy in the social system" (MacIntyre, 1971, p. 92). Thus his work was designed as a scientific structure of theory to aid the accomplishment of socialist revolution. It is, therefore, not simply an academic study of economy and society: Marx studied it only in order to change it in a definite and conscious way.

Notes

1.   Marx's vision of social structures, the method of his analysis and exposition of that analysis can all be classed as *dialectical*. In all cases the main idea is that social phenomena are seen as existing in relation to each other, and continually developing in and through such relations so as to form, at various phases, contradictory forces that generate qualitatively new formations. Thus social reality is seen always as in a state of becoming something else. The term dialectical, therefore, expresses the general structure of historical processes of development, Marx's method of discovering concrete empirical laws in historically specific stages, and his exposition of them.

2.   See for instance, Aron (1965, pp. 161ff.) and McLellan (1971, pt 2, Ch. 4).

3.   The amount produced over and above the consumption requirements of the producers.

4.   Illustration of this argument as it applies to political economy can be found in Chapter 2, pp. 39—45.

5.   But see Chapter 7, where it is pointed out that Marx may have changed his mind in the late 1870s.

6.   This definition covers alienation in all its forms, but we deal here only with the economic alienation characteristic of capitalism. In his early works, however, Marx deals extensively with political and religious alienation. (Religious systems and state institutions are, in all cases, social products, but function as powers over society. Men, the creators, are thus controlled by their creations). In both the *Grundrisse* and *Capital* Marx deals directly only with the economic alienation of commodity producing systems, that is, the alienation of pre-capitalist forms of commodity production (or money) and the alienation of capitalist commodity production. The phenomena of religious alienation are referred to only as analogies to the consciousness (fetishism) of economic actors in alienated economic processes. The reason for this emphasis lies in Marx's view that economic alienation had become increasingly important with the development of capitalism and was, in certain ways, less obvious than other forms. Further, since in all cases Marx regards alienation as rooted in the structure of economic relations, the determinant of all alienation ultimately lies in this economic structure.

7.   On the nature of the workers' economic freedom in capitalism as Marx conceived it, see Ch. 2, pp. 44—5.

8.   There are other social relations of capitalist production, *i.e.* those comprising landed property, merchant and money-lending capital, but following Marx these are for the time being abstracted from as secondary.

9.   On the nature of economic motivation in Marx's theory, see Chapter 2, pp. 29—32.

10.   Marx uses the term "centralization" for what in orthodox theory is termed "concentration", and the term "concentration" simply to refer to an increase in the size of capitals.

11.   "All of Marx's statements throughout his writings, upon the 'abolition' (*aufhebung*) of religion, the state, alienation or capitalism as a whole, have to be understood in the light of the threefold connotation of the verb *aufheben* (to abolish, to preserve, to raise up). Thus the 'abolition' of religion involves, not its eradication in any simple sense, but its dialectical transcendence" (Giddens, 1971, p. 7).

12.   In *GI* Marx notes that, "The apparent stupidity of merging all the manifold relationships of people in the *one* relation of usefulness, this apparently metaphysical abstraction arises from the fact that, in modern

bourgeois society, all relations are subordinated in practice to the one abstract monetary-commercial relation" (p. 109). "The economic contest gradually turned utility theory into a mere apologia for the existing state of affairs, an attempt to prove that under existing conditions the mutual relations of people today are the most advantageous and generally useful. It has this character among all modern economists" (p. 114).

2

The sociological method
of Marx's economics

2.1 Introduction

In this chapter we deal with the major aspects of Marx's method as it relates to his political economy. It will emerge (especially in section 2.5) that it is in the nature of the case impossible to present the methodological aspects of his thought in complete isolation from his substantive theory. We have taken advantage of this by introducing certain important elements of the Marxian theory of value, which form a springboard for the following chapters. This chapter, however, does seek to deal with Marx's method as a topic worthy of treatment in its own right. In order to bring out certain distinctive traits of Marx's method we have at some points compared it with the methodological principles of orthodox economic theory.

Section 2.2 builds on Chapter 1 in discussing Marx's view of economic causation and the scope of his economics; 2.3 uses this to outline his definition of capitalism, and also briefly considers the origin of this mode of production. Further light is shed on the nature of capitalism in 2.4, which explains how Marx develops a theory of economic motivation, mainly with reference to the capitalist.

Section 2.5, probably the most difficult in this chapter, analyses Marx's concepts and seeks to show their specific properties. This in turn helps us to understand his distinction between "appearance" and "reality" in 2.6. This is important for explaining his view of social science and his theory of ideology.

Section 2.7 provides a thumbnail sketch of Marx's method of exposition in *Capital*. It also provides a guide for readers who wish to undertake the mammoth task of reading *Capital* themselves. Sections 2.8 and 2.9 constitute an analysis of Popper's famous criticism of Marx's view of science, and a discussion of how Marx unites science and values. We conclude in 2.10 with some brief remarks on the usefulness of Marx's method for economic theory today.

2.2 Economic causation and the definition of economics

The major theoretical problem for any economist is that of causation: why are economic phenomena as they are, and why do they change over time (if in fact they do)? Marx's answer to this question follows from his general social theory, as outlined in Chapter 1. He argues that the economic laws applicable to each stage of historical development result from the social relations of production which characterize that stage. Economic phenomena (methods of resource allocation, the distribution of income, dynamic laws of economic development), are what they are because of the nature of the relations between economic agents. When these relationships change so do the economic laws to which they give rise.

Consequently Marx defines economics as the science which studies how historically specific systems of economic relations originate, operate and change (see, for example, *Grundrisse*, pp. 852–3). Marx does not simply seek to undertake this task qualitatively; that is, to show how different economic relations underlie different forms of resource allocation, distribution and types of development. He also seeks, wherever possible, to undertake the task quantitatively; in the case of capitalism, for example, to show how the historically specific set of capitalist economic relations determines the quantitative exchange ratios between commodities, and the quantitative proportions of total income received by different classes.

Thus he makes no sharp distinction between sociology and economics. Economics is defined sociologically in terms of the social relations of production. Furthermore, since the materialist conception of history emphasizes the causal importance of the economic structure for all social phenomena, economics is for Marx the most basic of all social sciences. For example, he maintained that it was only after the economic analysis of property incomes in capitalism had been undertaken that the prevailing forms of consciousness in bourgeois society could be understood (see below, pp. 39-45).

This view of economic causation, with its related definition of economics, is very different from that of other schools of thought. These do not attribute the same critical importance to social relationships. And where such relations are dealt with there is a strong tendency to abstract from their historically specific form.

This is very clear in the Ricardian laws of distribution: the highpoint of classical political economy. The two basic assumptions for this analysis are *diminishing returns* (the "niggardliness of nature"), and the *Malthusian population principle*, derived from the innate biological drives of the species[1]. On the interaction of these two laws of nature Ricardo derives his results. Marx was severely critical of Ricardo's emphasis on the importance of these laws, not just by questioning their validity on simple empirical grounds, but more fundamentally in terms of his sociological perspective (see Chapters 3 and 4). Marx's own distribution theory is based squarely on the historically specific social relations of capitalist commodity production (see Chapters 5 and 6).

The major emphasis of neoclassical economics is placed on *scarcity*. This is clearly stated by Robbins (1946, p. 16), in his now classic outline of neoclassical theory: "the economist studies the disposal of scarce means", so that economics is "the science which studies human behaviour as a relationship between ends and scarce means which have alternative uses". All neoclassical theory is based on this idea, and its analysis is focused on the way in which economic actors "rationally" handle scarcity. Neoclassical theory is thus held to be universally applicable, and "institutional" factors are generally introduced only at the level of empirical research.

Marx himself was very much aware of the problem of scarcity:

"Every child knows ... that the mass of products corresponding to different needs require different and quantitatively determined masses of the total labour of society. That this necessity of distributing social labour in definite proportions cannot be done away with by the particular form *of social production, but can only change the* form *it assumes is self evident. No natural laws can be done away with"* (SC, p. 209).

Here is a clear recognition of the importance of scarcity for the structure of economic organization. Marx, however, adds to the above passage the important point that

"What can change, in changing historical circumstances, is the form in which these laws operate. And the form in which this proportional division of labour operates in a state of society where the interconnection of social labour is manifested in the private exchange *of individual products of labour is precisely the exchange value of these products"* (ibid.)[2].

The analysis of scarcity in commodity-producing economies is thus an important part of Marx's theory of value. But he argues that this is a historically specific form of dealing with scarcity, and that the mechanism it embodies cannot be extended as an explanation of the operation of other and different systems of production. Other systems of production have allocated resources in completely different ways (*Capital* I, 355f). The key to understanding these historical methods is the study of the social relations of material production in such societies. The theory of value relates to a historically specific method of resource allocation, because the social relations it embodies are themselves historically specific. As we shall see, Marx's labour theory of value shows how prices and distribution patterns are functionally related to the social relations of commodity production. Depending on their precise structure — simple or pre-capitalist, early or advanced capitalist commodity production — price and distribution patterns vary in predictable and meaningful ways (Meek, 1973).

Keynes's economic theory, and orthodox Keynesian economics, also abstract from the social relations of capitalist production[3]. This is quite clear, for instance, in the definition of the key concepts. The propensity to consume, liquidity preference, the entrepreneur's "animal spirits", and the marginal efficiency of capital are defined in asocial, ahistorical terms. It is not specified which classes, in which types of economic structures, these relate to. As a consequence the historical reference of the General Theory is highly ambiguous[4]. Marx, on the contrary, is quite explicit on the historical applicability of his own theory of overproduction. It applies only to capitalism, because he sees the causes as stemming from the social relations specific to this system. Marx argues that crises are "possible" in commodity-producing systems generally, but he stresses that this possibility does not become an actual occurrence (at least a regular periodic occurrence) until the social conditions of capitalist production emerge; this question is further discussed below (pp. 119—22).

Although this section is only an outline, from one particular perspective, of a large body of economic theory, it does highlight a crucially important difference between Marx's political economy and orthodox economics. We return to this question in more detail in Chapter 4.

2.3 The definition and origin of capitalist production

Marx's own economic analysis deals most extensively with the capitalist mode of production, defined in terms of a historically specific set of social relations. As we have seen (above p. 15), the main elements in its definition are the existence of the producers as propertyless wage labourers, and the fragmentation of the owning bourgeois class into autonomous competing units which employ the proletariat through periodic exchange in the market. Furthermore, the bourgeoisie employs capital with the primary aim of acquiring wealth or, more strictly, of accumulating more capital (see below, pp. 29—32).

This last aspect is of crucial importance. It means that capitalism as defined by Marx is not geared to the immediate personal consumption of the capitalists. Marx was impressed by capitalism's development of the means of production, and built his model on the assumption of a strong drive toward capital accumulation[5]. This means that if wage labour is employed solely or predominantly to serve the immediate consumption requirements of the capitalist class, the system is *not* capitalist, even though the other defining characteristics may be present (see, for example, *Grundrisse*, p. 334; *Capital* II, 123).

Marx's definition and economic theory of capitalism relates to no particular concrete example. But he did take England to be the clearest empirical case which conformed to the theoretical model (*Capital* I, 8, 240, 648), adding that "the country that is more developed industrially only shows, to the less developed, the image of its own future" (*ibid*, I, 8—9). Marx's main concern was to analyse capitalism as a fully developed system, the operation of which is unimpeded by the survival of pre-capitalist economic relationships. He does, however, deal with some of the processes by which it became established in Western Europe, particularly in England, under the title of "primitive accumulation"[6].

Marx summarized the main points in his theory of primitive accumulation as follows:

"In themselves money and commodities are no more capital than are the means of production and of subsistence. They want transforming into capital. But this transformation can only take place under certain circumstances that centre on this, viz., that two kinds of commodity-possessors must come face to face and into contact; on the one hand the owners of money, means of production, means of subsistence, who are eager to increase the sum of values they possess, by buying other people's labour-power; on the other hand, free labourers . . . in the double sense that neither they themselves form part and parcel of the means of production as in the case of slaves or bondsmen, etc., nor do the means of production belong to them, as in the case of peasant proprietors; they are, therefore, free from, unencumbered by, any means of production of their own. . . . The process, therefore, that clears the way for the capitalist system, can be none other than the process which takes away from the labourer the possession of his means of production; a process that transforms on the one hand, the social means of subsistence and of production into capital, on the other, the immediate producers into wage labourers" (Capital I, 714).

The actual mechanisms of this process to which Marx gives emphasis are the forcible expropriation of the agricultural population through enclosures; state legislation which forced the dispossessed into the labour market and out of crime and vagrancy; and conditions which swelled mercantile and usurers' profits, including piracy, colonization, and the slave trade, and led to the accumulation of monetary wealth which could be used to purchase both means of production and labour power[7].

Marx's analysis of primitive accumulation is probably open to objection on points of empirical detail. Nevertheless, his general conclusion has not lost its relevance:

"This primitive accumulation . . . is supposed to be explained when it is told as an anecdote of the past . . . there were two sorts of people; one the diligent, intelligent, and, above all, frugal elite; the other, lazy rascals, spending their substance, and more, in riotous living. . . . Thus it came to pass that the former sort accumulated wealth, and the latter sort had at last nothing to sell but their own skins. . . . Such insipid childishness is every day preached to us in defence of property. . . . In actual history it is notorious that conquest, enslavement, robbery, murder, briefly force, play the great part" (Capital I, 713—14).

2.4 The motivation of economic actors

Consistent with his sociological view of economic theory, Marx analyses motivation in terms of the social division of activity which constitutes the historically specific economic structure under consideration. So far as most historical modes of production are concerned, this entails conceiving motivation in terms of the class position of the individual, and thus in terms of the social relations by which that position is defined:

"Society does not consist of individuals, but expresses the sum of interrelations, the relations within which these individuals stand" (Grundrisse, p. 265).

"In the course of our investigation we shall find, in general, that the characters who appear on the economic stage are but the personifications of the economic relations that exist between them" (Capital I, 85).

"Here individuals are dealt with only in so far as they are the personification of economic categories, embodiments of particular class-relations and class-interests" (ibid., I, 10).

Motivation is thus traced back to the operation of economic structures which exist and function independently of the conscious control of the individuals of which they are composed. This does not imply that economic actors are inert and non-conscious. But it does imply that activity and consciousness is only that of the individual *as he fills a social role.*

It is possible to indicate Marx's meaning more fully by referring to his conception of the capitalist, for whom

"the expansion of value . . . becomes his subjective aim, and it is only in so far as the appropriation of ever more and more wealth in the abstract becomes the sole motive of his operations, that he functions as a capitalist. . . . Use value must therefore never be looked on as the real aim of the capitalist" (Capital I, 152; see also ibid., I, 592).

This is not a "natural" expression of a universal economic impulse. Such an action pattern is not even characteristic of other economic actors in a *capitalist* society, let alone of other forms of society. The capitalist's motivation arises in a historical process prior to the domination of capitalist production. Crucially important here, according to Marx, were the developments associated with the growth of the medieval European towns: the movement for municipal autonomy and the creation of a money economy which grew out of the expansion of trade. In this process the towns became emancipated from the stultifying communal ethics and restrictions of the feudal system. The extension of money relationships promoted the rational acquisition of "wealth in general" by providing a means by which heterogeneous qualities can be reduced to a common standard; a standard, moreover, which has no effective limits imposed on its acquisition.

However, as capitalist production itself develops, the capitalists' drive to accumulation is intensified through competition. This social relation of capitalist to capitalist "brings out the inherent laws of capitalist production, in the shape of external coercive laws having power over every individual capitalist" (*Capital* I, 270). For example, each capitalist must keep constantly extending his capital in order to "build technical progress into his productive organism" (*Capital* II, 123)[8].

In so doing the capitalist is forced to engage in a struggle with the workers he employs to increase the degree of exploitation through increasing the intensity of the labour process and the length of the working day. Marx stresses that in this process of conflict between capital and labour "the dice are in the long run very heavily loaded against the workers" (Meek, 1967, p. 117). In this situation, he argues, "capital is reckless of the health or length of life of the labourer, unless under compulsion from society" (*Capital* I, 270). "What", Marx asks, "could possibly show better the character cf the capitalist mode of production than the necessity that exists for forcing upon it by Acts of Parliament, the simplest appliances for maintaining cleanliness and health?" (*ibid*, I, 481). He notes, however, that although the capitalist is thus painted "in no sense *couleur de rose*", one cannot "make the individual responsible for relations whose creature he socially remains, however much he may subjectively raise himself above them" (*ibid*, I, 10).

The reduction of "individuals" to social positions, and in particular to *class* positions, did not preclude Marx from recognizing the unique character of the individual biography in actual life. The "personal life" does exist for Marx, and it affects the way in which individuals interpret and act out their social roles[9]. There are two main points to consider here. First, Marx clearly realized that the motivations ascribed to economic actors in theory may not correspond to the motivations which individuals would themselves accept as governing their behaviour. This is clear from his theory of false consciousness and ideology. Marx argues that, historically, individuals have generally been unaware of the real driving forces behind their actions (see above pp. 13f and below pp. 54–5). However, the "personal" motives existing in the actual consciousness of the individual economic actors are, in Marx's view, also a necessary product of their class position, and have a definite relation to the motives attributed to them in theory.

· Secondly, Marx's reduction of individuals to class positions is not meant to deny that individuals may act from other bases than this (social or otherwise). Consequently he accepts that theory is a simplification, and that empirical deviations away from theoretical propositions will exist to some degree. However, in the case of developed capitalism at least, Marx did not expect the deviations to be very large:

"In theory it is assumed that the laws of capitalist production operate in their pure form. In reality there exists only approximation; but this approximation is the greater, the more developed the capitalist mode of production, and the less it is adulterated and amalgamated with survivals of former economic conditions" (*Capital* III, 175).

Needless to say, these points create certain methodological problems, but the problems are by no means peculiar to Marx's political economy. All economic theory is similar in this respect, abstracting from the personal life and basing its analysis on abstract economic actors.

What is distinctive about Marx's economic method is its explicit concentration on the socially and historically specific nature of motivation. The uniqueness and significance of Marx's procedure can be shown more clearly by an examination of neoclassical methodology.

The motivation of economic actors in neoclassical theory is expressed through the concept of *preferences*, and economic phenomena (for example distribution of income, choice of production technique, relative prices and capital accumulation), are explained by the interaction of actors' preference patterns with various types of constraints. Preference is taken to mean what the economic actor under consideration (for example, the consumer or the entrepreneur) *prefers*. This was originally analysed in terms of utility theory, but is increasingly accepted as revealed by what the actor does (that is, "revealed preference theory").

These motivations, as expressed in preference mappings, are consciously made abstract by neoclassical theorists in order that the theory not be tied to particular preference structures and thus to particular results. The consequence of this is that these preferences are assumed to be *exogenous* to the economic system, and comparative static equilibrium procedures simply alter preferences when their effect on the theoretical economic system is to be analysed.

One assumes that few neoclassical economists actually believe that preferences are exogenous to the economic system, since the evidence is quite clearly to the contrary. Neoclassicists justify the exclusion of such sociological considerations by pointing to the generality of the theory that they are constructing. The crucial point is, however, that once abstracted from sociological considerations they cannot easily return to be incorporated in applications of the general theory. In short, it is not possible to make preferences endogenous to the economic system without generating severe shocks which irreparably damage the neoclassical theoretical structure.

This is particularly true of that part of neoclassical theory which attempts to judge the efficiency of economic systems in terms of their capacity to satisfy preferences. The efficiency of economic systems can only be evaluated if the standards of judgment (preferences) are independent of what is being judged (the economic system itself). Thus if one builds into such a theory the sociologically endogenous nature of preferences the theory collapses.

More damaging still is the problem that an asocial and ahistorical conception of motivation short-circuits explanation. Joan Robinson (1964, p. 48) expresses this criticism succinctly when she writes that, in neoclassical theory, "*utility* is a metaphysical concept of impregnable circularity; *utility* is the quality in commodities that makes individuals want to buy them, and the fact that individuals want to buy commodities shows they have *utility*". The modern development of "revealed preference theory" is even more futile, amounting to a complete rejection of the view that the motivations of economic actors are important.

Thus the neoclassical asocial and ahistorical approach to motivation turns out to be barren. As such it helps to highlight the importance of Marx's own procedure. More generally it illustrates the rather obvious methodological point that if one seeks to carry out social science it is not advisable to abstract from the social nature of motivations.

2.5 Marx's economic concepts

Marx's view of the nature of economic causation and his definition of economics forms the basis for an understanding of his economic concepts. Since economic laws result from the historically specific structure of social relationships between economic actors, and it is the task of economics to study such relations, each concept of Marx's political economy relates to a set of social relationships. There are, however, a number of difficulties in the way of understanding this point. These lie partly in the nature of economic relationships themselves, especially in commodity-producing systems, of which capitalism is an example. But difficulties also arise because of the way in which Marx sees these relationships. We outline these difficulties first of all in general terms, and then illustrate them by examining Marx's concepts of commodity, value and capital. Sections 2.7 and 2.10 throw further light on the issues raised here.

The first reason why the social relationships of commodity-producing systems are difficult to understand is because they interpenetrate with relations between *things*. Engels states this with clarity when he writes that "economics deals not with things but with relations between persons, and in the last resort, between classes; these relations are, however, always *attached to things* and *appear as things*" (*SW* I, 514)[10]. This point is central for an understanding of Marxian economics. In Marx's view it is the social relations of production which govern the way in which things enter the economic process. If these social relations are attached to things and appear as things this in no way detracts from their status as social relations.

Given the primacy of social relations in causation, Marx considered it both illegitimate and confusing to consider them simply as relations between things (see below pp. 35—9). However, where social relations are attached to things it is possible to use the concept which embodies the social relationship also to cover these things, in so far as they are attached to the social relations in question. This is Marx's practice, and it explains his habit of referring to things as "definite social relations".

A further difficulty arises because Marx sees a fully developed stage of social production as comprising an organic unity of elements:

"While in the completed bourgeois system every economic relation presupposes every other in its bourgeois economic form, and everything posited is thus also a presupposition, this is the case with every organic system. This organic system, as a totality consists precisely in subordinating all elements of society to itself, or in creating out of it the organs which it still lacks. This is historically how it becomes a totality" (*Grundrisse*, p. 278).

Each part of bourgeois society is what it is because of its relations to the whole. As a consequence particular aspects of the whole only become fully intelligible when they are viewed in terms of the whole[111]. So too, therefore, Marx's conceptual structure displays this property of organic interconnection. Each aspect of reality, and each concept which reflects it in the conceptual structure when fully defined, is conceived as a different aspect of one whole, and as implying or including the other aspects. Each, therefore, has many different facets and can be treated from many different angles. The whole, real or conceptual, is contained in each of its parts. (On this see Ollman (1971) and *Grundrisse*, pp. 512—14.)

This further implies that each social factor is related to the processes of change, past and potential, associated with the whole. As such, each social factor is "related to its own past and future forms, as well as to the past and future forms of the surrounding factors" (Ollman, 1971, p. 18). This again is paralleled in the conceptual structure of political economy, for theoretical categories are only simplified, one-sided representations of their subject matter (*Grundrisse*, p. 106).

This means that Marx's concepts are unstable. Engels pointed this out when he warned against expecting "fixed, cut to measure once and for all applicable definitions in Marx's works", and noted that:

"It is self-evident that where things and their interrelations are conceived not as fixed, but as changing, their mental images, the ideas, are likewise subject to change and transformation; and they are not encapsuled in rigid definitions, but are developed in their historical and logical process of formation" (*Capital* III, 13—14; see also below, pp. 45—52).

In a literal sense, then, Marx's economic theory is contained in his concepts. These convey the theory by their own definitions and structure. This is one of the reasons why Marx found the exposition of his theory so difficult. It is clear that Marx's relational view of reality and the method by which he studies it is very different from that of most social science, which proceeds as if the factors it conceptualizes are logically independent of each other.

This set of points has been partially illustrated in the last section in terms of Marx's conception of the capitalist. It can be further exemplified by examining the major aspects of Marx's key economic concepts: *commodity*, *value*, and *capital*. First, then, we examine the concept of a commodity. In orthodox economic theory this is synonymous with the term "good", that is, an object of utility, and is thus seen to apply to all modes of production. The utility aspect of this definition is incorporated in Marx, for whom a necessary condition for a thing to be a commodity is that it have "use value". This, however, is not the most important defining characteristic, precisely because it does not encompass a social relation:

"Articles of utility become commodities only because they are products of the labour of private individuals or groups of individuals who carry on their work independently of one another . . .[and] do not come into social contact with each other until they exchange their products" (Capital I, 72—3; see also *ibid.,* I, 42 and 624).

Engels points out that such a product is "a commodity solely because a relation between the two persons or communities attaches to the *thing,* the product, the relation between producer and consumer who are no longer united in the same person" (*SW* I, 514)[12].

Such relations of material production are in no sense natural or universal. This is most clearly seen if we take in contrast those

"small and extremely ancient Indian communities, some of which have continued down to this day . . . [which are] based on possession in common of the land, on the blending of agriculture and handicrafts, and on the unalterable division of labour . . . each forms a compact whole producing all it requires. The chief part of the products is destined for direct use by the community itself and does not take the form of a commodity. . . . In those of the simplest kind, the land is tilled in common and the produce divided among the members. At the same time, spinning and weaving are carried out in each family as subsidiary industries. . . . If the population increases, a new community is founded, on the pattern of the old one, on unoccupied land" (Capital I, 357—8).

Production for Marx is always social production, but the mutual exchange of activities takes the form of market exchange of products only with *commodity* production—the most developed form of which is capitalism. It is this specific relational aspect which is embodied in the concept "commodity".

Further analysis of the concept of a commodity leads directly on to the concept of *value* — the most important, but least understood, of all Marx's economic concepts. Commodity producers, in exchanging their products, create a quantitative relation between things (or, as we can now call them, commodities). This quantitative relationship between commodities Marx calls their *exchange value;* it is generally expressed in terms of money where there is a developed system of exchange. However, since in commodity production the "social" character of production is expressed through this exchange of commodities, these exchanges are simultaneously exchanges of the activities of the producers within the division of labour. Thus the relation between the commodities (*things*) is simultaneously a relation between men (commodity *producers*). Marx's concept of *value* represents this social relation of commodity production. Since the relationship takes place through relations between commodities, the concept has to express the social relations of the producers as relations between commodities (things). As Marx puts it, "value is a relation between persons expressed as a relation between things" (*Capital* I, 74). (As such *value* must be distinguished from the related concepts of *exchange value* and *use value*, as defined above.)

Marx's reasoning is as follows. In commodity production, production is social because producers work for each other by embodying their labour in things which they exchange on the market for other similarly produced things (commodities). If we abstract from the non-social physical aspects of commodities and consider them solely as the products of commodity producers, then the only quality they have in common is that of being the products of human labour.

To do this is to abstract the social relations of commodity producers from the material objects to which these social relations are attached and as which they appear. Human labour thus possesses the property of being able to represent the social relations of commodity producers. Human labour is in fact the *only* property of a commodity that can embody the social relations of commodity production, since it is the only property left when we abstract from the non-social, material properties of commodities.

In expressing the social relations of commodity production, then, the concept of value refers to the commodity conceived as a product of human labour; and the quantitative magnitude of value is the *amount* of labour embodied in it (measured in "socially necessary" units)[13]. Value is thus a property of the commodity, but it is not a physical property. It is the property which is socially attributed to objects because they are the products of a historically specific form of social labour (*Capital* I, 47).

The concept of "value", then, is identical to that of "commodity" when it is conceived abstractly as expended labour. As we have seen, to be a commodity an object must also have utility; this is clearly so for all objects intended for human consumption, irrespective of the social context. However, only commodities can possess value, simply because value is a property given to a thing by virtue of its production by human labour in a certain set of social relations.

The "use value" of a commodity, on the other hand, as with the use value of all things irrespective of social context, stems from those properties of things which we ignore when we consider the commodity as a "value", that is, its physical, non-social features (*Capital* I, 37—8). It follows that although value exists only in objects possessing utility, the magnitude of use value does not affect the magnitude of value. This follows directly from the definition of these concepts. "Value" is a concept expressing a relation between men in production, while "use value" refers to the relation between the consumer and the thing consumed.

Marx's concept of value is, of course, very different from that of orthodox economics. Here the term simply means "price", or the ratio in which one good exchanges for another at any point in time and space. Marx reserves for this the term "price" or "market price", and "price of production" for its long-run equilibrium level, and often uses the term "exchange value" to refer to either or both, depending on the context. The "magnitude of value" determines such "prices of production", but the precise relationship between them cannot be stated for commodity production *per se*. The precise form of the relationship between value and price of production depends, as we shall see, on the *type* of commodity production, whether capitalist or pre-capitalist and, if the former, on the various stages of capitalist development. Marx's labour theory of value is a complex set of statements which show how the social relations of production determine relative prices in the whole range of commodity-producing societies found in historical development (Meek, 1973; and below pp. 45–52).

Thus Marx's concept of value is also very different from that of classical political economy, which itself had a "labour theory of value". In qualitative terms this school of economists made no explicit and systematic attempt to use the concept of value in order to analyse the social relations of commodity-producing systems. In quantitative terms, they identified "value" with what Marx was to term "price of production" (see below pp. 103–111).

The concepts of "commodity" and "value" relate, therefore, only to commodity production. Capitalism is just one specific form of commodity production; not all systems of commodity production are capitalist[14]. The production of commodities is common to many forms of society. Its purest non-capitalist form, Marx argued, was colonial America, where the settlers were independent artisans and farmers who owned their own means of production, worked on their own account, and marketed their own surpluses as commodities (*Capital* I, ch. xxxiii).

The concept of "capital" applies only to the historically specific social relations of capitalist society. Capitalism is a unique form of commodity production: it is only here that the "labour power"[15] of the producers is sold as a commodity to a capitalist who then uses it in the process of production, which he controls. The capitalist–labourer relation is a distinguishing characteristic of capitalist commodity production. Marx's concept of "capital" refers to this relation[16].

"Capital", then, refers to a particular form of the social division of labour. Since it is through this form of the social labour process that the capitalist exploits the labourer, the term "capital" is extended to cover this historically specific form of exploitation (see below pp. 42f). The concept of "capital" can also be extended to cover the social properties of things. The capitalist can only exploit the worker because he possesses the means of production which the worker must use in order to produce at all. The definition of capital, then, extends to include "the means of production monopolized by" the capitalist class (*Capital* III, 815).

Capital is *not* the means of production as such, but the means of production used in the capitalist–labourer relation: "Capital is not a thing but rather a definite social production relation belonging to a definite historical formation of society, which is manifested in a thing and lends that thing a specific social character" (*Capital* III, 814). In commodity production products take the form of commodities, and these commodities are values. Thus capital is made up of commodities, and can be represented as a *value* which can be measured in socially necessary labour units. It is therefore also "stored up labour", which raises the physical productivity of wage labourers in the production process.

So far the focus has been static. But capital changes its form as the economic process unfolds. The capitalist's capital initially takes a money form, which he then exchanges for commodities (means of production and labour power). These are set to work to produce new commodities, which are then sold. If everything has gone according to the capitalist's expectation, he receives from the sale a larger quantity of money than he began with. Capital in this process of circulation takes four forms:

MONEY → COMMODITIES → COMMODITIES → MONEY

At each stage capital changes its form, but in each case it is still capital. Thus Marx uses the term "capital" to cover this process of circulation, as well as each of its elements; or, to put the point differently, to refer to money that circulates in this way (*Capital* I, 147).

All this lies in a different world from that of orthodox theory. Here capital is defined simply in terms of things themselves, that is, as the produced means of production. Marx explicitly rejected such a definition of capital because of its non-relational, ahistorical character. Such a definition could only serve to conceal the specific nature of capitalist exploitation, income distribution, relative prices and the whole accumulation process.

Clearly one major problem in coming to terms with the political economy of Marx is the difficulty encountered in deciphering his concepts. Concepts such as value and capital are defined as *relations* and thus contain "in themselves, as integral elements of what they are, those parts with which we tend to see them externally tied" (Ollman, 1971, p. 15). Only so long as the requisite relations hold in reality is the concept applicable. Hence the concept *capital* is not applicable to the feudal economic system, for example, because here the capitalist—labourer relation is non-existent.

Perhaps more than anything else the difficulty springs from the multidimensional character of these concepts. In the concept of capital, for example, we see that the capital—labour relation can be treated as part of the definition of capital. This is possible because the concept of capital refers to many references simultaneously, and such a conceptualization is possible only because Marx views capitalism as an organic relational whole.

All this indicates how Marx unifies what would now generally be considered to be sociological factors (that is, social relations) and economic factors (relative prices, "factor shares", the accumulation process, and so on). It should be clear that this is no simple unification in terms of, for example, framing mutually compatible propositions or of suggesting that "sociological" factors affect "economic" variables. Marx builds up his economic theory directly from the structure of social relationships.

2.6 Appearance and reality

It should be clear from the previous section that Marx's view of social reality is not a simple description in terms of reality as it appears. In Marx's view, in fact, appearances are illusory; "reality as it appears" to social actors is deceptive. He talks of "reality" as hidden or concealed by "appearance"[17]. It is the role of scientific political economy to penetrate through appearances to the reality, and to make appearances scientifically comprehensible[18]. Only when viewed in terms of this underlying structure is the perception of appearances a *true* perception, as opposed to *false consciousness*.

Furthermore, Marx argued, contemporary political economy was concerned with appearances only; and it is in fact in the domain of political economy where the greatest difficulties exist for scientific work[19]. This is because its subject matter, being predominantly commodity production, is exactly that form of production where social relations are attached to things and appear as things. Thus relationships between things are not perceived for what they really are: social relations "for which the material elements of wealth serve as bearers"; instead they appear as, and are conceived as, stemming from the "properties of these things themselves" (*Capital* III, 826).

This constitutes Marx's theory of commodity fetishism, a state of affairs in which "a definite social relation between men . . . assumes in their eyes, the fantastic form of a relation between things" (*Capital* I, 72). Or, to put it another way, "their own social action takes the form of the action of objects which rule the producers instead of being ruled by them" (*ibid*, I, 75). Thus, instead of seeing their own social relations as they are, producers see them only as they appear, as the independent activities of inanimate material objects.

This fetishistic form of appearances corresponds to an objective state of alienation. The atomization of commodity producers and their consequent lack of social control means that their own interactions become independent forces that dominate and control them. Each producer's economic power over others, and his simultaneous control by society, is exercised through the prices and quantities of things (commodities). Thus, because atomized social interaction takes place through things in this way, things actually *do* control men. Material domination replaces personal domination (*Grundrisse*, pp. 156–60).

This fetishism of commodities, therefore, has its origin in the "peculiar social character of labour that produces them" (*Capital* I, 72), and all "forms of society, in so far as they reach the stage of commodity production and money circulation take part in this perversion" (*Capital* III, 826–7). Marx goes on to say, however, that "under the capitalist mode of production . . . this enchanted and perverted world develops still more" (*Capital* III, 827; see also Meek, 1973, pp. xi–xiv).

The fetishism which specifically attaches to the capitalist system of commodity production can best be seen in the economic actors' perceptions of capital and profit. The crucial feature of this perverted perception is that capital is conceived as a thing which produces or earns profit as a result of its productivity. (The marginal productivity theory is the most sophisticated form of this theory.) Marx does not, of course, deny that material objects are productive of "wealth", or use values. But he rightly argues that the physical or technical properties of things logically cannot produce social categories like profit. In the fetish perspective social properties are made the properties of things, and the social relations of production are thus "naturalized" (*Capital* III, 816–7). As Marx says of interest-bearing capital, "it becomes a property of money to generate value and yield interest, much as it is an attribute of pear trees to bear pears" (*ibid.*, III, 392).

Marx's point is not to deny that capitalist property does lead to a profit for the capitalist in capitalist society. This, however, is a very different statement. Capitalist property is a *social object* through which the historically specific capital–labour relation is acted out. Such a social object can yield the social category of "profit on capital". The fetishism of the "productivity" theories of profit lies precisely in their conversion of the "social, economic character impressed on things in the process of social production into a natural character stemming from the material nature of those things" (*Capital* II, 229). If profit does exist, it must result from the social qualities of objects, and thus from the social relations of material production in capitalism.

For Marx, however, the false world of appearance is not limited to the fetish perspective outlined above. The capital—labour relation appears as an ordinary relation of exchange, and Marx is adamant that this appearance in itself leads to illusions that form part of the ideological structure of bourgeois society. The essential feature of the capital—labour relation is the exploitation of the labourer by the capitalist which forms the basis of profit, and this is not apparent in the appearance of that relation as an ordinary exchange relation. It is clear, for instance, that the incomes of the slave-owner and the feudal lord derived from political force and legal custom. But capitalism is characterized by personal freedom and competition on the open market, with determinate prices that all are forced to pay because no one controls them. The capital—labour relation appears as a social relation of exchange, a quantitative exchange of market-determined equivalents: so much labour supplied for so much received as a wage per hour or per piece produced, and so on. It thus appears only as a particular example of the larger category of free and equal exchange relations:

"In so far as the commodity or labour is conceived only as exchange value, and the relation in which the various commodities are brought into connection with one another is conceived as the exchange of these exchange values, as their equation, then the individuals, the subjects between whom this process goes on, are simply and only conceived as exchangers. As far as the formal character is concerned, there is absolutely no distinction between them. . . . Each of the subjects is an exchanger; i.e. each has the same social relation towards the other that the other has towards him. As subjects of exchange, their relation is therefore that of equality. It is impossible to find any trace of distinction. . . . Thus, if one individual accumulates and the other does not, then none does it at the expense of the other . . . if one grows impoverished and the other grows wealthier, then this is of their own free will and does not in any way arise from the economic relation, the economic connection as such, in which they are placed in relation to one another" (*Grundrisse*, pp. 241—7).

This argument is important, not merely in ideological terms but also theoretically: if it is true, it implies that there is no need for a specific political economy of capitalism. The capital—labour relation is of itself not economically significant, and merely reflects a particular initial endow-ment pattern and preference structure. One can use the economic theory applicable to any society, or at least any *exchange* society, to analyse capitalism[20]. Marx was a severe critic of this argument.

There is one major problem with the above argument. This con-cerns the receipt of profit: the receipt by property owners of an income which is unrelated to any social effort or social cost which they incur. How can property owners appropriate such an income in a situation where economic relationships are apparently those of equality based on the exercise of free will, and where exchange is an exchange of equivalents?

Marx systematically reviews economic theory in his search for a correct scientific answer to this question (see Chapters 3 and 4). He finds only hints, not an adequate explanation. Marx himself solves the problem by showing how the appearances which we have discussed actually *conceal* reality. The illusion results from looking at the capital—labour relation as a simple exchange relation[21]. What the capitalist buys from the labourer is not what he appears to buy. The capitalist does not buy the worker's *labour*, but his *labour power*. He does not buy the worker's productive activity, or what the worker creates in a specified period of time. He buys his labour power, the worker's capacity for labour, or control over the worker's creative capacity for a specified time period.

This insight forms the basis of Marx's theory of exploitation. He maintains that the economic forces of capitalist society are such that there is *a difference between the exchange value of labour power and the exchange value of what is produced by its employment (that is, the exchange value of the product); and this difference is the source of the capitalist's profit.*

This can be put in the terms used by Marx in volume I of *Capital*. Assume that the exchange value of commodities is proportionate to their values. On this assumption we can clearly see that the labourer's time is split into two parts: (1) that period during which the magnitude of the value that he creates is equal to the value of the commodities he receives (indirectly) from the capitalist through his wage: this Marx terms "necessary labour time"; (2) that period during which he creates value over and above that received via wages: this Marx terms "surplus labour time". The ratio of surplus to necessary labour time is termed the rate of exploitation.

We can now see that, in capitalism, the value of a commodity is made up of three components. The first part represents the value of the raw materials and machinery used up in its production. The second part is that which replaces the value of the workers' labour power (that is the first part designated above); and the third part is made up of the surplus labour (the second part designated above). From the viewpoint of the circulation of capital, the first component is termed *constant capital* (c), since it "does not in the process of production undergo any quantitative alteration of value" (*Capital* I, 209), but merely passes its value on to what it produces. In contrast the second component is termed *variable capital* (v), because the capitalist's purchase of labour power allows value to expand through the creation of the third component. This third component is *surplus value* (s): "its receipt by the capitalist requires no further extension of his capital" (*ibid*).

The division of capital into constant and variable components is unique to Marx's political economy. The distinction is made neither by classical nor by any other branch of non-Marxian economics, where the only distinction made is that between fixed and circulating capital. Marx also makes use of this latter distinction[22], but argues that the constant–variable dichotomy is much more significant for economic theory. He argues in particular that it is only in these terms that the nature of surplus value can be fully comprehended. Thus this distinction is crucially important in much of Marx's own substantive theory, and forms the basis for his criticism of other schools of political economy (see Chapter 4). It is only the expenditure of capital on "living labour" (v) which leads to the *creation* of value, and hence to the production of surplus value. Means of production — machines and raw materials representing materialized or "stored-up labour" — merely *transfer* the pre-existing value which they have to the commodity. Means of production do not produce new value; they only replace their own value.

All this is fully compatible with Marx's concept of value, which embodies the key social relationship of commodity production. Relations between material objects (for example, the relation of means of production to physical output) are not social relations but technical relations between things. Means of production obviously increase physical output, but they do not create value; they merely pass on their value in the process of production.

Thus surplus value is created in the production process by the performance of unpaid labour. Given the rate of exploitation, its magnitude depends on the quantity of living labour (variable capital) employed, and *not* on the quantity of constant capital that is used. Constant capital does not produce value, and cannot, therefore, produce surplus value. Commodity values, at any level of aggregation, can be written as $c + v + s$. Surplus value forms the source of the capitalist's profit, and this in turn derives from surplus (or unpaid) labour. While there appears to be equality in the labour market, with all labour being paid labour, there is in reality exploitation; some labour is unpaid labour (*Capital* I, 539—40).

During the course of his analysis Marx also undermines another illusion created by the capitalist process of exchange: that the worker disposes of his labour power according to his free preferences. Marx argues that in an important sense he is forced to sell his labour power, and thus his labour is "forced labour". The compulsion acting on the worker is not political, nor legal, nor overtly coercive, as in pre-capitalist societies. It is precisely in a negation that the compulsion lies. It is the producers' *non-ownership* of the means of production which compels them to sell their only asset, labour power, to the capitalist class which monopolizes the means of production[23].

The source of this second illusion again lies in the appearances of exchange, where one sees free contractual agreements with particular capitalists. Only when the analysis penetrates beneath this appearance does it become clear that the workers' "free choice" is exercised within a social structure which compels production within the exploitative capital—labour relation. Free choice in the labour market is therefore limited to choosing which *particular* relation, which *particular* capitalist to work for.

Having undermined these twin illusions created by the appearances — the exchange relations — of capitalist commodity production, Marx's analysis necessarily leads beyond consideration of the process of exchange or circulation:

"The relation of exchange subsisting between capitalist and labourer becomes a mere semblance appertaining to the process of circulation, a mere form, foreign to the real nature of transaction, and only mystifying it . . . what really takes place is this — the capitalist again and again appropriates, without equivalent,"

the surplus labour of the producers *through the process of production*, by putting the labour power which he has purchased to work (*Capital* I, 583).

The change in perspective from the "phenomenal form" to the "hidden substratum" is, therefore, also a process in which the analysis shifts from exchange relations to those of production. The illusions arise from the appearances of the circulation process; the reality is uncovered by the scientific analysis of the production process. Hence Marx condemns any economic theory which limits itself to consideration and rationalization of the appearances of exchange and emphasizes the importance of supply and demand, competition and the market. Marx called such economic theory "vulgar", in the literal sense that it is concerned only with superficial appearances. In Marx's view it was only by probing beneath exchange to production that one could place exchange in a scientific perspective

(*Capital* III, 337). Only thus was it possible to understand how the social relations of material production, as expressed in the concepts of value and surplus value, underlie the familiar concepts of prices, profit, rent, interest, and so on.

The mere consideration of appearances lay at the basis of the whole ideological superstructure of bourgeois society[24]. Marx considered it a prime purpose of his analysis that these ideological distortions be unmasked (see Chapter I, pp. 20—1). It is important to note that his distinction between appearance and reality does *not* refer to a distinction between phenomena that are in principle non-observable and those that are. The concepts of value and surplus value have direct empirical references, and can in principle be measured without difficulty. The appearances which are relevant in this context are the perceptions of certain economic actors and economic theorists; Marx regards them as false because they are not correctly related to the causal connections revealed by scientific analysis. The distinction between appearance and reality is thus a sociological rather than an epistemological question[25].

Marx concludes that social theory requires a political economy of capitalism as opposed simply to a political economy of commodity production. The capital—labour relation cannot be subsumed in the analysis of exchange relations: "Capital is the all dominating economic power of bourgeois society" (*Grundrisse*, p. 107). Hence the theoretical structure of a political economy that seeks to analyse bourgeois society must be based on this relation.

Now this capital—labour relation is itself a relation of a commodity-producing society. Thus the key concepts used for the analysis of commodity production need not be rejected, merely modified. Marx analyses capital in terms of the concept of value, and extends his argument through the use of the concept of surplus value, on which basis he makes the division of capital into its constant and variable components. The capitalist mode of production is thus seen, not simply in terms of the production of value, but above all as the production of surplus value (*Capital* I, 197). Hence Marx asserts the historical specificity of the capitalist's motivation, as we have seen.

2.7 The structure of *Capital*[26]

As we have seen in the last section, Marx argues that the key to the scientific comprehension of capitalism lies in processes which are concealed from the economic actors themselves. Thus once he has uncovered the *reality* beneath the *appearances* it is incumbent upon him to show the connection between the two; to show how appearances can be derived from the underlying reality. Since in developed capitalism profits accrue to the capitalist through the exchange phenomenon of "prices of production" which cannot be assumed to equal values, Marx's theory of value and surplus value must be shown to underlie these relative prices and profits.

Marx's analytical procedure is that which modern theorists have termed the method of "successive approximation". This consists of "moving from the more abstract to the more concrete in a step by step fashion, removing simplifying assumptions at successive stages of the investigation so that theory may take account of and explain an ever wider range of actual phenomena" (Sweezy, 1946, p. 11). For Marx the "abstract" consists of the underlying reality of value and surplus value relationships, which are concealed by the "phenomenal form" of appearances (exchange relationships, prices of production, market phenomena, and so on). Only by successively approximating the latter on the basis of the former through a series of logical steps is it possible scientifically to comprehend the appearances for what they actually are (Grundrisse, pp. 100–1).

Marx's method is not, however, simply one of abstraction and successive approximation. He argues that the logical stages in this successive approximation correspond to historical stages in the development of capitalism. This has been aptly called a "logical-historical method" (Meek, 1967, p. 96). Marx integrates the logical analysis and historical development of capitalism in this way since "in history . . . development as a whole proceeds from the most simple to the most complex relations" (SW I, 513). Both logical and historical development can also be characterized as "dialectical" (ibid, p. 514). Bourgeois society is the most complex of all historical societies. In Marx's view it becomes more complex as it develops, so that its earlier historical forms and the elements of its structure which existed prior to its emergence can be analysed, simultaneously, both logically and historically (Grundrisse, pp. 100–8).

But Marx's logical analysis of capitalism is not simply a mirror image of the actual course of its historical development. He abstracts from certain historical developments, and history is therefore "corrected" by the logical analysis. This abstraction and correction is made "according to the laws furnished by the real course of history itself" (SW I, 514). Since in bourgeois society capital is the "all dominating economic power" (Grundrisse, p. 107), as the determinant of the organic interconnections of that society, the logical analysis of capitalism must hinge on this relation. Thus, although historically some relations of bourgeois society – landed property, merchant and money-lending capital – existed before the development of the capital–labour relation, it is only in terms of the latter that their place in bourgeois society can be understood (Grundrisse, pp. 107–8). Consequently they are brought into the logical-historical analysis towards the end (in Capital III, Parts IV–VI), even though, chronologically, they appear prior to bourgeois society. Thus in Marx's logical-historical methodology it is the logical analysis which dominates the concrete historical development. However, each logical stage is still seen as a historical stage of development, in so far as it is considered in terms of the subject of the analysis, that is, the organic connections of modern bourgeois society (*Grundrisse*, pp. 107–8, 460–1).

This body of theory attempts to show how the relations of material production in systems of commodity production underlie, both qualitatively and quantitatively, the ratios in which commodities exchange and the distributional shares received by the various types of producer and exploiter. In particular Marx is concerned to show how changes that take place in the social relations of production lead to changes in these other factors as the analysis moves through successive logical and historical stages (Meek, 1973, pp. 152–3, 180f). He is especially interested in the analysis of the emergence of the capital–labour relation, and the series of effects which result from its historical and logical development.

His procedure can best be understood in the light of a typology of historical stages outlined in *Grundrisse* (p. 158):

"*Relations of personal dependence . . . are the first social forms, in which human productive capacity develops only to a slight extent and at isolated points. Personal independence founded on objective [sachlicher] dependence is the second great form, in which a system of general social metabolism, of universal relations, of all round needs and universal capacities is formed for the first time. Free individuality, based on the universal development of individuals and on their subordination of their communal, social productivity as their social wealth, is the third stage. The second stage creates the conditions for the third.*"

Here Marx combines the non commodity-producing economic relations of pre-capitalist societies to form the first stage of the typology. Economic relations of *personal* dependence characterize this stage, which thus includes the dominant aspects of pre-capitalist systems of production. The feudal mode of production, for example, was characterized by the dependence of *particular* serfs on *particular* feudal lords.

The commodity-producing economic relations of all societies (capitalist and pre-capitalist) are brought together to form the second stage, which is based on *material* dependence. Here the relations of personal dependence which characterize the first stage are absent, and dependence may be described in terms of economic alienation and fetishism (see above pp. 39–41). The third stage relates to post-capitalist society, and is based on free individuality (see above pp. 7–8).

Marx's presentation of his theory in *Capital* does not start from the first stage of this typology. Instead he concentrates on the second stage, and shows how the third stage emerges from it. Marx has three related reasons for adopting this procedure. First, he wishes to concentrate on commodity production as such because capitalism is the most developed type of this more general form; second, he argues that many of the key features of capitalism historically developed from pre-capitalist forms of commodity production (see, for example, *Grundrisse*, p. 468, and *Capital* I, 334); third, and most important of all, he believes that these aspects of capitalism are logically best developed out of, and in contrast to, pre-capitalist commodity production (see *Grundrisse*, p. 259; *Capital* III, 14, and below pp. 49–52). Thus Marx concentrates on the second stage. In order to present his theory he divides it into a further series of logical-historical stages, starting with a theoretical model of pre-capitalist commodity production and building up from this successive stages of capitalist commodity production.

Marx recognizes that pre-capitalist forms of commodity production are extremely diverse, since they exist in most actual pre-capitalist societies which are predominantly based on relations of personal dependence[27]. Since, however, he is primarily concerned with a logical development of his theory as outlined above, he works from a model of pre-capitalist commodity production which he terms "simple commodity production". This theoretical construct incorporates certain empirical elements of pre-capitalist systems in a pure form. They are never found in historical reality in this form because they are transformed and exaggerated in a certain way; but this is not done arbitrarily. They are transformed and exaggerated in such a way as to make a logically precise and consistent whole, and this is done with the purpose of developing from them successive logical and historical models of capitalism[28].

Simple commodity production is a system in which there are no relations of personal dependence. Each producer owns his own means of production, and there is no wage labour. Furthermore, there are no *classes* as in capitalism. Individual producers work on their own account, and sell their commodities on a competitive market[29]. Marx argues that, in pre-capitalist commodity production, exchange ratios tend to equal—and in the theoretical model of simple commodity production do equal—their labour value ratios (*Capital* III, 177–9). This is because the capital–labour relation is absent, so that the category of profit is also absent. Consequently the category of an "average rate of profit" does not exist. As we shall see below (pp. 103–11), it is the creation of an average rate of profit in developed capitalism, where "capital–labour ratios" differ between industries, which is responsible for the deviation of prices of production from values.

The next stage of the analysis is concerned with the introduction of the capital–labour relation. This stage refers to capitalist commodity production[30]. It is, however, a particular stage in the development of capitalism, both logically and historically. It is a logical stage built on the assumptions that there is no change in the technical basis of production and that competition is confined within industries, so that there is no mobility of capital between industries. Marx suggests that this is how, historically, capitalism emerges. It does not take over all branches of production simultaneously, but sequentially. Capitalist competition, therefore, originally develops *within* each industry. Moreover each industry that is taken over initially continues to rely on the technical basis of handicraft labour bequeathed to it by pre-capitalist commodity production, even though increased labour productivity may result from the extension by the capitalists of the division of (handicraft) labour[31].

This logical stage corresponds to the historical stage which Marx terms the period of "manufacture". Given the assumptions, the only significant difference is the emergence of the capital–labour relation. Thus Marx argues that at this stage commodity exchange ratios again tend to equal – and in the pure model do equal – their labour value ratios. The only effect of the introduction of the capital–labour relation is the emergence of exploitation and surplus value, which forms the basis of the capitalists' profit[32].

The third stage builds on the second by introducing the social relations of free competition between all capitalists in *all* industries. This results in a tendency for profit rates to be equalized in *all* branches of production. When the ratio of constant to variable capital, the "organic composition of capital", differs between industries, this means that commodity exchange ratios differ from their labour value ratios. The profit of each capitalist is calculated as a percentage of his total capital. In consequence it must be true that in equilibrium (where profit rates are equal) the amount of profit received in each industry is no longer equal to the amount of surplus value extracted from the workers in that industry. It is here that Marx seeks to show how values are "transformed" into prices of production, and surplus value into profit on total capital (see Chapters 4 and 5). He argues that although neither values nor surplus values are observed by economic actors, who are only conscious of prices of production and profits, both prices of production and profits are determined by the social relations incorporated in the concepts of value and surplus value.

This third stage in the logical analysis is, Marx suggests, a theoretical model of an actual historical stage in the development of capitalism. He argues that the technical basis of manufacture gives way to that of "modern industry", through an "industrial revolution". Modern industry is characterized by factory production, power machinery and rapid technical change (*Capital* I, 368, 382—3; see also Chapter 6, section 2). What is more, it sees the development of capital mobility between industries and the establishment of the competitive forces making for the equalization of the rate of profit throughout the economy (*Capital* III, chapter x; Meek, 1967, pp. 93—112; Dobb, 1946). It is mainly in terms of this stage that Marx works out his dynamic laws of motion of capitalism: the theories of the industrial reserve army, declining rate of profit, crises and monopolization (*Grundrisse*, pp. 650—1; see also Chapters 4 and 6).

The fourth stage of Marx's logical analysis of capitalism introduces into the model of the third stage the relationships embodied in landed property, mercantile and money-lending capital. Marx's main concern here is to show the reallocation of surplus value which now takes place. Surplus value is no longer completely absorbed by the profits of the industrial capitalist, as in the second and third stages, for it now also provides the source of rent, merchant profit and interest (see Chapters 4 and 5).

Marx recognizes that landed property, merchant and money-lending capital existed prior to the historical development of the capital—labour relation. He argues, however, that they can only be understood theoretically as they operate *within* capitalism in terms of the capital—labour relation and, more specifically, when capitalism in characterized by free capital mobility and competition. This is because the "domination of capital" changes their economic roles within the totality of which they are part:

"Modern landed property . . . cannot be understood . . . [and] cannot exist without capital as its presupposition, and indeed appears historically as a transformation of the preceding historic stage of landed property by capital so as to correspond to capital" (*Grundrisse*, p. 252).

"The other kinds of capital, which appeared before industrial capital amid conditions of social production that have receded into the past or are now succumbing are altered in conformity with it . . . move solely with it as their basis, hence live and die, stand and fall with this basis" (*Capital* II, 57).

This stage in the analysis is therefore a historical stage of development, and not simply a logical stage[33] . This is where Marx's analysis of the theory of value and surplus value ends in *Capital* III. In plans for his future work, however, Marx outlined three major areas of analysis to follow those presented in *Capital*: the State, the international organization of production, and the world market. He never completed this work.

As we have seen, each stage in Marx's analysis is a logical stage in his analysis of capitalism, and also represents a historical stage in the development of capitalism itself. The theory of value and surplus value, then, was essentially a theory which linked the social relations of commodity production, both qualitatively and quantitatively, to ratios of commodity exchange and distribution as they *appear* in successive logical-historical stages of development (Meek, 1967, pp. 154—6). It thus connected the appearance with the underlying reality by showing how values determine prices and surplus value determines profit, rent and interest; and how necessary labour (expressed in value terms) determines the wages of the producers.

This outline probably gives the impression that the contents of *Capital* are more organized than they actually are. A note of qualification is warranted at this point. This section should be seen as making overt what Marx generally left covert. Furthermore, Marx frequently jumps between stages with little warning that he is doing so (see, for example, *Capital* I, 316). Thus, although the structure of *Capital* is correctly represented by the summary given in this section, the reader should bear these reservations in mind when reading *Capital* itself.

This largely accounts for certain misunderstandings concerning Marx's argument. Both Blaug (1968) and Samuelson (1957), for example, see Marx's logical-historical analysis as applying directly, without qualification, to actual historical development. Thus Blaug (1968, p. 238) states that:

"Taken at its face value ... [Marx's argument] is untenable: all societies that have ever approximated the conditions of 'simple commodity production' have been custom ridden. Competition was never allowed to equate skilled labour to so many units of unskilled labour, and hence the ratios at which products exchanged could not have corresponded to quantities of 'socially necessary simple labour' required to produce them. Moreover, what has happened to ... 'primitive accumulation'? Instead of capitalism arising out of colonial plunder, piracy, the slave trade, debasement of currency, and enclosures, we suddenly have an orderly historical process of the transformation of values into prices. The interesting implication of the argument, however, is that it admits that the labour theory of value can be operative when the sociological spectrum of capitalism is missing. ... 'Simple commodity production' is nothing else than Adam Smith's 'early and rude state of society' ... [but, unlike Smith, Marx] actually supposes that a precapitalist economy functions in the same way as a Smithian society of beaver and deer hunters."

On our interpretation of Marx, Blaug's criticisms are absurd. Simple commodity production was a highly abstract model; Marx does not give two different analyses of the actual origins of capitalism; and the labour theory of value was not intended to relate solely to the social relations of capitalism. For Marx all economic phenomena are the product of history. He therefore considered it important to make logical relationships and causes correspond to historical relationships and causes. It is, however, fundamentally incorrect to suggest that Marx confused the two, and substituted the former for the latter. At most Marx can be criticized for failing to state what he was doing sufficiently clearly, and for believing that pre-capitalist commodity exchange ratios more closely approximated labour values than they actually did. This is an empirical question on which neither Marx nor his critics provide evidence.

2.8 Historicism

An important methodological criticism of Marx is put forward by Popper (1961). It is based on the charge that Marx claimed to have uncovered *inevitable* laws of historical development which form the basis for *unconditional* predictions about the future course of events. In this sense Popper classes Marx as a "historicist". There is some factual support for Popper's view. In the preface to *Capital*, for example, Marx writes that:

"Intrinsically, it is not a question of the higher or lower degree of development of the social antagonisms that result from the natural laws of capitalist production. It is a question of these laws themselves, of these tendencies working with iron necessity toward inevitable results" (Capital I, 8–9).

There are many other similar statements in his work.

Such a view, Popper argues, is based on a false view of science. Historicists, he maintains, fail to see that any historical trend must depend on certain historical conditions which may not persist into the future. We cannot know *for certain* that they will persist, and it is therefore false to class anything as *inevitable*. If, for instance, we accept that knowledge affects the course of history, as Marx does, then in order to predict the future with certainty we must know the future development of knowledge. This, Popper observes, is logically impossible, for such knowledge would not then lie in the future. Popper is thus an *indeterminist*, arguing that a scientist can only make conditional predictions. There are no certainties which can be discovered by science.

But this is in fact all that is implied by the structure of Marx's own social and economic theory. A historicist view is "incompatible with Marx's own picture of the working class intervening to put an end to the trends of capitalist development by altering the conditions on which their continuation depends" (MacIntyre, 1969, p. 182). Nor is historicism consistent with

Marx's own analysis of key phases in historical development. Thus Marx insists against a critic that

"The chapter on primitive accumulation [Capital I, Part VIII] does not pretend to do more than trace the path by which, in Western Europe, the capitalist order of economy emerged from the womb of the feudal order of economy. It, therefore, describes the historic movement which by divorcing the producers from their means of production converts them into wage earners . . . while it converts into capitalists those who hold the means of production in possession. . . . My critic . . . feels obliged to metamorphose my historical sketch of the genesis of capitalism in Western Europe into a historico-philosophic theory of the marche generale [general path] imposed by fate upon every people whatever the historic circumstances in which it finds itself. . . . But I beg his pardon" (SC, pp. 312—13).

On the basis of a historical example of economic development Marx now argued that

"events strikingly analogous but taking place in different historic surroundings led to totally different results. By studying each of these forms of evolution separately and then comparing them one can easily find the clue to this phenomenon, but one will never arrive there by the universal passport of a general historico-philosophical theory, the supreme virtue of which consists in being super-historical" (ibid, p. 313; see also *Capital* III, ch. xxvi).

It was precisely the type of philosophical materialism usually attributed to Marx as underlying his "historicist" views that Marx criticized as early as 1845 in "Theses on Feuerbach" (*KM Phil.*, pp. 82f). Here Marx criticizes certain materialist ideas for the passive role which they assign to men in history; for putting forward mechanical ideas of cause and effect whereby human consciousness is regarded as a *reflection* of material reality. On this view something outside of and separate from man determines human activity, and history can therefore be explained in terms of purely objective processes. Historicist views clearly result from this type of materialism. But Marx is strongly critical of such views, and on the contrary asserts the importance of the dialectical *interrelation* between men and their environment. He stresses in particular how man progressively subordinates the material world to his own purposes and needs, in the social process of which are generated new forms of consciousness, new needs and activities (see above pp. 3—6). Marx's materialism, then, incorporates the activism of men which was, he believed, initially but inadequately developed by antimaterialist (idealist) philosophy.

Of course, Marx never says that "anything can happen". Generally he makes reasonably precise predictions which are backed up by scientific analysis; thus the logical structure of these predictions is such that they are conditional. As we have seen, however, he also states that there *are* inevitable trends. It does appear that he is ambiguous on the question of historicism. In consequence he was probably inconsistent in his views on the nature of historical development. "That he is totally committed to what is genuinely fallacious in historicism seems less clear" (MacIntyre, 1969, p. 182).

2.9 Science and values

As we have seen, Marx did not view his scientific work as a purely academic exercise. It was intimately bound up with an ethical critique of capitalist society and with revolutionary action. He therefore rejected the dualism, now current in social science, which asserts that science is one dimension, and values and political action represent another. This close relation which Marx posits between scientific comprehension and the demand for revolution derives directly from his scientific view of the world.

Crucially important here is Marx's belief that human nature is capable of scientific analysis. In particular, he argues that it is possible to state the social conditions which frustrate the realization of human potentialities, and thus to conceive of a social structure which allows individuals fully to develop themselves. He suggests, moreover, that this frustration of social actors prior to the development of such a structure is precisely the motivating force behind dialectical historical change.

In an important sense, therefore, *freedom* is the goal which social actors unconsciously strive to realize, and it is the form of its negation in their actual societies which dictates the direction of historical change. Aron (1965, p. 143) expresses this well when he writes:

"What is incontestably Marx's philosophical heritage is the conviction that the historical movement has a fundamental meaning. A new economic and social regime is not just a new event presenting itself after the fact to the detached curiosity of professional historians; a new economic and social regime is a stage in the evolution of humanity itself."

Post-capitalist society is "the goal, so to speak, of mankind's search for itself" (*ibid*, p. 139).

Marx scales down this abstract conception of the dialectic of social development into support for proletarian revolution. The integration of science and values, however, takes place at the higher level. As a result Marx believes, on the basis of his scientific research, that his own value commitment is, in the sense just outlined, that of all men. And in this sense there are no competing value systems to choose between. Scientific knowledge of the nature of history becomes the guide and impetus to action.

Some of these ideas are expressed in the following passage from *The Holy Family* (p. 176), written in 1845:

"[Materialism is necessarily] connected with communism and socialism. If man draws all his knowledge, sensation, etc. from the world of the senses and the experience gained in it, the empirical world must be arranged so that in it man experiences and gets used to what is really human and that he becomes aware of himself as man. If correctly understood interest is the principle of all morals, man's private interest must be made to coincide with the interest of humanity. If man is unfree in the materialist sense, i.e. is free not through the negative power to avoid this or that, but through the positive power to assert his true individuality, crime must not be punished in the individual, but the antisocial source of crime must be destroyed, and each man must be given social scope for the vital manifestation of his being. If man is shaped by his surroundings, his surroundings must be made human."

Marx's integration of science and values, then, has nothing to do with whether in the abstract it is possible logically to deduce a value proposition from a statement of fact. His position clearly implies that the validity of the integration depends on the scientific validity of his substantive theory. Thus there can be no question of having to accept certain moral propositions in order to understand his interpretation of capitalism; or that, when understood, it logically entails the acceptance of particular values.

2.10 Conclusion

As we have seen, Marx made some clear and unique decisions about the method to be employed in political economy. An important criterion for judging the fruitfulness of his approach is the validity of his theoretical results. Since we have not yet dealt with this question we cannot try to give any comprehensive evaluation, but there are a number of issues on which we can comment even at this early stage.

Marx's method is above all characterized by its sociological basis, and this seems to us to be a most useful approach to the problems of economic theory. The economic world is primarily sociological, which means that the form taken by economic structures and their historical change is largely determined by their *social* properties. In other words, the social relations which make up the elements of the economic structure are the main determinants of those forces which both sustain and change the economic structure of which they are parts. Consequently we accept that the explanation of the economic structure must be sought primarily within the structure itself.

It is impossible completely to isolate economic theory from sociological factors. It is also true that the sociological perspective is not the conscious organizing principle of most orthodox economists. Neoclassical theory analyses economic life on assumptions which, by their very nature, deny the relevance of many crucial sociological factors. We have already illustrated this point (above pp. 31–2); another instance can be seen in the assumption of perfect certainty[34]. With this built into a model there are no expectations, hence no process of forming expectations, no readjustment of goals when they are unrealized, no conscious and unconscious generation of misinformation, and so on. Thus areas of theoretical significance which must necessarily be sociological in focus are excluded as irrelevant. The assumption of perfect certainty is especially inappropriate for the analysis of capitalism, for its economic structure of autonomous competing capitals actually *creates* uncertainty (see Richardson, 1959).

Obviously the assumption of perfect knowledge may be an appropriate simplification in some circumstances. These circumstances are, however, historically specific, and indeed almost the converse of those which characterize capitalism; that is, economic structures which change very slowly over time and are relatively isolated from world history. Thus the validity or otherwise of the assumption of perfect certainty itself depends on sociological considerations.

It is because assumptions like that of perfect certainty, exogenous motivations (see above p. 32), and certain others (see below pp. 251–2) are used, and are used without a sociological analysis of their validity, that economic theory has generally been formulated in terms which imply, or at least do not deny, a universal applicability. We regard this as unjustified by the most obvious facts of economic history. This is so even if we dismiss pre-twentieth-century history as irrelevant and uninteresting. The last fifty years have provided experiences, in the form of different types of totalitarian economic structures, which suggest just how frighteningly wide the limits of economic action are.

This criticism of orthodox theory is, of course, not new. Marxists and many other non-Marxist social scientists have repeatedly taken neoclassical economists to task on this issue. We are now perhaps beginning to see the possitive effects of this criticism with the development of new types of theory which are more sociologically based[35]. However, the historical and continuing predominance of neoclassical patterns of thought in the face of such criticism must rank as a major sociological problem in its own right.

This is not to suggest that Marx's method is completely above criticism. The way in which he conceptualizes reality is certainly open to question. He interrelates concepts to an excessive degree. According to his method of conceptualization, the full definition of a concept requires a complete specification of the totality of which it is a part. Since the totality changes the concepts do not have fixed meanings (see above pp. 33f). This obviously creates ambiguity unless each concept is fully specified each time it is used. More generally, to make concepts "contain" the substantive theory in this way makes exposition of the theory extremely difficult (as Marx himself found).

It would thus appear appropriate to distinguish in logic, as far as possible, the substantive theory from the conceptual scheme in which it is expressed. This requires that we *change* our concepts when reality changes, rather than including in the full definition of those concepts the future development of reality itself.

Furthermore, although one can view the world as an organic unity of elements and still talk in terms of causation (see above pp. 33—4), this is not the case when one uses Marx's method of conceptualization. If one uses Marx's concepts in their full complexity it becomes difficult, if not impossible, to talk in terms of causation, because each concept "includes" or "implies" all the others. The fact that Marx himself does talk in terms of causation means that he does not always use his concepts in their full complex definitions. Instead he often uses them only in their more simple direct or primary definitional sense.

Overall, then, although it is acceptable and useful to view reality in terms of organic interconnection, it appears more useful, contrary to Marx's procedure, to define concepts in terms which as far as possible maintain conceptual independence. A sociological method, and the principle of historical specificity, by no means entail that we should be bound by Marx's method of conceptualization.

At this stage we can also say something about his logical-historical method. We consider this not only as a brilliant expository device, but also as providing a useful means of developing economic theory. In fact it includes the method of comparative statics and comparative dynamics of orthodox theory, and applies it to economics conceived sociologically. Thus in orthodox theory, in order to discover the properties of a model, we alter relevant variables or parameters and then analyse the effects of these changes. In a growth model, for example, one problem is to find out how the level of the capital—output ratio required for steady state growth is affected by changes in the rate of population growth. The logical-historical method in effect carries out a similar procedure with respect to changes in social relationships. In Marx's own theory we saw how he successively introduced the capital—labour relation, the relations of landed property, and other relations into a model where they were previously absent, keeping as far as possible other elements unchanged, so as to discover the implications of their introduction. An extremely good recent example of this procedure can be found in Robinson and Eatwell (1973, pp. 61—88).

The logical-historical method has the further property of helping us to comprehend theoretically the actual process of capitalist or other types of economic development. This is the case if we build models which logically introduce social relations, or change them, in the sequence in which they actually develop historically. In this way processes of logical development in theory construction become very relevant for the analysis of actual historical processes. This method, therefore, has the potentiality of focusing theoretical economics onto the study of economic history.

Thus, irrespective of Marx's own substantive conclusions, there are a number of reasons for regarding his analysis of the sociological character of economic action as a major contribution to economic theory.

Notes

1. The sociology of "moral restraint" never caught on in the theory construction.

2. In the *Poverty of Philosophy*, p. 78, Marx notes that "in principle, there is no exchange of products—but there is the exchange of labour which co-operated in production. The mode of exchange of products depends on the mode of exchange of the productive forces".

3. "Neo-Keynesians" are more inclined to base their analysis on such social relations. This is, however, connected with the study of Marx (for example in the case of Joan Robinson).

4. See Tsuru (1954), Klein (1947), and Meek (1967, pp. 179—95).

5. On this see in particular Chapter 6. Marx's rationale for this assumption lay in the historically specific nature of the capitalist's motivation, and the historically specific form of capitalist competition (see above pp. 29—31).

6. For Marx's analysis of the development of capitalism outside Western Europe see Chapter 7.

7. For a more detailed analysis of primitive accumulation see *Grundrisse*, pp. 497–515; *Capital* I, pt viii; III, chs. xx,xxxvi,xxxvii,xlvii; also Hobsbawm (1964) and Dobb (1946).

8. See also *Grundrisse*, pp. 414, 517, 552, 650–1; *Capital* I, 592.

9. In some cases it involves a choice of the position which they occupy within a given structure. In *GI*, p. 94, for instance, Marx states that it is possible for the "communist consciousness" to "arise among the other classes ... through the contemplation of the situation of the [proletariat]".

10. Although Engels here makes this the definition of "economics" it is clear from the context that he means "economics of commodity production".

11. This is not incompatible with Marx's materialist conception of history, which emphasizes the causal importance of the economic structure. Marx argues that the economic structure determines the other phenomena of bourgeois society, not only as the predominating factor within a mutual interaction of all elements, but also because it determines the reciprocal relations, or patterns of interaction, between the various social elements that make up the whole. On this see, for example, *Grundrisse*, pp. 99–100, and the enlightening, if rather dogmatic, statement in *Capital* I, 81–2.

12. Where there are no unproductive consumers, the relation between producer and consumer is also a relation between producers.

13. There are two aspects to the definition of socially necessary labour. It refers to that labour a) "required to produce an article under normal conditions of production, and with the average degree of skill and intensity prevalent at the time" (*Capital* I, 39); and b) required for producing the commodity in the amount demanded by the market when in long run equilibrium (*ibid.*, I, 107). It should also be noted that Marx uses the term "value" to refer to the commodity conceived *qualitatively* as the product of human labour, and *quantitatively* to refer to the "magnitude of value" (*ibid.*, I, 53).

14. Nicolaus (1973, p. 38) is quite wrong to assert that the category "commodity" is historically specific to capitalist production alone. On this point see also above pp. 45f.

15. For a precise definition of this term, see above p. 42.

16. The capitalist—labourer relation is *not* entailed by the production of commodities. It arises from a long process of historical development, referred to by Marx as "primitive accumulation" (see above pp. 27—9).

17. Marx draws this distinction in various ways: for example, essence—appearance, content—form, hidden substratum—phenomenal form.

18. He notes that "all science would be superfluous if the outward appearance and the essence of things coincided" (*Capital* III, 817).

19. "[That] in their appearance things often represent themselves in inverted form is pretty well known in every science except political economy" (*Capital* I, 537; see also *ibid.*, 4, 10, and 21).

20. This is the position of neoclassical economics; see for example Robbins (1946, pp. 19—20).

21. A more rigorous analysis of what follows here is given in Chapter 4.

22. The formal difference between the two typologies concerns the classification of raw materials. All variable capital is also circulating capital, and all fixed capital is constant capital. The raw material component of circulating capital, however, is constant capital.

23. Marx discusses the origins of this situation in his analysis of primitive accumulation (above, pp. 27—9).

24. Marx considered vulgar economy to be only one aspect of this superstructure; parallel distortions are found in politics, legal theory, religion, philosophy, and so on.

25. We return to this point later (pp. 160f) in our discussion of certain criticisms of the labour theory of value.

26. On this aspect of Marx's method see Meek (1967, pp. 93—112).

27. See, for example, *Grundrisse*, pp. 159, 204, 252, 673—4, 882; *Capital* I, 169—70, 359, 763f; II, 113; III, 174—7, 325, 880.

28. Readers familiar with work of Max Weber will see that Marx's procedure here comes very close to the construction of an "ideal type". Marx develops it from pre-capitalist forms of commodity production where exchange has become a *regularized* economic activity.

29. The pre-capitalist society which most closely approximates to Marx's theoretical model of simple commodity production is, he argues, colonial America (see above p. 37).

30. As we have seen (above pp. 27–9), Marx argues that the actual emergence of the capital–labour relation is the product of a long historical process of primitive accumulation. However, he initially introduces the capital–labour relation without any historical analysis. It is only at the end of *Capital* I that he deals with primitive accumulation, which is the actual historical counterpart to his logical development from simple commodity production to the first stage of capitalism (see, for example, *Capital* I, 623–4).

31. On this initial stage of capitalism see *Grundrisse*, pp. 510–12, 586–7, 725, 729–30; *Capital* I, 184, 248, 310, 314–15, 322, 338–9, 364, 368, 459; Meek (1967, pp. 93–112); Dobb (1946).

32. It is quite wrong to maintain, as does for example Blaug (1968, p. 279), that Marx assumes identical organic compositions in all industries throughout *Capital* I. Marx never makes such an assumption explicitly, nor is it implicit (see, for example, *Grundrisse*, p. 761, and *Capital* I, 306, 309, 405, where this is very clear).

33. The effect of the introduction of landed property, merchant and money-lending capital on the divergence of values from prices of production, and on the dynamic laws of motion of capitalism, were regarded by Marx as secondary. Thus there is little systematic exposition of their impact in *Capital*.

34. Blaug (1968, p. 471) rightly notes that the "fundamental theorems" of neoclassical analysis rest on this assumption.

35. We refer here primarily to developments which have often been called "neo-Keynesian" and "neo-Ricardian"; see, for example, Nell (1967 and 1972).

3

Classical political economy

3.1 Introduction

Marx was as well versed in the literature of economics as any of his
contemporaries. The scope of his reading is witnessed by frequent
references to earlier works, some famous and many obscure, throughout
his economic writings; and by his detailed dissection of those of his
predecessors whom he deemed to be of greatest importance in the three
volumes of *Theories of Surplus Value*. Marx's own economic theory, and
the model of capitalism from which this was derived, reflect a continuous
critique of classical political economy.

He was not unselective in his choice of adversaries. He distinguished
very clearly between that he termed the "scientific" and the "vulgar"
economists. The former correspond to classical political economy: a strand
of thought originating in France with Boisguillebert and in Britain with
Petty, and culminating in the work of Adam Smith and David Ricardo[1].
The latter were seen by Marx as essentially a product of heightened class
tension after 1830, and as mere apologists for capitalism; neither he nor
Engels paid very much attention to the developments in economic theory
which took place after this date[2].

For Marx, then, a decisive break in the history of economic thought
occurred in the 1830s, a decade in which methodological rigour and
scientific honesty, characteristic of classical political economy, began to
succumb to a superficial and trivial apologetic. Though the culmination of
this trend may be seen in the so-called "marginalist revolution" of the
1870s, Marx placed the fundamental watershed some forty years
earlier[3]. Most modern economists would agree with Schumpeter (1954)
that the rise of the marginal utility doctrine in the 1870s was the major
climacteric in the history of nineteenth-century economic thought, and

that it represented a genuine scientific advance. Dissenting voices have never been entirely absent, and are beginning to increase in number and vociferousness[4]. We shall see later that the disintegration of neoclassical capital theory has led to a substantial revival of interest in classical political economy, and especially in Ricardo as representing the peak of its achievement.

In any case, it is not our intention here to provide a full account of the origins, achievements and demise of classical political economy. Instead we pose two more modest questions: how did Marx himself view classical political economy? and how strong was its influence on him? Moreover, our discussion is centred on Ricardo, as the commanding figure of the school: more penetrating and consistent as an abstract theorist than, for example, Adam Smith[5].

In looking at classical economics through Marx's eyes we are on contentious, if not dangerous ground. Many neoclassical writers have attempted to rescue classical political economy, and above all Ricardo, from such a Marxian interpretation, arguing instead that their aims, methods and analysis were seriously misunderstood by Marx, and were in essence akin to those of modern orthodox economics. The classical example of this piece of revisionism is that of Marshall (1890, Appendix I), itself heavily influenced by Mill (1848); Dobb (1973, ch. 5), emphasizes the lasting significance of Mill's highly misleading interpretation of Ricardo.

The risk is, in our view, well worth taking. Firstly, whatever the *merits* of Marx's interpretation of classical political economy, we intend to show that this interpretation played a major role in determining the structure and content of his own economic theory. Even if mistaken, it cannot be glossed over or ignored. Secondly, however, we shall argue that Marx's interpretation is substantially correct; as a corollary, we suggest that Marx's criticisms of classical economics are, in the main, valid and important ones[6]. Thirdly, we wish to correct what we believe to be a mistaken emphasis in some recent work, both "pro-" and "anti-Marx" in nature, which exaggerates the similarities and minimizes the differences between Marx and classical political economy[7]. The balance can best be restored by examining Marx's own view of his relation to classical economics.

This relationship can be seen most clearly in terms of three issues: the methodologies which they employed; the fundamental problems which they set themselves; and the answers which they supplied to these basic problems. The first two aspects refer to what Schumpeter (1954, pp. 41–2) described as the "vision" of society, and the role of economic theory within it, which economists hold. The third refers to the theoretical apparatus used to develop and implement this vision, and to solve these fundamental economic problems.

Most non-Marxian accounts of the relationship between Marx and classical political economy restrict their scope to this latter technical aspect. It will be clear from what we have said in Chapters 1 and 2 about the distinctive nature and overriding importance of Marx's methodology that such a treatment is inevitably inadequate. Marx studied classical economics so seriously precisely because he saw it as the first attempt, even if it was only an implicit one, to ground the study of economics in the specific social relations of capitalism. He argued that only in this way, and only if it pursued this essential methodological requirement rigorously, could the technical analysis of classical political economy claim either relevance or logical validity.

Marx's view of society differed markedly from even the more sophisticated versions presented by the classical economists. The three-class model of capitalist society — landlords, capitalists and workers — originating with Smith and preserved intact by Ricardo, becomes in Marx, by an explicit act of abstraction (above, pp. 46–7) a simple polarization between capitalists and workers. The landlords are reduced, in effect, to minor parasitic appendages of the capitalists. Class conflict, absent from Smith except very obliquely[8], was of course fundamental to Marx. But it was a different type of conflict from that postulated by Ricardo, for whom industrial struggle between capitalist employers and their workers played a subsidiary role in a more basic conflict between the landlords and the rest of society. Agriculture is never for Marx the prime mover in the economy, as it is for Ricardo. Indeed, the whole of the first two volumes of *Capital*, and much of the third volume, explicitly abstract from "landed property".

Nor is Marx's view of capitalist society different from that of classical political economy only because of his insistence on the importance of secondary rather than primary industry. He distinguishes between two stages in the development of secondary industry (*Capital* I, 364–8 and 486–8; see also Chapters 2, pp. 49–50 and 6, pp. 181–2). The first, which he terms "manufacture", is based on traditional skills, without significant advances in the mechanization of production, but with the division of labour developed to a higher degree than in the feudal economy. But "handicraft skill is still the foundation of manufacture" (*Capital* I, 367). The second stage is that of "modern industry", in which production is organized in factories, and mechanization develops rapidly. Industrial concentration, rapid technical progress and the formation of the industrial reserve army (*ibid.*, I, 487)[9] are all features of this second stage: "Modern Industry never looks upon and treats the existing form of a process as final. The technical basis of that industry is therefore revolutionary, while all earlier modes of production were essentially conservative" (*ibid*, I, 486). Marx argues that classical political economy concentrates exclusively on the earlier, "manufacture" stage, and ignores "modern industry". This has important consequences for the analysis of, for example, economic crises, which cannot be fully understood without an understanding of "modern industry" (see below, pp. 210f).

Despite these differences Marx respected classical political economy for having pioneered what he considered to be a vital methodological breakthrough: the establishment of the principle of historical specificity as the linchpin of economic theory[10]. His praise was, however, qualified, as may be seen in an early assessment of the Ricardian theory of value[11]:

"Ricardo's investigations are concerned exclusively with the magnitude of value, and regarding this he is at least aware that the operation of the law depends on definite historical pre-conditions. He says that the determination of value by labour-time applies to 'such commodities only as can be increased in quantity by the exertion of human industry, and on the production of which competition operates without restraint'. This in fact means that the full development of the law presupposes a society in which large-scale industrial production and free competition obtain, in other words, modern bourgeois society. For the rest, the bourgeois form of labour is regarded by Ricardo as the eternal natural form of social labour. Ricardo's primitive fisherman and primitive hunter are from the outset owners of commodities who exchange their fish and game in proportion to the labour-time which is materialized in these exchange-values. On this occasion he slips into the anachronism of allowing the primitive fisherman and hunter to calculate the value of their implements in accordance with the annuity tables used on the London Stock Exchange in 1817" (*Critique*, p. 60).

Thus Marx criticized even Ricardo, "who gave to classical political economy its final shape" (*Critique*, p. 61), for his failure to apply his own methodological principles consistently. Ricardo's tendency to see capitalism as an "eternal, ahistorical" form of social production, and hence wage-labour as "the eternal natural form of social labour", had serious consequences for his theoretical work. It led him to fall back on universal "laws of nature" to explain phenomena which, in Marx's view, resulted from the specific organisation of capitalist production, and were hence as transient as capitalism itself. This is especially clear, as we shall argue in Chapter 4 (esp. pp. 96—7; 118—9), in Ricardo's theory of wages and in his account of the falling rate of profit.

In terms of the fundamental problem facing political economy, however, Marx was at one with the classical economists. For both the critical issue was to account for the origins, magnitude and historical trend of what Marx was to term surplus value: the difference, *in value terms*, between social input and social output. Ricardo's famous statement of the objects of political economy, made in a letter to Malthus in 1820, is relevant here:

"Political Economy you think is an enquiry into the nature and causes of wealth—I think it should rather be called an enquiry into the laws which determine the division of the produce of industry amongst the classes who concur in its formation. No law can be laid down respecting quantity, but a tolerably correct one can be laid down respecting proportions. Every day I am more satisfied that the former enquiry is vain and delusive, and the latter the only true objects of the science"(Ricardo, 1819–21, pp. 278–9).

This question was vital to classical political economy for two reasons. Firstly, the distribution of the social product obviously plays a major role in the class structure of society, and is thus a significant problem in its own right. Secondly, both the classical economists and Marx were deeply interested in "the laws of motion of capitalist society" (*Capital* I, 10, from the Preface to the first German edition, 1867), and saw the property share in total income as the basic determinant of the pace of capital accumulation[12].

The content of classical political economy, and in large part also of Marx's economic theory, emerged from these underlying problems. If we are dealing with a single-commodity world, in which only (say) corn is produced, the measurement of the property share in total output is very simple: total profits are paid in corn, and can easily be calculated as a proportion of the total net output of corn. Once a variety of different commodities are produced the problem is much more complicated, since the *values* of the various commodities which make up total output must now be calculated. A theory of value, which was superfluous when only one commodity was produced, is now an urgent necessity.

Classical political economy, and Marx, attempted to derive a measure of the value of commodities which would remain constant when distributive shares changed. If this criterion were not met, they argued, it would be impossible to provide a satisfactory analysis of changes in income distribution: a shift in distribution would lead to a change in the standard of value, hence to a change in the value of total output, and thus to a further change in distributive shares[13]. This problem, as we shall see below (p. 149), has been found to arise in the neoclassical theory of value. The classical labour theory of value was derived in order to avoid it.

Thus the scope of Marx's economic theory very largely mirrors that of classical political economy, in an attempt to produce a logically consistent and empirically satisfactory labour theory of value, and to build a model of growth on it. Marx argued that these two problems, first posed by classical economics, had not been solved. His dialectical critique of the methodology and theoretical analysis of classical political economy was the means by which he hoped to find the solutions.

3.2 The classical theory of value

There is very little agreement among modern historians of economic thought about the theory of value in classical political economy. At one extreme, it is possible to argue, as in effect does Marshall (1890), that the labour theory of value was for the most part an irrelevance, and that Ricardo's main achievement in the *Principles* was to abandon it. At the other extreme, many share Marx's view of classical economics, arguing that its entire history represents progress towards an acceptable and internally consistent labour theory of value, which in turn provided the foundations for the rest of classical economic theory.

As already suggested, two related problems formed the core of the classical theory of value. One concerned the historical and analytical origins of non-wage incomes in the capitalist mode of production, or (in Marx's terminology) of surplus value. The other dealt with the perfection of a measure of value in terms of which both social output and the surplus product could be quantified. Our statement of the issues is itself in Marxian terms. In attempting to justify Marx's interpretation of the classical labour theory of value, we analyse first the origins of the theory in the period preceeding the publication of the *Wealth of Nations*[14]; secondly the vacillations of Adam Smith; and finally the refinement of Smith's arguments undertaken by Ricardo, and the latter's alleged abandonment of the labour theory of value in his *Principles*. We conclude with a brief discussion of the underlying rationale of the classical labour theory of value, in terms of the purpose which it was intended by its authors to serve.

From the viewpoint of the twentieth century, pre-Smithian economics can easily appear as the metaphysical fantasies of a bygone age. It is difficult to take seriously the Mercantilists, who believed that the way to riches lay through the accumulation of vast stores of bullion; or the Physiocrats, who regarded only agriculture as productive, and saw industry as an encumbrance. Yet both can be seen as intelligible products of their time. More important, both schools of thought were engaged in the same quest which, we have argued, lay at the heart of classical political economy: the analysis of the origins and magnitude of surplus value.

The most dynamic and profitable sector of the late seventeenth- and early eighteenth-century British economy was its foreign trading sector. Trade and colonization offered the largest and the quickest profits, and provided the major stimulus to economic growth. Industrial capital was very much a junior partner, and the factory system was almost completely unknown. At the same time, Britain was even then much less an agricultural nation than any of her international rivals, and the economic theory of Mercantilism reflected very closely the problems and interests of the growing class of commercial capitalists.

The fetishist stress on bullion found in Mercantilism indicates the deeply felt problems of balance of payments crises and currency shortages which haunted the British economy at the time. But the economy was above all a growing one, in which an investible surplus was being generated at an increasing pace and invested most notably in the commercial and trading sector. It was thus entirely understandable, if fundamentally mistaken, for the Mercantilists to locate the source of the social surplus in this sector.

At the same time they recognized the essential importance of labour in the economy, and came to view the value of commodities as determined by the cost of the labour embodied in them[15]. Such a "wage-cost" theory of value was obviously very difficult to reconcile with the existence of non-wage incomes. If the value of a commodity depended solely on the labour costs incurred in its production, it could not both be sold at its value *and* yield incomes to the capitalists responsible for its production. How, then, could the existence of profit, rent and interest — especially the first — be reconciled with such a crude labour theory of value? In essence, as we shall see in several places below, this is the most fundamental problem to be confronted by the adherents of a labour theory of value, and one which Marx found to be unsolved even by the most advanced classical economists.

The Mercantilists' answer to this question was derived from what we have suggested were the fundamental characteristics of the economy which they observed. They argued that profit arose, not from the production process, but in the act of exchange. Commodities were sold at prices higher than their labour values, and the difference represented what Marx was later to term surplus value. As we shall see, both the Physiocrats and the later English classical economists rejected this view, but it recurred well into the nineteenth century. Marx was later to take both Proudhon and Malthus to task for similar errors[16].

The issues are raised very clearly in Marx's criticism of Destutt de Tracy:

> *"[Capitalist] A may be clever enough to get the advantage of B or C without their being able to retaliate. A sells wine worth £40 to B, and obtains from him in exchange corn to the value of £50. A has converted his £40 into £50, has made more money out of less, and has converted his commodities into capital. Let us examine this a little more closely. Before the exchange we had £40 worth of wine in the hands of A, and £50 worth of corn in the hands of B, a total value of £90. The value in circulation has not increased by one iota, it is only distributed differently between A and B. What is a loss of value to B is surplus-value to A; what is 'minus' to one is 'plus' to the other. The same change would have taken place, if A, without the formality of an exchange, had directly stolen the £10 from B. The sum of values in circulation can clearly not be augmented by any change in their distribution, any more than the quantity of the precious metals in a country by a Jew selling a Queen Anne's farthing for a guinea. The capitalist class as a whole, in any country, cannot overreach themselves.*
>
> *Turn and twist then as we may, the fact remains unaltered. If equivalents are exchanged, no surplus value results, and if non-equivalents are exchanged, still no surplus value. Circulation, or the exchange of commodities, begets no value"* (Capital I, pp. 162–3)[17].

Marx's point here is a very simple one. It is impossible for everyone to cheat everyone else, and for everyone to make a net gain in the process. One man's gain is another's loss, and on balance they must cancel out. Capitalists may get more than the value of their commodities when they sell them but in aggregate they will have to pay just as much more for those commodities which they buy.

There are three ways out of this dilemma. One was taken by the Mercantilists who, while accepting the validity of this argument for *internal* trade, pointed out that it does not apply to international commerce. It is entirely possible for one nation to enrich itself by systematically cheating its trading "partners", and this indeed forms at least one strand of the Marxian and post-Marxian theory of imperialism. Thus the Mercantilists came to view *foreign* trade as the only source of surplus value and thus of economic growth. Protection, rigid control over the economic activities of the colonies, and a desire for balance of payments surpluses follow as necessary corollaries.

The alternative solutions both reject this approach. Although capitalism is not in practice found in the context of a closed economy, there is no obvious *logical* reason why non-wage incomes should be impossible without foreign trade. If surplus value arose in the process of production, and was merely "realized" in the act of exchange[18], there would be no need to resort to as narrow a view of its origins as did the Mercantilists. Moreover, it might then be possible to reconcile the existence of property incomes with adherence to a labour theory of value *and* to the view that commodities were in general sold at, rather than above, their labour values.

Smith and Ricardo, followed by Marx, develop this line of reasoning to the point where they see industrial profit as resulting from industrial production. But the third form of escape from the Mercantilist dilemma, that of the Physiocrats, represents an intermediate position of considerable interest. For the Physiocrats, surplus value is derived from *agricultural* production. Industrial profit is then explained in a manner similar to that of the Mercantilists, by the cheating of the farmers by the industrial capitalists.

To understand the way in which the Physiocrats arrived at the conclusion that agriculture was the only form of productive activity, we must again refer to the economic climate in which they wrote. Late eighteenth-century France was a predominantly agricultural nation, with a relatively small commercial sector, small, low profit and largely handicraft manufacturing industries, and a large parasitic bureaucracy prone to subsidizing and protecting the few large industrial monopolies. Now the surplus product in agriculture was directly visible as a *physical* surplus of corn output (the harvest) over corn input (seed and food for farm workers). It is easy to understand how agriculture came to be viewed as the only productive sector of the economy. Marx cites a curiously convincing summary of the Physiocrats' argument:

"Give the cook a measure of peas, with which he is to prepare your dinner; he will put them on the table for you well cooked and well dished up, but in the same quantity as he was given, but on the other hand give the same quantity to the gardener for him to put into the ground; he will return to you, when the right time has come, at least fourfold the quantity that he had been given. This is the true and only production" (TSV I, 60)[19].

Industry is thus seen as "sterile", in the sense that it could not produce a surplus like agriculture, but merely "cook" the raw materials supplied by agricultural activity.

Any surplus accruing to industry must thus be the result of the sale of manufactured goods to the farmers at prices higher than their values, that is, the result of the process of cheating we have already discussed. On the assumptions made by the Physiocrats, industrial profit represented a deduction from the surplus value available for productive use in agriculture. Hence, for example, their insistence on laissez-faire, which amounted less to a charter of freedom for industrial capital (as it was intended by, for example, Adam Smith) than to a demand for the abolition of state protection for an essentially parasitic monopoly manufacturing sector.

But this was not a theoretical apparatus likely to survive the emergence of a large, highly competitive and obviously dynamic industrial capitalism. It was clearly his perception of the beginnings of the industrial revolution which led Adam Smith to regard industry as being as productive as agriculture, and to extend the production of surplus value "to all spheres of social labour" (*TSV* I, 85). It then became possible to analyse the origins of industrial profit, which both classical political economy and Marx saw as the most important form taken by surplus value, in the context of a theory of value which did not require manufactured commodities to be sold (in aggregate) at prices greater than their values in order for any profit to result.

Marx made explicit what Smith's critique of the Physiocrats had left implicit. In historical terms, he observed that their model of society was an uneasy mixture of feudalism and capitalism (*TSV* I, 50), and in analytical terms he argued that they were mistaken in the only grounds which they could consistently use to justify the unique position attributed to agriculture. This, Marx argued, was the identification of surplus *value* with surplus *product*, seeing the former as a simple physical surplus of output over input. Such a view was perhaps tenable in a purely agricultural society, when both inputs and outputs consisted of the same commodity (for example, corn in the case quoted above). But what meaning did it have in an advanced industrial economy, where a range of different commodities enter into production and the output is quite distinct in its physical characteristics from any one of them?

Marx thus criticized the Physiocrats for failing to distinguish between "riches" and "value". Physical output, he pointed out, is a quite separate concept from the value of that output. This confusion led the Physiocrats to attribute the social surplus to the "bounty of nature", and thus to ignore the social relations which give rise, in capitalist economies, to property incomes (*TSV* I, 52). They were led to this error by their insistence that free competition would completely eliminate industrial profit, with its implication that the continued existence of agricultural profit, and rent, required the surplus product to be viewed as a "gift of nature". We shall see below that for both Ricardo and Marx competition played a much less important role.

In the last resort, the Physiocrats had no theory of industrial profit. What, then, had they achieved? As Marx points out, "the Physiocrats transferred the inquiry into the origins of surplus value from the sphere of circulation into the sphere of direct production, and thereby laid the foundation for the analysis of capitalist production" (*TSV* I, 45). Once it was recognized that property incomes arose in the production process, it was no longer necessary to argue that commodities had to sell at prices higher than their (labour) values in order for profit to be possible. The demolition of this aspect of Mercantilism was a necessary condition for the derivation of a viable labour theory of value.

The distinction between productive and unproductive activity, which lay at the heart of Physiocratic theory, also exists in classical and Marxian theory. If surplus value originates in production rather than in exchange, it is vital to be clear as to what exactly constitutes "production". If trading or money-lending is to be regarded as "productive", then all the problems arising from Mercantilist theory must be encountered all over again. It is to the Physiocrats' credit that they did distinguish clearly, albeit wrongly, between "productive labour" (in agriculture), and "unproductive labour" (in all other forms of economic activity). Such a distinction has almost disappeared from orthodox economic theory, which in effect defines as productive any activity which is paid for.

Some of the essential groundwork for the analysis of surplus value, and for the derivation of the labour theory of value, had thus been done by the Physiocrats. They had raised some of the most significant theoretical problems later to be faced by classical political economy, and by Marx.

How far was Adam Smith able to build on these foundations? As we have seen, Smith accepted the Physiocrats' argument that surplus value arises in production rather than in exchange, and thus cannot be explained in terms of the general sale of commodities at prices higher than their values. Moreover, he went beyond the Physiocrats in showing that the production of surplus value was not restricted to agriculture; indeed, industry plays the major role in his treatment of productive and unproductive labour. As Marx observed, Smith attributed surplus value to the activity of social labour, and not to the bounty of nature (*TSV* I, 85). As Meek has emphasized, Smith is the first economist to base a labour theory of value explicitly on a particular analysis of the nature of society (Meek, 1973, ch. 2).

This he does, articulating what is perhaps the first clear labour theory of value, in his famous example of the deer and the beavers:

"*In that early and rude state of society which precedes both the accumulation of stock and the appropriation of land, the proportion between the quantities of labour necessary for acquiring different objects seems to be the only circumstance which can afford any rule for exchanging them for one another. If among a nation of hunters, for example, it usually costs twice the labour to kill a beaver which it does to kill a deer, one beaver should naturally exchange for or be worth two deer. It is natural that what is usually the produce of two days or two hours labour, should be worth double of what is usually the produce of one day's or one hour's labour"* (Smith, 1776, p. 53).

Smith proceeds to locate the origins of property incomes in the development of capitalism:

"As soon as stock has accumulated in the hands of particular persons, some of them will naturally employ it in setting to work industrious people, whom they will supply with materials and subsistence, in order to make a profit by the sale of their work, or by what their labour adds to the value of the materials. In exchanging the complete manufacture either for money, for labour, or for other goods, over and above what may be sufficient to pay the price of the materials and the wages of the workmen, something must be given for the profits of the undertaker of the work, who hazards his stock in this adventure. The value which the workmen add to the materials, therefore, resolves itself in this case into two parts, of which the one pays their wages, the other the profits of their employer upon the whole stock of materials and wages which he advanced . . . in this state of things, the whole produce of labour does not always belong to the labourer. He must in most cases share it with the owner of the stock which employs him" (ibid., pp. 54—5).

Here Smith begins by analysing a model of simple commodity production, in which production is carried on for exchange rather than to satisfy the personal needs of the producer himself, but in which capitalist class relations are absent. In this case not only does all income accrue to the producers, but the ratios at which the different commodities exchange depend solely on the ratios of labour embodied in them, or required for their production. In this "early and rude state of society", profit and rent do not exist; the labour theory of value applies without modification.

Smith then considers the consequences of the emergence of capitalist class relations within such a society. Ownership of the means of subsistence, and of the raw materials required, passes from the hands of the producers themselves into the possession of a minority of private individuals. In Marx's terminology, this class monopoly of the means of production[20] allows the emergence of surplus value. A separate category of income, unknown in simple commodity production, springs into being: the capitalists now obtain *profit* from their capital. Marx regarded this analysis as a major theoretical advance: "thereby", he wrote, "he has recognized the true origin of surplus value" (*TSV* I, 80).

In the process, however, Smith is driven to reject the labour theory of value as inapplicable to capitalism. The two sentences following on from the passage just quoted make this very clear:

"Neither is the quantity of labour commonly employed in acquiring or producing any commodity, the only circumstance which can regulate the quantity which it ought commonly to purchase, command or exchange for. An additional quantity, it is evident, must be due for the profits of the stock which advanced the wages and furnished the materials of that labour" (Smith, 1776, p. 55).

A similar problem is posed with the emergence of rent once land becomes privately owned. Smith's justly famous conclusion is obviously inconsistent with the labour theory of value which he had developed in the context of simple commodity production:

"The real value of all the component parts of price, it must be observed, is measured by the quantity of labour which they can, each of them, purchase or command. Labour measures the value, not only of that part of price which resolves itself into labour, but of that which resolves itself into rent, and of that which resolves itself into profit. In every society the price of every commodity finally resolves itself into some one or other, or all of those three parts; and in every improved society, all the three enter more or less, as component parts, into the price of the far greater part of commodities" (ibid., p. 56).

Thus Smith argues that the very existence of property incomes invalidates the labour theory of value. The value of the labour *embodied* in a commodity is now less than the value of the labour which it can *command* (that is, for which it can be exchanged). Suppose that two hours of labour are necessary to "produce" a beaver, and that the value of an hour of labour – the hourly wage – is 50p. The "labour-embodied" value of a beaver is then £1. The capitalist's profit is 25p per beaver, so that it sells for £1.25. But at the prevailing wage £1.25 will buy 2½ hours labour, so that "labour-commanded" exceeds "labour-embodied".

This is, in effect, the very same problem which confronted the Mercantilists. They attempted to solve it by retaining a primitive labour theory of value, and arguing that commodities in general sell at prices in excess of their values. Smith, as we have already seen, rejects this position and is therefore forced to reject the labour theory of value itself[21]. He replaces it with what is in essence a rather naïve cost-of-production theory. Rent and profit are viewed as costs of production, on a par with wages, and form part of the value of commodities. Commodities can thus be sold at their values, *and* yield profit to the capitalist and rent to the landlord;

but these values no longer depend solely on the quantity of labour required to produce them. Labour now figures only as one constituent part of the "costs of production", and as a *measure* of value; it is no longer the sole *source* of value.

The change is a major one. Property incomes, instead of being *derived from* the labour used to produce commodities, are seen as costs additional to it. Instead of resulting from the value of the commodity, which is defined in terms of embodied labour alone, they become a *component part* of that value. Sraffa (1951, p. xxxv) aptly describes Smith's conclusion as an "adding-up theory of value". Smith thus arrived at something similar to the Marshallian theory of long-run equilibrium price, and quite alien to the labour theory of value. It is evident that the reconciliation of the existence of property incomes (and thus of capitalism itself) with the labour theory, is really the crucial problem in classical value theory. Ricardo's efforts to solve this problem form the next stage in the development of that theory.

Marx distinguishes between "the esoteric and the exoteric part of [Smith's] work" (*TSV* II, 166; see also *Capital* II, 223, 382), and in particular emphasizes a theme which runs through all his work on the theory of value: the low level of abstraction (and therefore of theoretical significance) to be attributed to the operation of competition:

"Smith himself moves with great naivety in a perpetual contradiction. On the one hand he traces the intrinsic connection between economic categories or the obscure structure of the bourgeois economic system. On the other, he simultaneously sets forth the connection as it appears in the phenomena of competition and thus as it presents itself to the unscientific observer just as to him who is actually involved and interested in the process of bourgeois production. One of these conceptions fathoms the inner connection, the physiology, so to speak, of the bourgeois system, whereas the other takes the external phenomena of life, as they seem and appear and merely describes, catalogues, recounts and arranges them under formal definitions. With Smith both these methods of approach not only merrily run alongside one another, but also intermingle and constantly contradict one another" (*TSV* II, 165).

At one moment Smith is developing a theory of value, and also of surplus value, which has pretensions to scientific rigour and is therefore not at all obvious to the casual observer. The next moment he is merely reflecting the appearance, to such an observer, that the value of a commodity is simply the sum of its "cost-of-production". Since the capitalist pays wages and rent, and makes a profit, he naturally assumes that the value of his commodity is simply the sum of these costs. Hence the emphasis, in neoclassical price theory and as early as Smith's "exoteric" moments, on the importance of the process of exchange and of market competition. Marx's methodological conclusions on the relationship between appearance and reality in economic theory (above, pp. 39–45) are applied ruthlessly in his criticism of Adam Smith.

Ricardo proves to be a much more consistent abstract theorist. He did share with Smith certain basic preconceptions. He preserved the classical view that surplus value originates in production, and was far more consistent than Smith in relegating competition to a subsidiary role. Smith was praised in the *Principles* (Ricardo, 1821, p. 92) for limiting the role of competition to that of equalizing the market prices of commodities with their "natural prices" (by which Ricardo meant values) when the two happen to diverge as a result of "accidental causes". While Ricardo invariably took this position, and dismissed competition forthwith, this is true of Smith only in his more "esoteric" moments[22]. Ricardo was equally quick to see the basic circularity in any cost-of-production theory of value, a circularity exposed by Marx's cogent criticism:

"[Smith] makes the exchange-value of labour the measure for the value of commodities. In fact, he makes wages the measure; for wages are equal to the quantity of commodities bought with a definite quantity of living labour, or the quantity of labour that can be bought by a definite quantity of commodities. The value of labour, or rather of labour-power, changes, like that of any other commodity, and is in no way specifically different from the value of other commodities. Here value is made the measuring rod and the basis for the explanation of value – so we have a vicious circle"(TSV I, 70–1).

Costs of production are *themselves* values, and no explanation of value is provided by any cost-of-production theory.

Ricardo criticizes Smith in similar terms, and thus attacks that part of *The Wealth of Nations* where Smith is most vulnerable: the connection between value and distribution, the logical hiatus in the classical theory of value. Ricardo's aim was to reconcile the existence of property incomes in a capitalist society with a logically valid labour theory of value.

One of the fundamental propositions of the Ricardian system is relevant here. This is the argument that wage increases alter the distribution of income, and *not* the general price level. In this Ricardo is fundamentally at odds with Smith. In terms of Smith's cost-of-production theory of value, an increase in wages represents a cost increase; since, therefore, one of the component parts of the values of commodities has risen, their values must also rise.

Ricardo, however, was a forceful critic of this seemingly innocuous proposition. A general wage increase can have only one effect consistent with the labour theory of value: a *reduction in profits*. Ricardo's argument here is logically impeccable. The value of a commodity depends solely on the labour time which is required to produce it; a wage increase has no effect on embodied labour requirements; therefore commodity values will remain unaffected by increases in wages[23].

Now this statement clearly makes sense in the context of a labour theory of value. In Ricardo's theory of rent, his break with Smith was equally apparent. For Smith rent was a component part of value, and thus one of the determinants of the value of a commodity. Ricardo opens his chapter on rent with a very significant statement of intent:

"It remains, however, to be considered, whether the appropriation of land, and the consequent creation of rent, will occasion any variation in the relative value of commodities, independently of the quantity of labour necessary in production" (Ricardo, 1821, p. 67).

His theory of rent provided him with the necessary means for giving a negative answer to this highly important question.

Ricardo takes corn as the representative agricultural output. The value of corn is determined by the amount of labour needed to produce it under the *least* favourable conditions, where *no* rent is paid. Rent, says Ricardo, "is always the difference between the produce obtained by the employment of two equal quantities of capital and labour" (Ricardo 1821, pp. 71–2)[24]. As such, it is a pure surplus, and does *not* form a component part of the value of corn:

"If the high price of corn were the effect, and not the cause, of rent, price would be proportionally influenced as rents were high or low, and rent would be a component part of price. But that corn which is produced by the greatest quantity of labour is the regulator of the price of corn; and rent does not and cannot enter in the least degree as a component part of its price" (ibid., p. 77).

In modern terminology, rent is price-determined and not price-determining. Adam Smith was, in Ricardo's view, quite wrong to contend otherwise.

Ricardo's analysis of income distribution is thus geared to his adoption of a labour theory of value. This theory itself he accepts as the basis for his treatment of value right from the beginning of the *Principles*, and brusquely dismisses any possible alternatives. Thus he distinguishes carefully between use value and exchange value, immediately rejecting the former as irrelevant to a discussion of the latter (Ricardo, 1821, pp. 275–6). He argues that *value* and *riches* (or wealth) are quite separate concepts, and criticizes Say for confusing them (*ibid.*, ch. 20). Both these distinctions are discussed above (pp. 35—8; 71). As we have seen, he limits his discussion explicitly to those commodities which can be freely reproduced by human labour, excluding those in fixed supply[25].

But Ricardo, like Smith, was worried that the labour theory of value might no longer apply under conditions of advanced capitalism. It is to this problem that much of the crucial first chapter of the *Principles* is devoted. In free competition the rate of profit on capital tends to equality in all industries. But industries differ in the ratio of capital to labour which they employ, and also in the ratio of fixed to circulating capital. These differences lead Ricardo (1821, p. 32) to argue that the simple labour theory of value applies only if no capital is employed, or if factor proportions and capital durability happen to be the same in all industries.

Except under these improbable conditions, the relative values of commodities may change while the quantities of labour embodied in them remain unchanged. For example, a general wage increase tends to raise the price of goods and services produced by labour intensive industries relatively to those produced by capital intensive industries. Car servicing becomes more expensive relatively to the purchase of cars, timber relatively to plastics, postal deliveries relatively to telephone calls, and so on. Thus although the quantities of labour embodied, directly and indirectly, in different commodities remains unchanged, relative prices are altered by changes in income distribution[26].

It is not easy to judge just how seriously Ricardo took this as an objection to the labour theory of value. Certainly he argued that its quantitative effect would be slight[27]. Moreover, he continued until the end of his life to search for an embodied labour measure of "absolute value", which would remain invariant with respect to changes in distribution[28]. At the same time, Ricardo did make a significant retreat between the publication of the first and third editions of the *Principles*. He had begun by using Smith's model of simple commodity production to show the *historical* emergence of surplus value as capitalist property relations developed in a society previously free of them. In a controversy with Malthus, Ricardo became aware that this argument, which Marx was later to use, contained a serious ambiguity.

The problem is in fact very simple[29]. We have seen that Ricardo came to realize that his statement of the labour theory of value was inadequate when there were significant differences in capital intensity or durability between industries. But there is no *analytical* reason to suppose that, even in the "early and rude state of society" discussed by Smith, these differences might not be substantial. And, on Ricardo's own reasoning, if deer-hunting had a substantially higher ratio of means of production to labour than beaver-hunting, deer and beavers would no longer exchange at ratios determined solely by the quantities of labour required to produce them. The labour theory of value would then be invalid, *despite* the absence of capitalist class relations.

Thus it seemed that, even in simple commodity production, Ricardo's own arguments had undermined the coherence of the labour theory of value. In the third edition of the *Principles*, Ricardo no longer reasons in terms of what Smith had called the "early and rude state of society". Does this mean that he had, in the last resort, abandoned the labour theory of value? Sraffa (1951) attempts with considerable success to combat this suggestion. In the process, however, he quotes a letter written in 1818 by Ricardo to James Mill which seems to undermine his own argument:

"In opposition to [Torrens], I maintain that it is not because of this division into wages and profits — it is not because capital accumulates, that exchangeable value varies, but it is, in all stages of society, owing only to two causes: one the more or less quantity of labour required, the other the greater or less durability of capital: — that the former is never superseded by the latter, but is only modified" (Ricardo, 1816—18, p. 377; cited Sraffa, 1951, p. xxxvii. Stress added by present authors).

Here Ricardo finally abandons the model of simple commodity production in the face of these considerations. This gives rise to a serious ambiguity in his argument. Instead of one, there are now *two* causes of changes in commodity values; and this is true "in all stages of society". We may readily agree with Sraffa that Ricardo did not *intend* to abandon the labour theory of value in the face of these difficulties, as Smith had done. But, despite Ricardo's claim that different "capital-intensities" merely modify the labour theory of value and do not destroy it, it is clear that the argument is left in a very unsatisfactory state. It was Marx's achievement to show how this "modification" could be made *without* destroying the theory as a whole, in his analysis of the transformation of values into prices (below, pp. 105—10).

In conclusion, it is necessary to pose again the question of what purpose the classical theory of value was intended by its authors to serve. The simplest interpretation is that of Stigler (1958): that the theory provided a convenient *approximation* to a precise theory of price determination, one in which the margin of error, while recognized, was thought to be acceptably small for all practical purposes. Rather more deviously, it has been argued that the theory was never intended as a piece of scientific economics, but rather as a normative judgment about income distribution (see, for example, Gordon, 1959; Myrdal, 1953).

Sraffa, however, regards Ricardo's overwhelming emphasis on the analytical, rather than the ethical, problem of income distribution as the key. He argues that "the problem of value which interested Ricardo was to find a measure of value which would be invariant to changes in the division of the product" (Sraffa, 1951, p. xlviii). This is obviously not an ethical question; it involves no moral judgments about the rightness or wrongness of any particular income distribution. Moreover, it is at a higher level of abstraction than a theory of market price determination[30], although such an "invariable measure of value" would form the basis for a theory of market prices.

Stigler's interpretation is inconsistent with Ricardo's continuing quest for a measure of "absolute value". Nor can it easily account for his continued adherence to propositions which clearly make sense in the context of a labour theory of value, and are wholly superfluous to a labour *approximation* to a theory of value. Such propositions include, for example, his insistence that wage increases could have no effect on the general price level.

Adam Smith's assertion that the "toil and trouble" involved in labour is equal between different people and at different points in time (Smith, 1776, p. 34), could be used as a basis for measuring social cost, as the concept is understood by modern welfare economists. The social cost of different commodities would then depend on the quantities of labour embodied in them, *because* this represents a good measure of the "disutility" incurred, through work, in their production. This, however, is a little too ingenious. Certainly Ricardo never developed this aspect of Smith's argument. (We have already noted above, pp. 77, Ricardo's curt dismissal of use-value as irrelevant to the problem of exchange-value.)

There is a much better case for Sraffa's view. Ricardo was primarily interested in finding an invariable measure of value, to allow him to measure precisely changes in income distribution over time. In particular, Ricardo needed to be able to measure the profit share in national income, for on this depended, as we shall see, capital accumulation and therefore the rate of growth. This, however, is strikingly similar to Marx's interpretation of Ricardo as seeking a logically watertight theory of surplus value. Thus when we come to discuss the achievements and defects of the classical theory of value, we shall do so very much through Marx's eyes.

3.3. The classical theory of development
It was almost universally accepted in classical political economy that the long-run trend in the rate of profit was downwards. The search for the factors underlying the fall in the rate of profit was an important part of

Adam Smith's analysis, and became the cornerstone of the Ricardian theory of economic development.

At one stage Adam Smith concluded that the combination of rapid capital accumulation with vigorous competition was sufficient to bring about a decline in the rate of profit:

"The increase of stock, which raises wages, tends to lower profit. When the stocks of many rich merchants are turned into the same trade, their mutual competition naturally tends to lower its profit; and when there is a like increase in stock in all the different trades carried on in the same society the same competition must produce the same effect in them all" (Smith, 1776, p. 98).

This argument is clearly based on the Mercantilist fallacy that profit arises through the sale of commodities at prices higher than their values, that is, in the process of exchange rather than in production. It is only possible for competitive pressures to reduce the *overall* rate of profit if commodities in general and in the aggregate sell at prices higher than their values.

If a labour theory of value is adopted, however, the role of competition is the more modest one of equalizing throughout the economy a rate of profit determined by other factors at a higher level of abstraction. Thus Ricardo, like Marx, rejects Smith's argument as a general long-run explanation of the tendency of the rate of profit to fall[31].

Later in *The Wealth of Nations* (p. 375), Smith modifies his argument:

"As capitals increase in any country, the profits which can be made by employing them necessarily diminish. It becomes gradually more and more difficult to find within the country a profitable method of employing any new capital. There arises in consequence a competition between different capitals, the owner of one endeavouring to get possession of that employment which is enjoyed by another. But on most occasions he can hope to justle that other out of this employment, by no other means but by dealing upon more reasonable terms. He must not only sell what he deals in somewhat cheaper, but in order to get it to sell, he must sometimes too buy it dearer. The demand for productive labour, by the increases of the funds which are destined for maintaining it, grows every day greater and greater. Labourers easily find employment, but the owners of capital find it difficult to get labourers to employ. Their competition raises the wages of labour, and sinks the profits of stock. But when the profits which can be made of the use of a capital are in this manner diminished, as it were, at both ends, the price which can be paid for the use of it, that is, the rate of interest, must necessarily be diminished with them".

Here intense competition is seen as an effect, not as a cause. The fundamental problem, Smith argues, is a growing shortage of profitable investment opportunities. It would be too generous to attribute to Smith an embryonic theory of deficient aggregate demand. In fact he specifies no reasons to explain why "it becomes gradually more and more difficult to find within the country a profitable method of employing any new capital", and this can only be seen as a restatement of the problem. Ricardo attempts to solve it, as we shall see, in terms of the analytical framework provided by his theories of value and rent.

Smith's second argument concerns the effect of capital accumulation on wages: increased demand for labour pushes up wages and eats into profits. It is not clear that this is consistent with Smith's cost-of-production theory of value. In any case, Ricardo develops a subsistence theory of long-run wage determination in which increases in real wages from this source are impossible.

The Ricardian theory of capitalist development is based, more rigorously than Smith's, on the three-class model of society which originated with Smith himself. It is also based on the labour theory of value. Within this framework, Ricardo developed two models of the falling rate of profit: the simple, one-commodity "corn model", and the more sophisticated variant expounded in the *Principles*, which includes a manufacturing as well as an agricultural sector.

In both models, two principles underpin the entire analysis. The first fixes the long-run real wage at subsistence level, through the operation of the Malthusian population principle. Thus, contrary to Smith, Ricardo argued that an increase in the demand for labour could have only a short-run effect on the real wage. In the longer run, population would rise in response to higher wages, and the subsistence level would be re-established[32]. In Ricardo's time there was some basis in reality for such an argument: at the peak of the British industrial revolution, capital accumulation was rapid, population rose very fast, and real wages rose little, if at all.

Secondly, capital accumulation would lead to diminishing returns in agriculture. Increasingly infertile land would be taken into cultivation, and the marginal productivity of agricultural labour would fall. More labour would be needed to produce a given quantity of corn, so that the labour value of farm produce would rise. This proposition replaces Smith's vague suggestion that there would be an increasing scarcity of profitable investment opportunities, and forms the second basic tenet of Ricardo's theory of economic development.

The implications of these two principles can best be seen in the one-sector "corn model"[33]. Ricardo assumes that only circulating capital, which turns over every year, is used. This consists entirely of corn, stored up as a "wage fund" to feed the labour force over the year which elapses between seed-time and harvest[34]. The amount of capital per worker (the "capital—labour ratio") is thus equal to the annual wage per worker, and is constant at the subsistence level. Ricardo can therefore treat capital-and-labour as a single input. His procedure is to investigate the effects of employing increasing quantities of capital-and-labour on a given quantity of land, thus extending the "intensive margin of cultivation"; or, equivalent to this, extending the "extensive margin" by employing the same amount of capital-and-labour per acre on land of progressively diminishing fertility.

The wage, paid in corn, is fixed at the subsistence level. In the long run the employment of capital-and-labour will proceed up to the point where its price equals the marginal productivity of this composite input (that is, up to the point of zero profitability). Since Ricardo assumes that marginal productivity falls, average productivity must, at least after some point, be above it. The excess of the average output of corn per unit of capital-and-labour over the marginal output is paid to the landlords as rent. In the short run, marginal productivity will be higher than the wage, and the residual accrues to the capitalist farmer as profit.

The process can be illustrated diagrammatically[35]. In Fig. 3.1, ON units of capital-and-labour are employed. APL and MPL are respectively the average and marginal productivity curves of the composite input. The total

Fig. 3.1: The Ricardian corn model

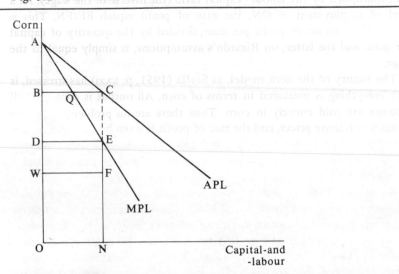

output of corn is given by the area under the MPL curve, OAEN; this is also equal to the product of the APL and the number of units employed, the rectangle OBCN. The wage is fixed at the subsistence level OW, and the total annual wage bill (equivalent to the wage fund, or the total stock of capital) is OWFN.

Now if competition prevails in the market for the composite input capital-and-labour, it will be paid its marginal product at the current level of employment. In Fig. 3.1, ON units of capital-and-labour are employed, at a payment per unit of EN. Here, at the margin, there is no surplus available for payment to the landlords as rent. But the employers of all *intramarginal* units of capital-and-labour are also paid EN, which is less than their marginal productivity. The first unit employed, for example, yields AD in rent (marginal product minus EN). Thus the rent generated and paid to landlords on any intramarginal unit of capital-and-labour is determined by the difference between the marginal productivity of that unit, and the marginal productivity of the no-rent unit at N. Total rent thus equals the area ADE, equal to the area BCED[36]. Total profits are shown by the area DEFW. Profit per man, and hence the rate of profit per unit of capital, is given by the ratio of the difference between marginal productivity and the wage (which represents profits), and the wage itself (which is equal to the stock of capital per man: this consists entirely of a stock of wage-goods, that is, corn to feed the workers). Thus, denoting profits by P, the capital stock by K, and the number of workers employed by L, then P/K (the rate of profit) equals $P/L \times L/K$: that is, profit per man multiplied by the labour—capital ratio (the inverse of the wage). At a level of employment of ON, the rate of profit equals EF/FN. This is clearly the amount of profit per man, divided by the quantity of capital per man; and the latter, on Ricardo's assumptions, is simply equal to the wage.

The beauty of the corn model, as Sraffa (1951, p. xxxi) has stressed, is that everything is measured in terms of corn. All output is corn, and all incomes are paid entirely in corn. Thus there are no problems involving changes in relative prices, and the rate of profit is given by the ratio of two quantities of corn: total profits, and total capital employed. Once the simple world of the one-commodity economy is left, the analysis is much more complicated.

As accumulation continues, and increasing quantities of capital-and-labour are applied to a given area of land (or increasingly infertile lands are taken into cultivation with a constant amount of capital-and-labour per acre; see above, pp. 82—3), it is evident from Fig. 3.1 that the rate of profit must fall. The decline would continue, Ricardo argued, until the rate of profit fell almost to zero. The economy would thus reach a stationary state, in which population, capital stock[37], total output and output per head would all cease to grow. The culmination of this process is shown in Fig. 3.2, in which population (and hence the input of capital-and-labour) has increased to ON'. Here profits have been eliminated altogether, leaving only wages (the area $OWJN'$) and rent (the area AWJ, which equals the area GHJW). The notion of the stationary state persisted at least as late as the work of John Stuart Mill; it is interesting to note that Mill's account of the reasons behind the falling rate of profit, as late as 1848 and quite unlike his theory of value, is almost identical to that of Ricardo (Mill, 1848, pp. 82–5, 112–13).

Fig. 3.2: The stationary state

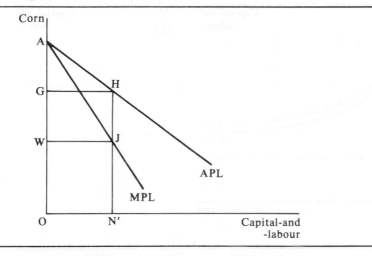

Two qualifications must be made at this stage, one of which was mentioned by Ricardo himself. He expected that the stationary state would set in before the rate of profit had reached zero. The "trouble and risk" attached to investment would lead it to dry up at a small, but still positive, rate of profit (Ricardo, 1821, p. 122). Secondly, it is possible for diminishing returns to apply without the rate of profit falling to zero, irrespective of the payment of any risk premium upon investment. This *may* be true if the APL and MPL curves fall at a decreasing rate; it can never apply when they fall at a constant or increasing rate. In Fig. 3.3A and B the latter two cases are illustrated, and on Ricardo's arguments a stationary state ensues. In Fig. 3.3C, however, the MPL curve is asymptotic to the x-axis at a level higher than the subsistence wage, and accumulation can continue indefinitely with a positive, though always declining, rate of profit.

Fig 3.3: The effects of capital accumulation

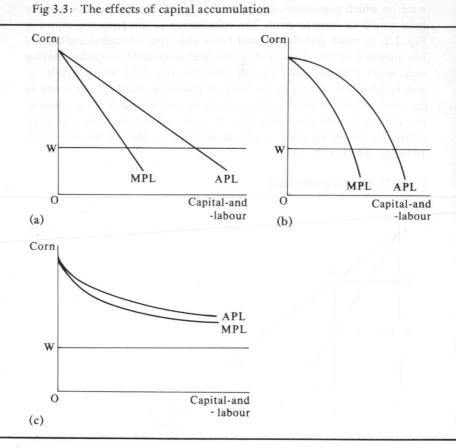

(a)

(b)

(c)

The introduction of a manufacturing sector makes the analysis more complicated, without invalidating it. At least two commodities are now produced, and it is no longer possible to measure everything in terms of quantities of one homogeneous commodity, corn. We must now proceed in *value* terms, and changes in the relative values of corn and industrial products play a major role in Ricardo's argument.

We shall make two simplifying assumptions, both rather stronger than Ricardo found necessary. Assume first that corn remains the only wage-good, so that workers do not consume manufactured products. Secondly, assume that corn is still the only "capital good" used by the farmers; there are, for example, no tractors. Then the effects of accumulation in agriculture are identical to those we have traced above. Wages are paid entirely in corn, and agricultural capital still consists entirely of corn. The rate of profit is still a ratio of two quantities of corn.

If either of our two assumptions are dropped, this is no longer true. Profit now represents the difference between the value of corn output (less rent), and the cost of heterogeneous inputs of corn, tractors, clothes for workers, and so on. The capital stock[38] depends on the values of these same heterogeneous inputs. Almost any change in the relative prices of corn and manufactured goods will thus alter the rate of profit, which no longer depends simply on a technically determined ratio of two quantities of corn.

Let us return to our simple case in which, as we have seen, accumulation has effects similar in agriculture to those in the one-sector corn model: the rate of profit in this sector must fall. Ricardo, however, assumes free competition, and thus free movement of capital between different sectors of the economy. This must imply, in the long run, that the rate of profit in industry will equal that in agriculture, or no capitalist would be willing to engage in agriculture. How is this to occur? Ricardo argues that the "internal terms of trade", the relative prices of agricultural and industrial commodities, must change. Corn, the value of which is now higher because of the increased amount of labour needed to produce it at the margin, must become more expensive in terms of cloth and tractors[39]. But industrial capitalists must feed their workers, and therefore have to pay higher wages, since the value of corn has increased[40]. This reduces the rate of profit in industry, which eventually falls to the same level as that in agriculture. Diminishing returns in agriculture thus lead to a reduction in the rate of profit throughout the economy.

Neither of our two simplifying assumptions is even remotely realistic. Ricardo (1821, p. 103) was well aware that workers consume manufactured goods as well as food. What he assumes is that there is no tendency for workers to substitute an increasing quantity of them for food as the relative price of corn rises. In other words, and ignoring income effects (as we are entitled to do, given that the real wage does not change, but stays at the subsistence level), the demand for corn is assumed to be totally price-inelastic (Pasinetti, 1960, p. 90). Ricardo then shows that, while the real wage remains at the subsistence level, the higher value of corn increases the value of the goods making up the subsistence wage. Now we have already seen (above, pp. 76–7) that, according to the labour theory of value, a wage increase does not affect the general price level, but instead reduces profits. Ricardo's argument can thus be summarized, this time in terms of *values*: decreased agricultural productivity leads to higher wages, which reduces profits, which lowers the rate of profit.

We must now consider the second complication, which concerns the composition of the farmers' capital. In industry both manufactured products (for example, machines) and corn (as a wage fund) will be required. In practice the same will be true of agriculture. Thus in both sectors the rate of profit becomes a ratio of two *values*, total profit divided by total capital.

In this case, as Ricardo realized, the value of the capital employed in each sector will be affected by changes in the relative prices of agricultural and manufactured commodities. Income distribution will also be affected; in Ricardo's words, "The landlord is doubly benefited by difficulty of production. First he obtains a greater share, and secondly the commodity in which he is paid is of greater value" (1821, p. 83; see also *ibid.*, pp. 117, 122). So the landlord receives, as we have seen, an increasing proportion of the corn which is not allocated to wages. And when he comes to exchange it for manufactured goods, he finds that a given quantity of corn will now exchange for a larger amount of the products of industry.

It is important to note that neither of these complications undermines Ricardo's basic conclusion. It remains true that, if there are diminishing returns in agriculture, and if the Malthusian wage—population theory is valid, the rate of profit in the economy as a whole must fall and is likely to induce economic stagnation. This is as valid in the multi-sector economy as in the simple one-sector model which Ricardo initially examines.

It is equally important to realize that Ricardo's argument in no way rests on Keynesian deficiencies in aggregate demand. In the course of an attack on Smith's proposition that accumulation itself, whatever the technical conditions of production, would lead to a falling rate of profit, Ricardo (1821, pp. 290—2) gives explicit support to Say's Law, and denies that general overproduction is possible. This suggests that the only way in which Smith's question-begging argument could have been correct was along Keynesian lines. Moreover we shall see below (pp. 210—13) that Marx points out that it *is* possible, if demand is inadequate to allow surplus value to be fully realized in the market, for commodities in the aggregate to sell at prices below their values, and for the rate of profit to fall as a result. But this is *not* Ricardo's argument.

Nor is it necessary for diminishing returns to apply in manufacturing. In fact Ricardo assumes constant returns outside agriculture. Moreover, the capital—labour ratio in Ricardo's agricultural sector remains constant; accumulation takes the form of "capital-widening" rather than "capital-deepening". It is possible for neoclassical economists to derive a falling rate of profit in the course of economic growth, on the condition that the capital—labour ratio increases and the production function is "well-behaved". Again, this is not the argument used by Ricardo.

Ricardo allowed for two offsetting factors which might operate against the tendency for the rate of profit to decline. One was the possibility of importing cheap agricultural produce from abroad, which could avert the rise in wages which he saw as inevitable if domestic farmers remained protected. But this would require modification of the Corn Laws, and would certainly meet with strong opposition from landlords. The second was technical progress in domestic agriculture. But this, Ricardo thought, was double-edged. The stimulus given by the higher rate of profit to capital accumulation would give a temporary boost to real wages, encourage population growth, and thus increase rent and depress the rate of profit once again. Thus "improvements in agriculture . . . are ultimately of immense advantage to landlords" (Ricardo, 1821, p. 81n). On balance, he remained pessimistic about the long-run prospects for economic growth, and predicted intensified social conflict between the landlords and the rest of society.

One important implication of Ricardo's analysis deserves some attention here. Only two types of productive activity have been considered: the production of wage-goods, consumed by workers as the necessary means of their subsistence; and the production of means of production, "capital goods" like tractors and industrial machinery. Ricardo argued that technical progress in either of these sectors would have important effects on the rate of profit.

But what about technical progress in the so-called "luxury" sector, producing commodities which serve neither as wage-goods nor as means of production, and which do not therefore enter as inputs into the productive process? It is one of the fundamental propositions of the Ricardian theory of value that changes in the conditions of production of such luxury goods can have *no* effect on the rate of profit; they merely alter the values of luxury commodities, relatively to those of wage-goods and means of production. This is a conclusion which is implicit in Marx's development of the labour theory of value[41], and in his, quite different, treatment of the falling rate of profit. As we shall see (below, p. 167), it has recently been brought back into prominence as a result of the revival in interest in classical and Marxian value theory.

Conflict between landlords and the rest of society was a reality in the period in which Ricardo was writing, and induced pessimism rather than shock or outrage. The latter reactions were, however, in evidence when Ricardo, in the famous additional chapter to the third edition of the *Principles*, entitled *On Machinery*, suggested good reasons for conflict between capitalists and workers.

Say's Law, which Ricardo supported, implied full employment, yet in this chapter he claimed that technical change could lead to unemployment among the working class, however profitable it might be for the capitalists. The essence of Ricardo's argument is that capital accumulation may *increase* output and *decrease* the wage fund, thus reducing the labour force employed at the same time as total output is growing. Whatever the merits of Ricardo's analysis, it appeared inconsistent with Say's Law, and it was seen as an incitement to workers to resist the introduction of new techniques.

The wheel has turned full circle. The division of labour, for Adam Smith the major stimulus to growth and the increased prosperity of all classes, became for Ricardo—and still more for Marx—a source of misery for the most numerous class of all. Smith had displayed a rather naïve belief in social harmony (tempered, it is only fair to add, by attacks on monopolists, unproductive labour and, occasionally, landlords). In Ricardo this belief has changed to a recognition of sources of acute class conflict. The chapter *On Machinery* may not enhance Ricardo's reputation for logical consistency; for Marx, at least, it was clear evidence of his integrity: "Chapter XX: 'On Machinery'. This section, which Ricardo added to his third edition, bears witness to his *honesty*, which so essentially distinguishes him from the vulgar economists" (*TSV* II, 555). (A long and detailed criticism of Ricardo's argument follows this tribute.)

Notes

1. Meek (1973, p. 1, n. 1) points out that Marx's definition of classical economics differs from that of modern historians of economic thought.

2. Exceptions are rare; John Stuart Mill, however, was regarded by Marx as greatly superior to most of his contemporaries.

3. It is difficult to agree with Blaug (1968, p. 276) that "the decade of the 1830s is the high-point of classical economics in terms of vigour of debate and appearance of new ideas".

4. See especially Meek (1967, pp. 51—74); Dobb (1940); Roll (1961).

5. We shall see that many of Ricardo's most important analytical achievements derived from his critique of Smith.

6. In correspondence with the authors, Maurice Dobb has pointed out that Marx's interpretation of Ricardo could not have been *entirely* accurate, since some of the latter's most important work remained unpublished (and thus unknown to Marx) until quite recently. This is

especially relevant in the case of Ricardo's letters (Ricardo, 1816—18, 1819—21), and his last paper on "Absolute and exchangeable value" (1815—23, pp. 361—412). We shall see below that Marx is occasionally unfair to Ricardo, albeit usually on quite minor points.

7. See respectively Walker (1971) and Nell (1967).

8. The "invisible hand" reflected Smith's belief in social harmony.

9. See pp. 199—203 for a detailed discussion of the sources and significance of the industrial reserve army.

10. Meek (1973, ch. 2; 1967, pp. 18—33) stresses Adam Smith's contribution in this regard, while in our opinion exaggerating the degree to which the principle was *consistently* applied in classical economics. Dobb (1973) argues persuasively that Ricardo was more consistent than Smith in this respect.

11. Marx continues this passage with praise for Ricardo's "theoretical acumen", "although encompassed by this bourgeois horizon".

12. It is interesting to note that this is a view which is increasingly shared by modern growth theorists; see the survey by Kregel (1971).

13. See Sraffa (1951, p. xlviii); Dobb (1940, ch. 1); Robinson (1965). While Marx used the labour theory of value for the same technical and analytical reasons as the classical economists, we have already stressed the wider significance of labour for his theory of historical materialism (see above, pp. 3—6; 36—52).

14. Our treatment of Mercantilism and Physiocracy, both of which were sophisticated and complex schools of thought, is deliberately short and simplified.

15. For a survey of the Mercantilist theory of value see Furniss (1920, ch. 7).

16. For Proudhon see *Poverty of Philosophy*; for Malthus see *TSV* III, ch. 1.

17. See also *Capital* II, 484—92; *TSV* I, 278—9. A similar, if more sophisticated, argument may be seen in Kalecki's "Marxian" degree-of-monopoly theory of distribution (see p. 138).

18.   What is involved here may be seen very clearly from Marx's analysis of the circulation process as: MONEY – COMMODITIES – COMMODITIES – MONEY (above, p. 38). This may be written as: $M - C - C' - M'$, where C' is greater in value than C, and M' than M. In the first stage $(M - C)$, the capitalist exchanges money for commodities (means of production and labour-power) of equivalent value. The second stage $(C - C')$ is the production process, in which these commodities are transformed into a finished product. The latter is not only qualitatively different from the original inputs, but is also *quantitatively* of greater value, since surplus labour has been absorbed in the course of production. This surplus value thus originates in the production process, and only there. In the third stage $(C' - M')$ the products are sold, realizing their value (M') and only their value. Like the first stage, this third stage involves an "exchange of equivalents". No *expansion* of value takes place between C' and M', any more than between M and C in the first stage; in both cases, there is simply a conversion of a *given* value into another form.

19.   Marx is here citing F. Paoletti, *I verri mezzi vende felici le societa* (1722), p. 197.

20.   The means of production themselves, it is important to note, have not changed, only their ownership. They remain very simple: Smith's example suggests that no machinery is used. The *only* difference between the two situations is thus the change in social structure.

21.   We shall see that Marx was able to show that this dilemma is only apparent, and that the "value of labour" is a meaningless concept. His distinction between labour and labour power (see p. 96) allows him to avoid the unpalatable consequences of a wage-cost theory of value, and to reconcile the existence of property incomes with a coherent labour theory of value.

22.   See p. 81, where this point is made again, this time in the context of Smith's analysis of the falling rate of profit.

23.   Ricardo did, however, allow that wage increases would affect the *relative* values of commodities. The grounds for this argument, and for its rejection by Marx, are discussed below (pp. 78; 109–10).

24.   This applies equally to both the "extensive" and the "intensive" margin (see note 32 to p. 83 on p. 94).

25.   See the passage quoted by Marx and referred to above (p. 65); and Ricardo (1821, pp. 382—5) where it is argued that supply and demand affected the long-run prices only of monopolized commodities.

26.   This is the so-called "Ricardo effect". We have followed Ricardo in using the terms "value" and "price" interchangeably. The essence of Marx's critique of Ricardo on this point is a clear and deliberate distinction between the two terms (see pp. 103—11).

27.   "The greatest effects which could be produced on the relative prices of these goods from a rise in wages could not exceed 6 or 7 per cent" (Ricardo, 1821, p. 36; see also Stigler, 1958).

28.   See the two drafts of Ricardo's last essay (1815—23, pp. 357—412); Sraffa (1951, pp. xlvi—xlvii); above, pp. 76—7.

29.   A very clear account is given by Moore (1966).

30.   In other words, it is closer to the "reality" than the "appearance" end of the spectrum. Smith's cost-of-production theory, and modern supply and demand theories, come at the other end.

31.   For Ricardo competition simply ensures that the prices of individual commodities do not permanently deviate from their values.

32.   Ricardo (1821, pp. 94—5) was careful to qualify this argument. If the pace of accumulation was rapid enough, he suggested, it was possible for the short-run "market wage" to exceed the long-run "natural" real wage for an indefinite period. Population might never catch up. Moreover, he defined subsistence in conventional, socially determined terms. Thus he wrote that "there can never be a better security against a superabundant population" than an expanding working-class "taste for comforts and enjoyments" (ibid, p. 100). However, the elevation of workers' tastes was expected to be a long-run process. In any particular historical period, Ricardo could thus treat the subsistence level as a constant. Marx's treatment of subsistence was quite similar (see below, pp. 97—8).

33.   See the "Essay on the influence of a low price of corn on the profits of stock" (Ricardo, 1815—23, pp. 1—41).

34.   This assumes, for reasons of simplicity, that seed inputs are negligible.

35. For a mathematical treatment, see Pasinetti (1960). In what follows we deal with the "intensive margin": that is, we examine the consequences of applying successive increments of capital-and-labour to a given quantity of land. Nothing but the terminology would need to be changed if, instead, we analysed the "extensive margin", and studied the effects of extending cultivation to virgin land of decreasing fertility, holding constant the quantity of capital-and-labour per acre.

36. This can be proved with the aid of a little simple calculus. Let total output be $y = f(x)$, where x is the amount of capital-and-labour employed. Then the average product is y/x, and the marginal product is $dy/dx = f'(x)$. Now the area OAEN is given by $\int dy/dx \, dx$, which equals y. This is, of course, the area under the marginal product curve. But the area OBCN is $y/x \cdot x$, which also equals y. A geometrical proof is also possible in the case illustrated in Fig. 3.1, where the APL and MPL curves are linear. It is well-known that in this case the MPL curve falls twice as fast as APL. MPL therefore bisects the line BC, so the BQ = QC. ABQ and QCE are thus similar triangles, with all three sides equal in length; they are therefore equal in area. But the area ADE is equal to BQED + ABQ; and the area BCED is equal to BQED + QCE. Thus ADE equals BCED in area.

37. This assumes that the landlords' savings propensity is zero.

38. Here we assume, with Ricardo, that capital turns over (that is, depreciates completely) exactly once a year, so that the value of capital *employed* equals the value of capital *used up* in the course of a year's production.

39. Ricardo assumes that embodied labour requirements remain constant in manufacturing (see below, p. 88).

40. Only money wages rise; the worker's real standard of living is unchanged.

41. Though, as we shall see (p. 177 n 41), Marx himself was inconsistent on this point.

4

Marx's critique
of classical political economy

4.1 Introduction

Marx's respect for classical political economy increased his determination to free it from its internal logical inconsistencies, and from the methodological defects which, in his view, were largely responsible for these shortcomings. He devoted great attention to the classical theory of value which, despite its major advances over earlier work, was still open to serious criticism. Since Marx attributed most of the other problems in classical economics to this source, we begin with an examination of his critique of the Ricardian theory of value. In the course of this discussion, the outlines of Marx's own theory will emerge.

4.2 The theory of value

A famous passage in the *Critique of Political Economy* summarizes the problems which Marx found in Ricardo's version of the labour theory of value[1]. Four fundamental criticisms are made; we deal with each in turn.

Labour and labour power
"One. *Labour itself has exchange-value, and different types of labour have different exchange-values. If one makes exchange-value the measure of exchange-value, one is caught up in a vicious circle, for the exchange-value used as a measure requires in turn a measure. This objection merges into the following problem: given labour time as the intrinsic measure of value, how are wages to be determined on this basis? The theory of wage labour provides the answer to this*" (*Critique*, pp. 61–2).

We have already encountered this problem, in a rather different form, in our discussion of the Mercantilists, whose wage-cost theory of value implied that the values of commodities were determined by the value of the labour embodied in them (above, pp. 67—9). As Marx saw, this is a circular argument: the values of commodities are made to depend on the value of another commodity, the value of which itself obviously cannot be determined in this way. Classical political economy never escaped from this dilemma. Either labour itself sold at its value, in which case the labour theory of value was meaningless; or it did not, and the sale of the most important commodity of all broke the law of value (*Capital* I, 535—8). It seemed logically impossible to adhere to the labour theory of value and to develop a consistent theory of wages at the same time.

Marx thus needed to show that while value depends on the *quantity* of labour embodied in a commodity, it does not depend on the *value* of that labour. He suggests that classical political economy is guilty of what modern philosophers would call a category mistake. Labour is an *activity*, not a commodity. It is not bought and sold, and therefore has no value, since the category "value" applies only to commodities. Thus " 'price of labour' is just as irrational as a yellow logarithm" (*Capital* III, 818). What is bought and sold in the "labour market" is human *labour power*, "the capacity for labour" (*ibid*, I, 168). And Marx quotes approvingly from Sismondi: "the capacity for labour ... is nothing if not sold" (*ibid*, I, 173).

The distinction Marx makes between labour and labour power is neither arbitrary nor trivial. It is found, for example, in the work of some careful modern labour economists, who refer to the "market for labour services" rather than to the "market for labour". And it is not simply a minor question of linguistic accuracy for, as we have seen, failure to make such a distinction fatally impairs any labour theory of value[2]. Having made it clear that it is labour power which is the commodity traded on the "labour market", Marx is able to produce a theory of wages — that is, of the value of labour power — which is fully consistent with his theory of value.

Let us recall Ricardo's theory of wages. The long-term equilibrium real wage, which Ricardo misleadingly terms the "value of labour", is maintained at the subsistence level by the operation of the Malthusian population principle. If real wages rise as a result of excess demand for labour, population will grow and the labour supply will increase, until the real wage returns to subsistence. Thus an inexorable biological law entails that the long-run supply of labour is perfectly elastic at the subsistence level.

Even on empirical grounds Marx had very little respect for this argument. He maintains, in line with modern anti-Malthusians, that the time lag in the response of the labour supply to wage increases is too long.

Escape from what development economists term the "low-level equilibrium trap" is thus entirely possible, even if the Malthusian population principle does operate in the long run (*Capital* I, 637–8). Marx accuses Malthus of confusing an erroneous macro-economic law with one which is valid at the micro level. The supply of labour to any one industry or occupation may be almost perfectly elastic even in the short run, but Malthus failed to prove that this will be true of the supply of labour *in aggregate* (*ibid*, I, 638–9).

Marx's main attack, however, was methodological. The classical theory of wages rests on a biological law which purports to apply to all economies. Even for Ricardo, who was careful to observe that the *level* of subsistence was socially determined and possibly variable in the long run, the Malthusian *mechanism* by which this level was enforced remained a natural one.

For Marx the category "wages" was a historically specific one, meaningful only within the capitalist mode of production. Therefore he sought a theory of wages which related specifically and exclusively to capitalist economies, and criticized classical political economy for its failure to provide such a law (*Capital* I, 637–9). Moreover the classical theory of wages isolated the labour market as a special case to which the theory of value does not apply. Ricardo explains the values of all commodities other than labour power in terms of a law specific to the social institutions of capitalism, while the "value of labour" was subject to a quite different analysis. For Marx this was unacceptable. Capitalism is *defined* by the status of labour power as a commodity, and it is this which distinguishes it from, for example, feudalism or simple commodity production. Labour power is thus the most important commodity of all.

Marx had therefore to develop a theory of wages which satisfied two criteria. He insisted that, since labour power is a commodity like any other, its value must rest on the same factors which determine the value of any other commodity (*Capital* I, 170–1; *SW* II, 56). First, then, Marx attempted to apply the labour theory of value *to distribution itself*[3]. Secondly, the mechanism by which the (long-run equilibrium) price of labour power was brought into equality with its value must be rooted firmly in the specific characteristics of the capitalist mode of production.

The first criterion is easily satisfied, once the crucial distinction is made between labour and labour power. According to the labour theory of value, the value of a commodity depends on the quantity of labour required, under the average prevailing technical conditions, for its production. The labour time needed to produce and reproduce human labour power is simply that necessary to keep the worker and his family alive and capable of working, It is this which determines the value of labour power, and thus the long-run equilibrium wage. Thus Marx, like Ricardo, had a subsistence theory of wages[4].

A major difference is at once apparent in the economic mechanism by which real wages, on average and in the long run, are maintained at subsistence level. Since labour power is not produced for profit by capitalists, this mechanism must be accounted for in some detail. Malthus's ahistorical law of population is replaced by Marx by a factor which is specific to the process of capitalist accumulation: the industrial reserve army of the unemployed. This is also a form of overpopulation, but it is quite different from the concept found under that name in classical economics:

"It is capitalistic accumulation itself that constantly produces, and produces in the direct ratio of its own energy and extent, a relatively redundant population of labourers, i.e. a population of greater extent than suffices for the average needs of the self-expansion of capital, and therefore a surplus-population" (Capital I, 630).

Later Marx observes that:

"This is a law of population peculiar to the capitalist mode of production, and in fact every specific historic mode of production has its own special laws of population, historically valid within its limits alone. An abstract law of population exists for plants and animals only, and only in so far as man has not interfered with them" (ibid, I, 632).

What, then, are the sources of the industrial reserve army? What forces produce and reproduce the unemployment of a substantial proportion of the working class? Marx argues that these forces are inherent in the nature of technical change and the accumulation of capital, which increases productivity through the growth of constant capital at a rate faster than that at which variable capital increases. The organic composition of capital thus rises, so that "capital increases its supply of labour more quickly than its demand for labourers" (Capital I, 632)[5]. Two further factors contribute, especially in the early stages of the development of modern industry, to the industrial reserve army. It is swollen, first, by the application of these same technical changes in agriculture, resulting in migration to the towns and a high degree of underemployment among those who remain; the latter form "a constant latent surplus-population" (ibid, I, 642). Secondly, there is the wretchedly exploited and irregularly employed section of the labour force which is still found in domestic industry, forming the "stagnant" part of the industrial reserve army (ibid, I, 643).

The existence of the industrial reserve army means that competition between workers for jobs prevents real wages from rising, in the long run, above the subsistence level. This whole analysis is very different from the classical theory of wages. No "abstract" law of population, applicable to plants and animals as well as to men, is invoked. Unemployment itself is only conceivable in an economy based on the *employment* of wage-labour. Smith's hunters, for example, could be *idle* for a number of reasons; they could not, under any circumstances, be described as unemployed. The classical economists had suggested that real living standards could not rise significantly for the mass of the population in *any* society for any length of time. Marx's treatment of the theory of wages deliberately and explicitly refers only to capitalism.

Marx is certainly able to satisfy the two criteria advanced above. His theory is wholly consistent with the labour theory of value. Note in particular that, although he can be interpreted as postulating a perfectly elastic long-run labour supply curve at the subsistence level, this in no way commits him to a supply-and-demand theory of wages:

"[Classical political economy] soon recognized that the change in the relation of demand and supply explained in regard to the price of labour, nothing except its changes, i.e. the oscillations of the market-price above or below a certain mean. If demand and supply balance, the oscillation of prices ceases, all other conditions remaining the same. But then demand and supply also cease to explain anything. The price of labour, at the moment when demand and supply are in equilibrium, is its natural price, determined independently of the relation of demand and supply. And how this price is determined, is just the question" (Capital I, 538).

But this is the pure theory of the long run. Relative overpopulation is "the pivot on which the law of demand and supply of labour works" (*ibid*, I, 639). The market prices of commodities may rise above, and fall below, their values as supply and demand fluctuate, and this applies equally to labour power. If, at the peak of a boom, unemployment temporarily disappears—and Marx argues that such a disappearance would be very shortlived — real wages may rise above subsistence for a while.

We can briefly summarize our argument so far. Marx found the distinction between labour and labour power to be necessary to correct a logical error in classical political economy, and to allow the reconciliation of the theory of wages with the theory of value. He developed a theory of the value of labour power which is specific to capitalism, without the ahistorical naturalism of the Malthusian population principle. Wages are maintained at subsistence by the operation of the industrial reserve army, itself an inherent result of the process of capital accumulation. It was not by accident that Marx's first line of attack on the classical theory of value was on the theory of wage-labour. This was to form the basis for his critique of the classical theory of surplus value, to which we now turn.

The theory of capital

"Two. *If the exchange-value of a product equals the labour-time contained in the product, then the exchange-value of a working-day is equal to the product it yields, in other words, wages must be equal to the product of labour. But in fact the opposite is true. Ergo, this objection amounts to the problem, — how does production on the basis of exchange-value solely determined by labour-time lead to the result that the exchange-value of labour is less than the exchange-value of its product? This problem is solved in our analysis of capital*" (*Critique*, p. 62).

This was the most acute problem facing political economy, and until it was solved no adequate theory of surplus value was possible. As we have seen (above, pp. 73—6), it drove Adam Smith to reject the labour theory of value itself when non-wage incomes of any sort existed[6]. The classical economists insisted that these incomes originated in production, not in exchange; that they resulted from the sale of commodities at, and not above, their values. But if labour was the only source of value, why does not the entire product accrue to the labourer? Labour power, after all, sells at its value like any other commodity. The Ricardian socialists were to raise this very question against classical political economy (Meek, 1973, pp. 124—5), and to provide an ethical answer: the working class, and the working class alone, was entitled to the full fruits of its labour. Marx, however, needed a *scientific* solution.

Like Smith, Marx proceeded by contrasting two different types of society: simple commodity production and capitalism. In simple commodity production, as in Smith's example of the deer and beavers, commodities exchange in ratios determined by the quantities of labour required to produce them, and only the producers consume them. The difference in definition between simple commodity production and capitalism is that in the latter labour power itself has become a commodity. For Marx, "capital" is above all the power of a minority class which monopolizes the means of production, over propertyless labourers:

"*Property in money, means of subsistence, machines, and other means of production does not as yet stamp a man as a capitalist if there be wanting the correlative — the wage-worker, the other man who is compelled to sell himself of his own free-will. . . . Capital is not a thing, but a social relation between persons, established by the instrumentality of things*" (*Capital* I, 766).

Associated with this difference in social structure is a difference in income distribution. Non-producers now share in the social product, in the form of rent, interest and profit.

But is this not inconsistent with the labour theory of value? Does it not imply, as Smith thought, that the prices of commodities are greater than their labour values, because profit is *added* to them? Not at all. Here Marx's distinction between labour and labour power is crucial. The value of labour power is determined, as we have seen, by the quantity of labour necessary to produce the subsistence requirements of the worker. But these bear no necessary relation to the product of his labour, which may be very much larger.

Thus in Ricardo's simple corn model the output of corn per worker, net of seed, is greater than that needed to feed the worker; the surplus product accrues in part to the landlord as rent, in part to the capitalist farmer as profit on his capital (above, pp. 80f). In the more sophisticated two-sector model, this surplus is expressed in value terms: surplus value is the difference between the value of labour power and the value of the worker's product, both measured in terms of labour time.

The argument may be put in a more direct fashion. Only part of the working day is required for the worker to produce enough to provide for the subsistence needs of himself and his family. During the remainder of the working day, he performs what Marx terms surplus labour: he produces for the benefit of his employer. In Marx's words:

"The fact that half a day's labour is necessary to keep the labourer alive during twenty-four hours, does not in any way prevent him from working a whole day. Therefore, the value of labour-power, and the value which that labour-power creates in the labour process, are two entirely different magnitudes; and this difference of the two values was what the capitalist had in view, when he was purchasing the labour-power" (Capital I, 193).

Surplus labour is an economic prerequisite for the existence of any class society. If technology, resources and knowledge were so limited that a full day's work yielded barely enough to keep the population alive, no non-producing class could survive; this, rather than Smith's example, is the true "early and rude state of society".

In all the other class societies which preceded capitalism, the fact that the producer is forced to perform surplus labour is blatantly obvious. No one would attempt to explain the opulence of the feudal lord or the slave-owner in any other way than by his exploitation of the mass of the producers. The nature of the wage bargain in capitalism, however, distorts and mystifies what for Marx is a fundamentally similar process which merely takes a different form. Labour power *does* sell at its value, and the commodities which the worker buys sell at their values; in this sense no one is being cheated. The worker is bound by no legal restrictions on the sale of his labour power, and unlike the serf or the slave is not directly and violently coerced into performing surplus labour. Marx traces this mystification back to the confusion of labour and labour power:

"But since the workman receives his wages after his work is performed, and knows, moreover, that what he actually gives to the capitalist is his labour, the value or price of his labour-power necessarily appears to him as the price or value of his labour itself. . . . A double consequence flows from this.

Firstly. The value or price of that labouring-power takes the semblance of the price or value of labour itself, although, strictly speaking, value and price of labour are senseless terms.

Secondly. Although one part only of the workman's daily labour is paid, while the other part is unpaid, and while that unpaid or surplus labour constitutes exactly the fund out of which surplus value or profit is formed, it seems as if the aggregate labour was paid labour.

This false appearance distinguishes wage labour from other historical forms of labour. On the basis of the wages system even the unpaid labour seems to be paid labour. With the slave, on the contrary, even that part of his labour which is paid appears to be unpaid. . . .

Take, on the other hand, the peasant serf, such as he, I might say, until yesterday existed in the whole East of Europe. This peasant worked, for example, three days for himself on his own field or the field alloted to him, and the three subsequent days he performed compulsory and gratuitous labour on the estate of his lord. Here, then, the paid and unpaid parts of labour were sensibly separated, separated in time and space; and our Liberals overflowed with moral indignation at the preposterous notion of making a man work for nothing" (SW II, 59—60; see also Capital I, 539).

It is thus the value form in which surplus labour appears in capitalism which is the source of all the difficulties. Because the worker is paid a wage, and seems to be paid for every hour that he works, the origins of surplus value in surplus labour are obscured.

It is for this reason that Marx gives great emphasis to the length of the working day. Once the value of labour power is determined, a longer working day means a longer time for the worker to provide unpaid labour for his employer. Ricardo's embryonic theory of surplus value is so elliptical precisely because of his failure to grasp this point:

"Ricardo starts out from the actual fact of capitalist production. The value of labour is smaller than the value of the product which it creates. . . . the *excess of the value of the product* over *the value of the wages is the surplus value . . . [but] the mere* possibility *of this surplus labour (i.e. the existence of that necessary minimum productivity of labour), does not in itself make it a* reality. *For this to occur, the labourer must first be compelled to work in excess of the [necessary] time, and this compulsion is exerted by capital. This is missing in Ricardo's work, and therefore also the whole struggle over the regulation of the normal working-day" (TSV* II, 405—6).

Ricardo does not deal explicitly with the length of the working day, and seems implicitly to assume that it is constant. Marx, on the other hand, stresses the continual pressure in capitalism for the working day to increase. The very long Chapter x of *Capital* I, for example, is devoted entirely to a historical discussion of this pressure, and the partly successful resistance to it of the working class. Nothing of this sort is found in Ricardo, who is criticized accordingly by Marx: "Important as it was, to resolve value into labour, it was equally important to resolve surplus-value into surplus-labour, and to do so in explicit terms" (*TSV* II, 405). This Ricardo had failed to do[7].

This failure had important repercussions on the classical theory of capital, which we have already outlined. Marx regarded his distinction between constant and variable capital — of which only the latter produced surplus value — as far more significant than the classical dichotomy between fixed and circulating capital. Marx's categories provide the missing link between the theory of capital and the theory of surplus value. He comments at some length, in Chapters x and xi of *Capital* I[8] on the failure of classical political economy to make the crucial distinction between constant and variable capital. It is significant that this is the only place in *Capital* itself where Marx develops his criticism of classical political economy so explicitly and at such great length. These objections, as we shall see, fundamentally differentiate his theory of the falling rate of profit, and his model of economic growth in capitalism, from Ricardo's treatment of these problems. They also form the basis of his third line of attack on the classical theory of value, to which we now turn.

The theory of competition

"Three. *In accordance with the changing conditions of demand and supply, the market-price of commodities falls below or rises above their exchange-value. The exchange-value of commodities is,* consequently, *determined not by the labour-time contained in them, but by the relation of demand and supply. In fact, this strange conclusion only raises the question how on the basis of exchange-value a market price differing from this exchange-value comes into being, or rather, how the law of exchange-value asserts itself only in its antithesis. This problem is solved in the theory of competition" (Critique, p. 62).*

There are two dimensions to this problem. The classical theory of value was attempting to explain the determinants of the exchange ratios of commodities in the long run under free competition. In the short run, market prices would differ from values because of fluctuations in demand and supply, but these fluctuations in no way invalidated the labour theory of value. Although, as we have already seen (above, pp. 75—6), Adam Smith was not entirely consistent on this point, Ricardo would certainly have agreed with Marx that "absolutely nothing can be explained by the relation of supply to demand before ascertaining the basis on which this relation rests" (*Capital* III, 181—2). Supply and demand determine the variations in the short-run market price of a commodity. In the long run the labour theory of value comes into its own. Marx had no dispute with Ricardo on this.

The second dimension causes far more serious problems. We have seen above (p. 78) that Ricardo was worried about the implications of differences in the ratio of "fixed" to "circulating" capital. Now the assumption of free competition means that capital is free to move from industry to industry in search of the highest rate of profit. Thus in the long run the rate of profit will be the same throughout the economy. But, except in very special circumstances, this is not consistent with the sale of commodities at their labour values.

Ricardo (1821, p. 37) uses the following example to illustrate the difficulties posed by differences in the ratio between fixed and circulating capital between industries. A rate of profit of 10 per cent paid on an investment of £2 000 for one year yields £200. If £1 000 is invested at the start of the first year, and another £1 000 at the start of the second year, the yield at the end of the second year is not £200, but £210 (10 per cent of £2 100, which is the total amount invested at the beginning of the second season).

If the annual wage is £50, then £2 000 will employ forty men for a year, perhaps as agricultural labourers. Equally, it will employ twenty men for two years, perhaps spending the first year in building a machine and the second year operating it. The *value* of output is the same in both cases, since the same forty man-years have been spent in each activity. But one sector is now more "capital-intensive" than the other, and the *prices* at which their outputs are sold must differ if the same rate of profit is to prevail in each.

If this is not so then the rate of profit will be lower in the mechanized sector. Suppose that the output of the mechanized sector (say, the textile industry) sold at £2 200 like that of the farmer. Then the rate of profit in textiles would be only 6.5 per cent[9], and capitalists would move to agriculture in search of the higher rate of profit being paid there. Without an increase in the relative price of textiles, textile production would eventually cease altogether[10].

Ricardo's treatment of this problem was ambivalent, as we have seen (above, pp. 78–9). He argues at one stage that the theory of value must be changed: long-run equilibrium prices still equal values, as before, but these values no longer depend solely on quantities of embodied labour. On the other hand, he clings to theoretical propositions (for example, the assertion that a wage increase will reduce profits rather than increasing the price level) which clearly apply to the context of the unmodified labour theory of value. In the last resort Ricardo failed to reconcile the operation of supply and demand with the labour theory of value[11].

This is the notorious "transformation problem" which Marx poses, and attempts to solve, in the third volume of *Capital* (*Capital* III, chs. viii–xii). There, however, his attack on Ricardo is usually only an implicit one. It is made explicit, and developed at some length, in a very important section of *Theories of Surplus Value* (*TSV* II, 173–216). Marx proceeds from his theory of capital. Only variable capital produces surplus value, and a given amount of variable capital will produce the same quantity of surplus value in any industry. But constant capital is also used, and this does not produce surplus value.

The ratio between constant and variable capital, which Marx terms the "organic composition of capital", normally differs between industries. Thus equal quantities of capital produce different amounts of surplus value whenever organic compositions differ. If commodities are sold at their values, rates of profit will be highest in those industries with the lowest organic compositions of capital, and vice versa. But this is inconsistent with the mobility of capital which is required by the assumption of free competition. Profit rates cannot differ in the long run.

For Marx this is the crux of the problem, and the question of differing degrees of durability of constant capital — which, as we have seen, consists partly of "fixed" and partly of "circulating" capital — is a matter of subsidiary importance[12]. Marx's solution is a bold one. He argues that differences in the organic composition of capital entail that long-run equilibrium prices differ *systematically* from labour values, in such a way as to equalize the rate of profit throughout the economy. Only in the aggregate are values and "prices of production" equal. Individual commodities sell at long-run equilibrium prices which are higher than their labour values if they are produced with an above-average organic composition, and vice-versa. Ricardo's error was to identify price and value *for each individual commodity.*

Marx criticizes Ricardo for confusing the two dimensions of competition distinguished above. The mobility of capital takes place at two different levels:

"The first migration occurs in order to establish cost-prices *which differ from* values. *The second migration occurs in order to equalize the* actual market-prices *with the cost-prices — as soon as they rise or fall above the latter. The first is a transformation of the values into cost-prices. The second is a rotation of the actual market-prices of the moment in the various spheres, around the cost-price, which now appears as the* natural price, *although it is different from the value and only the result of social action"* (*TSV* II, p. 209)[13].

It is the "first migration" which we have been discussing, and to which Marx attributes primary significance. The "second migration" merely reflects the tendency for short run differences in the rate of profit to be eliminated in the long run as the "natural price", or long-run equilibrium "price of production", is established. What Ricardo failed to realize is that this natural price is inevitably *different* from value[14].

The technique Marx uses in transforming values into prices rests on severely restrictive assumptions, which we discuss below (pp. 143—9). It may however help to illustrate his argument if we analyse an example which he provides in *Capital* III, 155—7. Equal quantities of capital are used in each of five industries, but the ratio of constant to variable capital employed is different in each. Assuming free mobility of labour the rate of surplus value must of course be equal in each, since the quantity of surplus value produced depends exclusively on the amount of variable capital used. Thus different quantities of surplus value are produced in industries with the same total capital. If these commodities were sold at their values, the rate of profit would thus be different in each industry.

Now the total surplus value produced is 110, and the total capital employed is 500. The average rate of profit is thus 22 per cent, and prices will deviate from values in each industry by an amount which allows each to obtain this average rate of profit. Industry I, for example, used 80 units of constant capital, which turns over rather slowly so that only 50 is used up in the course of a year's production[15]. It employs 20 units of variable capital, which Marx assumes to turn over exactly once a year[16]. A rate of profit of 22 per cent is paid on total capital employed $(80c + 20v = 100)$, and the *price of production* of industry I is therefore $50 + 20 + 22 = 92$. The *value* of its output, however, is equal only to 90:

Table 4.1 The transformation of values into prices

Industry	Constant capital (c)	Variable capital (v)	Total capital (c +v)	Rate of exploitation (s/v)	Surplus value (s)	Constant capital used up in a year (αc)	Value (c + v + s)	Cost price (c + v)	Profit at 22%	Price of production	Price − value*
I	80	20	100	100%	20	50	90	70	22	92	+ 2
II	70	30	100	100%	30	50	110	80	22	102	− 8
III	60	40	100	100%	40	52	132	92	22	114	−18
IV	85	15	100	100%	15	40	70	55	22	77	+ 7
V	95	5	100	100%	5	10	20	15	22	37	+17
Total	390	110	500	−	110	202	422	312	110	422	0

Note The reader will notice that two minor alterations have been made to Marx's figures (for industries II and III). These in no way affect the argument; our reason for making them are explained below.
* Note that the figures in this column are identical with the differences between profit and surplus value in each industry.

the sum of the dead labour (constant capital) transferred into the commodity in the course of the year (50), and the living labour embodied in the product in the same period (20 paid, as variable capital, and 20 unpaid, as surplus value). Industry I, which has an organic composition of capital slightly higher than the average for the five taken together, thus sells its output at a price rather higher than its value, and receives more in profit than it has produced in surplus value. Industry II, where the organic composition is lower than the average, sells at a price below its value, and receives a smaller sum in profit than it has produced in surplus value.

Note that the *sum* of values produced equals the sum of the prices, and the *sum* of the surplus values produced equals the sum of the profits. Thus while Marx distinguishes prices from values, and profits from surplus value, he argues that the labour theory of value is still required to *determine* prices and the rate of profit. All that is involved is a redistribution of surplus value from industries where the rate of profit would otherwise be higher than average to those where it would otherwise be lower:

"As far as profits are concerned, the various capitalists are just so many stockholders in a stock company in which the shares of profit are uniformly divided per 100, so that profits differ in the case of the indivual capitalists only in accordance with the amount of capital invested in the aggregate enterprise, i.e., according to his investment in social production as a whole, according to the number of his shares" (Capital III, 158).

We shall deal later with the controversy which has arisen concerning the validity of this procedure, and with the proposition that the labour theory of value is rendered superfluous in the course of the transformation (below, pp. 143f). At this stage, we merely wish to note that Ricardo failed to formulate the problem as clearly as Marx, still less to provide any solution[17]. This failure, in turn, was a direct result of the defects in his theory of capital.

Marx takes the argument a step further. The transformation of values into prices, he suggests, is not merely a formal problem in the abstract theory of value. It is also a historical problem, bound up with the development of capitalism (see above, pp. 49–50). Thus "it is quite appropriate to regard the ˙ˑˑes of commodities as not only theoretically but also historically *priu*˷ to the prices of production" (*Capital* III, 177).

In primitive societies, in which production for exchange is only a marginal activity in an otherwise self-contained economy, the ratios at which products are exchanged are governed more by accident than by any law of value. In simple commodity production, which is based on production for the market, exchange becomes regularized. As in Smith's deer and beaver example, commodities are traded at their labour values. The essential social relationship between capitalists and workers which characterizes capitalism is absent, therefore the transformation problem does not arise. In Marx's sense, as a social relation between the owners of the means of production and a propertyless working class, capital does not exist. All incomes stem directly from the sale by the producers of the products of their labour, and accrue to them alone. There is no surplus value, hence no profit, and thus no rate of profit to be equalized. It is only when capitalistic features begin to develop that these categories become relevant. The process of the transformation of values into prices is itself the product of the development of capitalism.

Note that this argument does not depend on the prevalence of "labour intensive" techniques in simple commodity production. Marx in fact discusses a situation in which techniques differ considerably in the proportions of dead to living labour which they require, but concludes that "in these circumstances [of simple commodity production] a difference in the rates of profit would therefore be immaterial" (*Capital* III, 177). These producers are not capitalists, and their aims, motives, and entire outlook towards production are fundamentally different. Marx claims that the concepts of profit and surplus value apply specifically, and exclusively, to capitalism. The transformation is a historical process: "The exchange of commodities at their values, or approximately at their values, thus requires a much lower stage than their exchange at their prices of production, which requires a definite level of capitalist development" (*Capital* III, 177).

He is thus able to dispose of another problem which defeated Ricardo, and to which we have already referred (above, pp. 78–9). Ricardo came to realize that differences in techniques between industries, leading, in Marx's terminology, to different organic compositions of capital, could be substantial even in simple commodity production. He concluded that, for this reason, the unmodified labour theory of value was inapplicable even in the "early and rude state of society". Marx, as we have seen, took the opposite view: the unmodified labour theory of value applied *only* in simple commodity production[18]. This is a significant point, for the efforts made by classical political economy to derive surplus value from capitalist class relations had been based on the ideal type of simple commodity production which, it seemed, had been destroyed by this argument. Marx was able to show that this problem was a false one, based on an application of economic categories from one form of production to another, in the context of which they were meaningless.

Failure to appreciate the significance of the transformation of values into prices led, in Marx's view, to a series of important errors. The price of production of a commodity is the sum of its "cost price" – comprising the constant and variable capital needed to produce it – and profits, which depend on the average rate of profit in the economy as a whole. Some economists came to interpret this as implying that the cost price was in fact the value of the commodity, to which profit was added. On this interpretation profit arises in exchange, through the sale of commodities *in general* at prices higher than their values. This is simply the Mercantilist fallacy which Smith and Ricardo had exposed. Writers such as Proudhon and Torrens, Marx argued, had fallen into the same trap (*Capital* III, 37–40).

Others, seeing that the profits actually achieved by the individual capitalist were proportional to the *total* capital he employed, and oblivious to the distinction between constant and variable capital, enshrined "capital" as the source of profit, as a separate "factor of production". An embryonic marginal productivity theory of income distribution emerged from this error:

"It is then only an accident if the surplus value, and thus the profit, actually produced in any particular sphere of production, coincides with the profit contained in the selling price of a commodity. As a rule, surplus value and profit, and not their rates alone, are then different magnitudes. At a given degree of exploitation, the mass of surplus value produced in a particular sphere of production is then more important for the aggregate average profit of social capital, and thus for the capitalist class in general, than for the individual capitalist in any specific branch of production. It is of importance to the latter only insofar as the quantity of surplus value produced in his branch helps to regulate the average profit. But this is a process which occurs behind his back, one he does not see, nor understand, and which indeed does not interest him. The actual difference of magnitude between profit and surplus-value — not merely between the rate of profit and the rate of surplus-value — in the various spheres of production now completely conceals the true nature and origin of profit not only from the capitalist, who has a special interest in deceiving himself on this score, but also from the labourer. The transformation of values into prices of production serves to obscure the basis for determining value itself" (Capital III, 167—8).

Again, Marx argues, appearances differ from, and conceal, reality. The rate of profit differs from the rate of surplus value. It may rise or fall, as the organic composition of capital increases or decreases, with no alteration in the rate of surplus value. Nor is the amount of profit accruing to the capitalist equal — except in the special case where he operates with an organic composition of capital equal to the social average — to the amount of surplus value which he himself has extracted from his labour force. As Marx's own example illustrates, the very nature of the transformation process entails that they differ systematically from each other. The individual capitalist, in attributing his profit to some mysterious power of the capital he employs, loses sight of the origins of profit in surplus value, and of surplus value in surplus labour. He makes the same mistake as the worker, who comes to believe that he is paid for every hour that he works for his employer, failing to see the unpaid part of the working day from which surplus value, and hence profit, is derived.

These comments are not directed specifically against Ricardo, for whose breadth and depth of vision Marx had great respect. His criticism of Ricardo is nevertheless a severe one. Ricardo had failed to recognize that commodities do not, in capitalism, sell at their values. He had therefore failed to give a clear and explicit distinction between surplus value and profit, and was thus unable to argue convincingly that the latter is a *derivative* of the former and is incomprehensible without it.

This has immense consequences for Ricardo's analysis of the falling rate of profit (*TSV* II, 215–16; below, pp. 116–7). But Ricardo's theory of the falling rate of profit depends on his theory of rent. Until the middle of *Capital* III Marx explicitly abstracts from all features of capitalist society except the fundamental polarity between employer and worker[19]. Now he introduces the landlord. His attack on the Ricardian theory of rent, which he bases on the transformation of values into prices, is Marx's fourth and final criticism of the classical theory of value.

The theory of rent

"Four. The last, and apparently decisive objection, unless it is advanced, as commonly happens, in the form of curious examples, is this: if exchange-value is nothing but the labour-time contained in a commodity, how does it come about that commodities which contain no labour possess exchange-value, in other words, how does the exchange-value of natural forces arise? This problem is solved in the theory of rent" (*Critique*, p. 63; see also *TSV* II, 247).

One of Ricardo's major achievements was to have shown that the existence of rent is not incompatible with the labour theory of value. For Ricardo the value of corn is determined by the quantity of labour needed to produce it under the least favourable conditions. Intramarginal land, requiring a lower labour input to produce the same output of corn, yields rent to the landlords. The more fertile the land in relation to that at the margin of cultivation, the higher the rent. Rent is thus a purely differential payment, and no rent is paid at the margin. Ricardo's reconciliation of the theory of rent with the labour theory of value forced him to deny the existence of "absolute rent".

Marx praised the logical consistency of this argument, which disposes of Smith's analysis of rent as one of the component parts of the value of corn (*TSV* II, 347–53, 130 and 242). He suggests, however, that it is too restrictive. It is perfectly possible for rent to be paid at the margin – in Ricardo's terms, for absolute rent to exist – without any inconsistency with the labour theory of value, so long as the transformation from values into prices is taken into account.

The essence of this problem, which Marx discusses at some length in *TSV* II, may be put rather differently:

"The farmer who grows wheat makes the same profit as all the other capitalists. This proves that, like all the others, he appropriates that portion of labour-time for which he has not paid his workers. Where, on

top of this, does the rent come from? Why should surplus-labour in agriculture resolve into profit and rent while in industry it is just profit? And, how is this possible at all, if the profit in agriculture equals the profit in every other sphere of production?" (TSV II, 32).

Agriculture, Marx argues, operates with a lower organic composition of capital than industry. The price of production would therefore be lower than the value of corn. The profits realized by capitalist farmers would be less than the surplus value produced in agriculture, so that the rate of profit here would be equal to, and no higher than, that in the rest of the economy[20].

Land is not, however, a commodity in the strict Marxian sense, since it cannot be reproduced by human labour. Free competition, and the resulting capital mobility, will ensure that the rate of profit in agriculture will not be higher in the long run than that in industry. But it cannot ensure that corn will sell at its price of production, and therefore below its value:

"Those who derive rent from monopoly are right. Just as it is the monopoly of capital alone that enables the capitalist to squeeze surplus-labour out of the worker, so the monopoly of land ownership enables the landed proprietor to squeeze that part of surplus-labour from the capitalist, which would form a constant excess profit. But those who derive rent from monopoly are mistaken when they imagine that monopoly enables the landed proprietor to force the price of the commodity above its value. On the contrary, it makes it possible to maintain the value of the commodity above its average price; to sell the commodity not above, but at, its value"(TSV II, 94).

An example which Marx provides may help to illustrate his argument (*TSV* II, 316). Suppose that agriculture and industry use the same total quantity of capital (100), but that this is divided between constant and variable capital in different proportions; 80 : 20 in industry, and 60 : 40 in agriculture. Let the rate of exploitation be 50 per cent. Then the value of the output of the two sectors would be as follows:

Industry : $80c + 20v + 10s = 110$

Agriculture : $60c + 40v + 20s = 120$

In the standard case, the values would be transformed into prices of production in order to equalize the rate of profit in both sectors. Both would sell at 115, and the same average rate of profit (15 per cent) would be paid in both. Agricultural output would thus sell at less than its value. But this is only possible if land is not privately owned. Under normal conditions in capitalism the landlords are able to maintain the price of agricultural output at a level equal to its value. Corn then sells at 120, and the landlords take 10 of the 20 units of surplus value in rent. The capitalist farmers retain 10, giving them the same rate of profit as their industrial counterparts. The actual selling price of corn is not forced *above* its value by the private monopoly in land, and the consequent payment of rent. On the contrary, corn sells at a price *equal* to its value, and therefore higher than the price of production which would have prevailed had the transformation process applied in agriculture[21].

Several important differences between Marx's theory of rent and that of Ricardo are easily seen. The existence of "absolute rent", paid on the least fertile land, is entirely consistent with the labour theory of value (*TSV* II, 43). In fact rent is paid *because* corn sells at its labour value. Differences in fertility between different types of land are no longer the reason for the *existence* of rent; they play a subsidiary role, simply explaining why some lands pay more rent than others (*ibid*, II, 18). It is unnecessary for agricultural productivity to *fall* as accumulation proceeds, in order that a theory of rent may be developed. The lower organic composition of capital on the farm simply means that productivity rises there at a slower rate than in industry, but it does still grow (*ibid*, II, 18–19, 43, 243). Rent does not form part of the value of corn, as Smith mistakenly inferred, nor even part of its price of production; but it does form part of its actual selling price, which would otherwise equal the (lower) price of production. Ricardo was in this sense wrong to argue that rent is price-determined rather than price-determining (*ibid*, II, 316–8).

Marx sees a certain irony in the fact that Ricardo at one stage articulates a theory of rent identical to his own, only to reject it as inconsistent with the labour theory of value. The error may be traced directly to Ricardo's failure to pose, still less to solve, the problem of the transformation of values into prices:

"The question is reduced to the following: Does an absolute rent *exist? That is, a rent which arises from the fact that capital is invested in agriculture rather than manufacture; a rent which is quite independent of differential rent or* excess profits *which are yielded by capital in better land?*

It is clear that Ricardo correctly answers this question in the negative, *since he starts from the* false *assumption that* values *and* average prices *of commodities are identical" (TSV* II, 242)[22].

By "average price" Marx here refers to the price of production (cost price plus the average rate of profit), which is established through the process of transformation. Ricardo ignores this process, and thus develops an unnecessarily restrictive theory of rent.

The implications of all this are considerable. For Marx, unlike Ricardo, the theory of rent "is not a law of nature, but a social law" (*TSV* II, 96). The landlord is a parasitic appendage of capitalist society, who could be abolished — for example, by the nationalization of the land — without any adverse effects on the operation of the system as a whole (*ibid*, II, 44). Moreover, as rent is the product of a particular set of historical circumstances, it may disappear altogether if these circumstances change. "Rent arises from an *historical difference* in the organic component parts of capital which may be partially ironed out and indeed disappear completely, with the development of agriculture" (*TSV* II, 105; see also *ibid*, II, 93, 103, 244). As modern technology is applied more rapidly to agriculture, Marx argues, the organic composition in this sector may rise to the social average. Value would then be no greater than price of production, and absolute rent would disappear.

Marx's theory of income distribution in general is significantly different from that of classical political economy. For Marx the crucial distinction is that between wages and surplus value, paid-for and unpaid-for labour:

"Profit of capital (profit of enterprise plus interest) and ground-rent are thus no more than particular components of surplus-value, categories by which surplus-value is differentiated depending on whether it falls to the share of capital or landed property, headings which in no whit however alter its nature. Added together, these form the sum of social surplus-value" (*Capital* III, 821).

Part of the total surplus value accrues to the landlords as rent, and the remainder forms the profits of the capitalists. In turn, part of the capitalists' profits accrues to financiers as interest; the remainder is "profit of enterprise". These categories are specific to capitalist production. We have already seen that rent may disappear altogether as technology in agriculture reaches the same level of development as in industry. The rate of interest, for Marx, is determined purely by the supply and demand for money-capital: "By the natural rate of interest, people merely mean the rate fixed by free competition. There are no 'natural' limits for the rate of interest" (*Capital* III, 364). The rate of interest is not a determinant of saving or the rate of accumulation.

But Marx was less interested in what might be called the "quantitative" aspect of distribution, dealing with the *proportion* of the aggregate surplus value accruing to each of these groups of claimants upon it. His main concern in criticizing Ricardo's theory was with the "qualitative" aspect: tracing the emergence of surplus value through the performance of surplus labour, and its division between landlords, money-capitalists and industrial capitalists[23]. Here, he argued, classical political economy had gone seriously wrong. Like his theory of wages, Ricardo's theory of rent was based on natural rather than on historical laws, on the innate character-istics of the land and its fertility, rather than on the social relations of production.

Ricardo was, however, never entirely consistent on this point. At one stage he traced the origins of rent to the emergence of private ownership of land, writing of "the appropriation of land, and the consequent creation of rent" (Ricardo, 1821, p. 67). Then he attributed rent to the intrinsic qualities of land itself: "the labour of nature is paid, not because she does much, but because she does little. In proportion as she becomes niggardly in her gifts, she exacts a greater price for her work" (ibid, p. 76). It would be difficult to wish for a better example of commodity fetishism, attributing to the properties of inanimate objects phenomena which are in reality the product of social relationships.

Whatever his own intentions, Ricardo had thus laid the foundations for the marginal productivity theory of distribution, in which physical objects — "capital", defined as the "produced means of production", and land — contribute to the production of value on an equal footing with human labour. The basic error lay in the use of ahistorical, natural laws to explain historical relationships which are specific to capitalism. Marx criticizes the "Holy Trinity" theory of income distribution on these grounds:

"In capital-profit, or still better capital-interest, land-rent, labour-wages, in this economic trinity represented as the connection between the com-ponent parts of value and its sources, we have the complete mystification of the capitalist mode of production, the conversion of social relations into things, the direct coalescence of the material production relations with their historical and social determination. It is an enchanted, perverted, topsy-turvy world, in which Monsieur le Capital and Madame la Terre do their ghost-walking as social characters and at the same time directly as mere things. It is the great merit of classical economy to have destroyed this false appearance and illusion, this mutual independence and ossification of the various social elements of wealth, this personification of things and conversion of production relations into entities, this religion of everyday life. It did so by reducing interest to a portion of profit, and rent to the surplus above average profit, so that both of them converge into surplus-value; and by representing the process of circulation as a mere metamorphosis of forms, and finally reducing value and surplus-value of commodities to labour in the direct production process. Nevertheless even the best spokesmen of classical economy remain more or less in the grip of

the world of illusion that their criticism had dissolved, as cannot be otherwise from a bourgeois standpoint, and thus they all fall more or less into inconsistencies, half-truths and unsolved contradictions" (*Capital* III, 830).

The links between the theory of distribution and the classical theory of economic development were so close that this criticism could not fail to be applicable also the latter, to which we now turn.

4.3 The theory of economic development
No more than classical political economy did Marx doubt that the falling rate of profit was an actual long-run tendency in capitalist economies. The problem was to explain this tendency, and to assess its consequences. Marx argued that the classical economists had done neither. His own analysis of the falling rate of profit was based on precisely those criticisms of the classical theory of value, and their methodological underpinnings, which we have already outlined. It follows that recent attempts (for example, Walker, 1971) to impute to Marx a Ricardian view of long-run trends in capitalist economic development can be shown, quite simply, to be false.

Marx's attack on Ricardo is based directly on the defects in the latter's theory of value:

"I have already shown that Ricardo's theory of rent is wrong. This then cuts out one of the grounds for his explanation of the fall in the rate of profits. But, secondly, it rests on the false assumption that the rate of surplus-value *and the* rate of profit *are identical, that therefore a fall in the rate of profit is identical with a fall in the rate of surplus-value, which in fact could only be explained in Ricardo's way. And this puts an end to his theory. The rate of profit falls, although the rate of surplus-value remains the same or rises, because the proportion of variable capital to constant capital decreases with the development of the productive power of labour. The rate of profit thus falls, not because labour becomes less productive, but because it becomes more productive"* (*TSV* II, 439).

This attack is repeated, and amplified, later in the same chapter:

"But if Ricardo identifies rate of surplus-value with rate of profit — and at the same time assumes, as he does, that the working-day is of a given length — then the tendency of the rate of profit to fall can only be explained by the same factors which make the rate of surplus-value fall. But, with a given working-day, the rate of surplus-value can only fall if the rate of wages is rising permanently. And this only if agriculture is constantly deteriorating, in other words, if Ricardo's theory of rent is accepted. Since Ricardo identifies rate of surplus-value with rate of profit, and since the rate of surplus-value can only be reckoned in relation to

variable capital, capital laid out in wages, Ricardo, like Adam Smith, assumes that the value of the whole product — after deduction of rent — is divided between workmen and capitalists, into wages and profit. This means that he makes the false presupposition that the whole of the capital advanced consists only of variable capital" (*TSV* II, 463—4).

Marx's argument here is a complicated one, for the very good reason that it involves nearly all his major points of disagreement with the classical theory of value. Ricardo does not make Marx's crucial distinction between constant and variable capital. In effect he assumes that all capital is variable (the wage fund). Thus when he refers to the "rate of profit" ($s/c + v$), he is really discussing the rate of surplus value (s/v). Ricardo's account of the tendency for the rate of profit to decline is really an analysis of a tendency for a decline in the rate of surplus value.

This may occur because of a decrease in s — for example due to a reduction in the length of the working day, or in the intensity of labour. But Ricardo does not deal with these factors. The rate of exploitation must thus fall because of an increase in v. But this happens only if wages rise, in other words if the value of labour power increases. For Ricardo food is the most important wage-good; thus his theory requires an increase in the value of food.

But, in terms of the labour theory of value, the value of a commodity will rise only if the quantity of labour needed to produce it goes up; that is, if the productivity of labour in agriculture falls. Thus Ricardo's account of the falling rate of profit hinges on a continual decline in the productivity of agricultural labour, so that an ever-increasing proportion of the working day must be devoted to reproducing the labourers' means of subsistence[24].

Marx's analysis is quite different. Assume that the organic composition of capital grows with the development of modern technology. Now the rate of profit is $s/c + v$. Divide both sides of this fraction by v, to get $(s/v)/(c/v + 1)$. The rate of profit is now equal to the rate of exploitation, divided by one plus the organic composition of capital. Marx argues that the numerator will rise less rapidly than the denominator (see below, pp. 203—10). But this is the result of an *increase* in the productivity of labour, and not, as Ricardo suggests, a decrease. Workers are transforming greater and greater quantities of constant capital (raw materials and machinery) into final products[25]. Thus Marx reverses the classical view of the falling rate of profit.

This argument is based, in part, on a realistic appraisal of the actual tendencies of capitalist production. Marx is highly sceptical of the proposition that labour productivity in agriculture can be expected to fall, though he is prepared to accept that, at least in the early stages of capitalism, it will grow less rapidly than in manufacturing[26]. But we have already seen (above, p. 114) that he considers it quite possible that rent will disappear completely as the organic composition in agriculture catches up with that in industry. This implies that agricultural productivity will eventually rise *faster* than in industry. In any case, agriculture plays a very minor role in Marx's economic theory: the really significant developments are taking place in industry[27].

This is more than an empirical question. Marx's attack on Ricardo rests also on the methodological position which determined his criticism of other aspects of classical economic theory. Ricardo's explanation of the falling rate of profit rests on two propositions, both of which purport to be ahistorical, natural laws not specific to capitalism. One is the theory of rent as the result of the "niggardliness of nature", and the other is the Malthusian population principle. As we have already seen, Marx rejects both as substantively and methodologically false. This represents a basic difference in attitude towards the long-run potentialities of capitalism. Ricardo and many of his followers (notably John Stuart Mill) saw an inevitable tendency for economic growth to peter out as the rate of profit fell to zero. They expected the emergence of a "stationary state" in which production, population and living standards would all remain stagnant.

For Marx this was to ignore both the contradictions and the potential of capitalism:

"Those economists, therefore, who, like Ricardo, regard the capitalist mode of production as absolute, feel at this point that it creates a barrier itself, and for this reason attribute the barrier to Nature (in the theory of rent), not to production. But the main thing about their horror of the falling rate of profit is the feeling that capitalist production meets in the development of its productive forces a barrier which has nothing to do with the production of wealth as such; and this peculiar barrier testifies to the limitations, and to the merely transient, historical character of the capitalist mode of production; testifies that, for the production of wealth, it is not an absolute mode, moreover, that at a certain stage it rather conflicts with its further development" (Capital III, 242).

Marx makes two important points here. First, he argues that the economic problems facing capitalism have nothing to do with "Nature", or with the expansion of physical production ("wealth")[28]. They are the results of its own characteristics as a mode of production, and will not exist in a society organized along different lines. Secondly, and derived from the first point, he argues that the life-span of capitalism is finite. Its economic contradictions ensure that it will be replaced by a different form of society which will not suffer from the same problems:

"The bourgeois mode of production is the last antagonistic form of the social process of production — antagonistic not in the sense of individual antagonism, but of an antagonism that emanates from the individuals' social conditions of existence — but the productive forces developing within bourgeois society create also the material conditions for a solution of this antagonism. The pre-history of human society accordingly closes with this social formation" (Critique, p. 21).

Capitalism does not stagnate, as the classical economists had thought. It transforms itself, through social conflict, into a classless society. It is in this sense that Marx refers to capitalism as the last period of the "pre-history of human society"[29]. And this transformation is not due to the existence of natural barriers to the expansion of production, but to the "social conditions of existence" characteristic of capitalism itself.

The same methodological objection is at the heart of Marx's attack on the second pillar of the classical theory of economic development: Say's Law. Say's Law may be given several, significantly different, interpretations (Clower, 1965). In modern Keynesian theory it is usually viewed as the claim that there exists an automatic endogenous mechanism which ensures *ex ante* equality of savings and investment at a "full employment" level of output. It is assumed that full employment of capital and labour are attained, if at all, simultaneously. This will *not* normally be the case for Marx, whose theory of the industrial reserve army (below, pp. 199f) implies substantial unemployment of labour even if the capital stock is fully employed. In Marx's theory full capacity utilization entails only that there are no "realization problems" of deficient aggregate demand, so that the total profits obtained from the sale of commodities equals the total surplus value produced in the economy. This, and not automatic full employment of *labour*, is what Marx refers to when he criticizes Say's Law. We use the term in this rather special sense, both here and in Chapter 6.

Marx implicitly assumes that Say's Law operates in his analysis of technical change, but he does so only in order to show that the problems of technical progress are *logically* independent of generalized crises of overproduction (Shoul, 1957). It does not prevent him from dismissing the "Law" as "childish babble" (*TSV* II, p. 502), and similarly strong attacks abound in Marx's economic writings. The first line of attack is obviously an empirical one: crises of overproduction (in modern terminology, of deficient aggregate demand) were too striking and regular a feature of nineteenth-century capitalism to be ignored. Ricardo's error, Marx argued, was mitigated by the relatively early period in which he wrote, when the trade cycle was very much in its infancy. But his theoretical mistakes were later uncritically adopted as a means of denying the very possibility of the cycle (*TSV* II, 497)[30].

In a barter economy, Marx argued, it is inevitably true that "supply creates its own demand"; in such an economy, "no one can be a seller without being a buyer or a buyer without being a seller" (*ibid*, II, 509). Since there is by definition no money, and therefore no store of value, products can only be exchanged for other products, and the very same act is one of supply *and* demand. But this type of exchange, to which Say's Law undoubtedly does apply, takes place only in primitive societies, where production is undertaken predominantly to meet the subsistence needs of the producer himself:

"In direct barter, the bulk of production is intended by the producer to satisfy his own needs, or, where the division of labour is more developed, needs that are known to him. What is exchanged as a commodity is the surplus and it is unimportant whether this surplus is exchanged or not" (*ibid*, II, 508—9).

In such an economy, market production is an insignificant sideline.

Once the bulk of production is undertaken for the market, for exchange rather than for direct consumption by the producer or his immediate family or tribal group, money begins to be used. It now becomes possible to sell without buying, to hoard the proceeds from the sale of commodities instead of instantly buying different commodities with the money obtained. Supply no longer necessarily creates its own demand, and aggregate demand may fall short of aggregate supply[31]. "The possibility of crisis therefore lies solely in the separation of sale from purchase" which is inevitable once money acts as the intermediary in the majority of transactions (*TSV* II, 508). Thus crises are *possible* even in simple commodity production.

But they are not at all probable. Marx repeatedly stresses that the *possibility* of crises does not entail their actual occurrence[32]. In practice, it is not until quite late in the development of capitalism, and long after the emergence of a largely monetarized economy, that crises occur (*TSV* II, 512). Though possible in simple commodity production, they are extremely unlikely. The motive for production in simple commodity production is very similar to that in a barter economy: the satisfaction of the needs of the producers. Smith's deer and beaver hunters exchange their commodities in the market, using money to facilitate their transactions. But the hunters work only in order to consume, if not their own products, the products of other hunters and the producers of food, clothing, and so on. If they feel no such needs, they will simply enjoy more leisure[33]. Use value is still the aim of production, and the simple commodity producer will be unlikely to supply deer, for example, unless he wishes to obtain beaver. Sale and purchase are formally separated, but are in practice directly and intimately related.

Capitalism is quite different. The ownership of the means of production, and thus control over the production process, is now in the hands of a minority class whose aim is the maximum possible profit. The consumption needs of the producers are irrelevant: "What after all has over-production to do with absolute needs? It is only concerned with demand that is backed by ability to pay" (*TSV* II, 506).

Nor is production carried out primarily to satisfy the consumption requirements of the capitalists themselves. The essential aim and basic motivation of capitalist production is *accumulation*:

"It must never be forgotten, that in capitalist production what matters is not the immediate use-value but the exchange-value and, in particular, the expansion of surplus-value. This is the driving motive of capitalist production, and it is a pretty conception that — in order to reason away the contradictions of capitalist production — abstracts from its very basis and depicts it as a production aiming at the direct satisfaction of the consumption needs of the producers" (*TSV* II, 495).

In contrast both to barter economies and to simple commodity production, exchange value and not use value dominates production[34]. Accumulation is a necessary condition for the survival of the capitalist, and this competitive compulsion, rather than "consumers' " habits and desires, motivates production. The capitalist's personal consumption of luxuries is a residual, and purely passive, category.

In the advanced stages of capitalism the most important source of demand is not for consumption, whether by employers or by workers, but to replace and expand the means of production. Output will not be increased, or even maintained at the same level, unless it is profitable to do so. The possibility of overproduction, which exists in any monetarized economy, become a probability and eventually almost a certainty (see below, pp. 210–9).

Marx's refutation of Say's Law may be regarded as a highly successful verification of his methodological principles. The application of a "law", which is valid in a barter economy, to a monetarized economy based on the profit motive and the accumulation of capital has been revealed to be absurd. Marx concludes that, in order to deny the possibility of crises of overproduction, Ricardo and his followers have been forced to deny the existence of capitalism itself (*TSV* II, 500–1). In a very penetrating passage, this conclusion is traced back to the inability of classical political economy to escape from its assumption that capitalism is eternal:

"All the objections which Ricardo and others raise against over-production etc. rest on the fact that they regard bourgeois production either as a mode of production in which no distinction exists between purchase and sale − direct barter − or as social *production, implying that society, as if according to a plan, distributes its means of production and productive forces in the degree and measure which is required for the fulfilment of the various social needs, so that each sphere of production receives the quota of social capital required to satisfy the corresponding need. This fiction arises entirely from the inability to grasp the specific form of bourgeois production and this inability in turn arises from the obsession that bourgeois production is production as such, just like the man who believes in a particular religion and sees it as the religion, and everything outside of it only as* false *religions" (TSV* II, 528−9).

In other words, Ricardo has proved unable to specify the difference between capitalism and other modes of production, and therefore cannot clearly express the essential characteristics of capitalism itself. Least of all is he able to recognize that "the bourgeois mode of production contains within itself a barrier to the free development of the productive forces" (*ibid*, II, 528). His error with respect to Say's Law stems from the same methodological mistakes as those which underlie his faulty analysis of the falling rate of profit.

4.4 Conclusions

In this chapter we have shown how Marx tried to expose four fundamental errors in the classical law of value: the confusion between labour and labour power, which Marx corrects in his theory of wages; the inability to explain the origins of surplus value, which is solved by Marx's theory of capital; the confusion between values and prices, clarified by Marx in his analysis of the transformation problem; and the inability to explain the emergence of rent (and especially the existence of "absolute rent"), for which Marx's solution to the transformation problem is a necessary prerequisite. We have suggested that a profound methodological criticism lies behind each of Marx's arguments about the defects of the classical theory of value, and that the same criticism forms the basis for his attack on the classical theory of economic development.

The relationship between Marx and classical political economy was thus double-edged. It is certainly true, in one sense, that Marx "used the Ricardian apparatus; he adapted Ricardo's conceptual layout and his problems presented themselves to him in the form which Ricardo had given to them ... criticism of Ricardo was his method in his purely theoretical work" (Schumpeter, 1954, p. 390). At the same time, Marx was never slow to attack the empirical implausibilities, logical defects and methodological weaknesses which he saw in classical economics. The corpus of economic theory which emerged from this critique was different in many respects from that which he had inherited from Ricardo. In the following chapters we develop the account of Marx's own economic theory which we have already outlined, and expose it to the criticism which it has incurred over the last century. We begin with the Marxian theory of value.

Notes

1.   For a lucid and perceptive account of this passage see Shoul (1967).

2.   Blaug (1968, p. 277) is quite wrong when he says that "the contrast between the two kinds of labour [sic] is purely terminological: labour as distinct from labour-power is a Marxian abstraction". The distinction is not between "two kinds of labour", but between a human activity and a commodity. It is certainly a "Marxian abstraction", and a necessary and valid one. Whether it is "purely terminological" is a question of pure terminology!

3.   Modern neo-Ricardians, as we shall see (p. 165), make no such attempt.

4.   He is equally careful to qualify it. The value of labour power, unlike that of other commodities, has both a natural and a "historical and moral element" (Capital I, 171), and thus depends in part on the prevailing social conditions. Like Ricardo, however, Marx treats this element as given in the short run, so that the concept of a fixed subsistence wage is valid within any particular historical period.

5.   This argument is put in a more rigorous form, and subjected to a critical analysis, in section 6.4

6.   It is to Smith's credit that he saw that there is indeed a problem here. Ricardo did not, as Marx observes (TSV II, 397).

7.   Trade union resistance to attempts to lengthen the working day, and demands for its reduction, are viewed by Marx far less ambivalently than efforts to raise the wage level (see below p. 135). Historically, Marx was correct in arguing that early capitalism had drastically increased the working day. Wilensky (1961) shows that total hours worked per year, which were much lower in 1950 than in 1800, had merely recovered to medieval levels. Further corroboration is provided by Bienefeld (1972, chs. 2–3).

8.   See also *Capital* I, 588–91; *TSV* I, 343–4. Schumpeter (1954, pp. 643, 680), also emphasizes the significance of this criticism. Meek (1973, p. 120) suggests that Ricardo's later work, unpublished until quite recently, reveals that he was groping towards this same distinction. In terms of the *Principles*, however, Marx's criticism is entirely justified.

9.   £1 000(1.065) + £1 000(1.065)^2 = £2 200 approximately.

10.   Ricardo's argument has been formalized by Samuelson (1959b, p. 221). Let the common rate of profit be r and the durability of capital in the two industries be b_1 and b_2. The common wage is w; a_1 and a_2 are the labour inputs per unit of output in each sector, and p_1 and p_2 the product prices. We can then write

$$p_1 = w \cdot a_1 (1 + r)^{b_1}, \text{ and}$$

$$p_2 = w \cdot a_2 (1 + r)^{b_2},$$

which yields the following expression for relative prices:

$$\frac{p_2}{p_1} = \frac{a_2}{a_1} (1 + r)^{(b_2 - b_1)}$$

which equals the ratio of the labour input coefficients only if $b_1 = b_2$.

11.   The "Ricardo effect" (above, pp. 103f) shows how a *change* in the wage, and corresponding inverse change in the rate of profit, alters relative prices when capital durability or "factor proportions" differ between industries. Thus we may credit Ricardo with an understanding of this problem. The "Ricardo effect" is, however, only *part* of the general problem of transformation, which was rigorously developed for the first time by Marx.

12.   If constant capital turns over less rapidly than once a year, the *stock* of constant capital will be greater than the *flow* which enters into the output produced each year, and vice versa. Such a case will be seen in our

discussion of Marx's numerical example of transformation (above, pp. 106—8); see also *Capital* III, ch. iv (by Engels), and Bajt (1970).

13.   In *Theories of Surplus Value* Marx uses the term "cost-price" in the sense in which he writes of the "price of production" in *Capital* III. In the latter, commodities sell at prices equal to their cost price *plus* the average rate of profit. The difference is a purely linguistic one.

14.   The only case in which they will be equal is the *special case* in which the industry concerned operates with an organic composition of capital equal to the average for the economy as a whole. For Marx this was the exception and not the rule.

15.   If constant capital consists only of machinery, this implies that the life of a machine is 1.6 years.

16.   Strictly speaking, this means that the capitalist must start production with a year's wages in hand. However, as we have observed, shorter turnover periods can be included in the model without difficulty.

17.   Marx praised Ricardo for "doubtless realizing that his prices of production deviated from the values of commodities", but then criticized him for failing to reveal these differences in a systematic fashion (*Capital* III, pp. 198, 203n).

18.   And also in the early stage of capitalist development (see above, p. 45f).

19.   See, for example, *Capital* III, 49; above, pp. 45—52. The structure of *TSV*, which deals with economists in roughly chronological order, requires Marx to drop this abstraction in places. He is, however, usually careful to make it clear just what his assumptions are.

20.   Agriculture is thus similar, in this respect, to industry II in Table 4.1.

21.   We suggest below (pp. 139—41) that there are serious difficulties inherent in Marx's theory of rent; in the present chapter we are concerned exclusively with his criticism of classical theory.

22.   Cf. *TSV* II, 244: "The whole blunder originates in the confusion of cost-price [i.e. price of production, see above, note 13] with value."

23. An obvious parallel exists here with Sweezy's (1946, p. 25) perceptive distinction between the qualitative and the quantitative aspects of the theory of value.

24. The rate of profit is P/K, which equals $P/L \cdot L/K$ (see above p. 84). Ricardo argues that P/L falls, while L/K remains constant. (The decline in P/L may, as we have seen, be offset by free trade in corn and, at least temporarily, by technical progress in agriculture.) Marx, as we shall see, proceeds from a fall in L/K, that is, a rise in K/L, the "capital–labour ratio".

25. Marx's conception of productivity is thus not identical with that of modern orthodoxy, which would exclude raw materials from measures of "value added per man".

26. See for example the historical account of the development of agricultural productivity in *TSV* II, 109–10.

27. For a different interpretation see Güsten (1965).

28. Cf. the analysis of scarcity in Marxian and in modern orthodox economics, above (pp. 25–7).

29. See Chapter 1, where Marx's argument is discussed in more detail. His analysis of the economic contradictions of capitalism is subjected to critical scrutiny in Chapter 6.

30. *TSV* II, 497. As we have seen (above, pp. 64–5), Ricardo is dealing with the "manufacturing" stage of capitalist production, rather than what Marx termed "modern industry". The pace of capital accumulation, and of technical and structural change, was much slower in this earlier stage. Marx saw the beginnings of the modern trade cycle in the slump of 1825 (*Capital* I, 14; this is Marx's *Afterword* to the second German edition, written in 1873).

31. "At a given moment, the supply of all commodities can be greater than the demand for all commodities, since the demand for the *general commodity*, money, exchange-value, is greater than the demand for all particular commodities, in other words the motive to turn the commodity into money, to realize its exchange-value, prevails over the motive to transform the commodity again into use-value" (*TSV* II, 505). Marx here anticipates what has become known as Walras's Law, which states that the

total demand for all $n + 1$ commodities equals the supply of those commodities, where the $n + 1$th commodity is money. Say's Law, on the other hand, stipulates that this equation holds for the n commodities *excluding money* (Baumol, 1970, pp. 96—8).

32. See, for example, *TSV* II, 509; also Sowell (1967). We discuss below (pp. 211—9) Marx's analysis of the concrete precipitating factors in crises.

33. The occasional miser may prefer to pile gold under his mattress, but in simple commodity production he will be very much the exception.

34. Schematically, simple commodity production can be represented as COMMODITIES−MONEY−COMMODITIES (C−M−C). The independent craftsman produces commodities, sells them (at their values) for money, and buys different commodities of an equal value for his personal consumption. This is his only motive for producing. Capitalism, as we have seen (above, p. 92 note 18) must be represented in a quite different way, as MONEY−COMMODITIES−COMMODITIES−MONEY (M−C−C′−M′). The capitalist's motive is the production of surplus value, and its conversion into money, which allows him to purchase means of production and labour power and thus to produce surplus value on an increasing scale. See also Sweezy (1946), and Tsuru (1952).

5

The labour theory of value

5.1 Introduction

There can be no doubt that Marx's analysis of the labour theory of value was greatly superior to that of any of the classical economists. As we have seen in Chapter 4, Marx was able to pose and, he believed, solve certain crucial problems in the classical theory of value. By a careful distinction between the various stages of pre-capitalist and capitalist society he was able to reconcile the labour theory of value, first with the existence of surplus value, and then with the existence of competitive forces which tended to equalize the rate of profit throughout the economy. None of the classical economists, not even Ricardo, had been so clear or methodical in their treatment of these key problems.

It would, however, be quite misleading to end a discussion of the Marxian labour theory of value at this point. Controversy has arisen not merely over Marx's relation to his predecessors, with which we have already dealt; but also in the context of continuing defects, real or apparent, in Marx's own statement of the theory. Logically, though not historically, these fall into two categories. First, there are a number of criticisms which are in principle independent of Marx's analysis of the transformation of values into prices, and which could therefore be advanced even if the latter analysis were entirely correct. These concern Marx's theories of wages, of monopoly price, of rent, and of productive and unproductive labour, and are discussed in section 5.2. Second, Marx's treatment of the transformation problem is incomplete and, as it has been outlined in Chapter 4, seriously at fault. Section 5.3 analyses the nature of this fault, and examines some of the remedies which have been proposed for it.

In 5.4 we outline the complete solution to the transformation problem which is implicit in the now classic work of Sraffa (1960). Section 5.5 deals with the complications resulting from the use of fixed capital, which seriously affect the generality of the labour theory of value. Section 5.6 assesses the labour theory of value in the light of these controversies. We show that the theory is not, as some have argued, based on meaningless metaphysical statements, but can be presented in operational terms so as to satisfy most positivists. This section concludes with a discussion of the usefulness of the labour theory of value in the context of the "neo-Ricardian" or Sraffian treatment of prices and distribution. Section 5.7 summarizes the arguments of the chapter as a whole.

5.2 Some initial problems

Wages
As Marx himself recognized, labour power is in one sense quite unlike any other commodity. It is not produced by capitalists for profit. The formal, legal freedom of the worker is a necessary condition for the development of capitalism itself. Why then should the labour theory of value apply to this peculiar commodity? Or, to put the point another way, why should not labour power sell at a price sufficiently high above its value to eliminate surplus value altogether?

Schumpeter poses this question against Marx (Schumpeter, 1954, pp. 650—1). He answers it in terms of the "abstinence" theory of capital, according to which the disutility involved in saving acts as the brake which prevents the rate of profit from falling to zero (*ibid*, pp. 655—9). Classical political economy, as we have seen, reaches the same conclusion by a completely different route, using the Malthusian population principle. Wolfson (1966, p. 100) attributes the survival of a positive rate of profit to inelasticities in the money supply.

For Marx these are all false solutions. He is scornful of the abstinence theory of capital[1], rejects Malthus, and treats interest as a *deduction* from total surplus value, so that an increase in the rate of interest means merely that the rate of profit paid to industrial capitalists is reduced (above, pp. 115—6). The formation and growth of the industrial reserve army, seen by Marx as an inevitable result of the accumulation of capital, prevents any long-run increase in real wages above the value of labour power. Thus, despite the fact that labour power is not directly produced by capitalists for profit, the law of value operates here too.

The *manner* of its operation is still contentious, and there are two further problems which merit discussion. The first concerns the elaboration which becomes necessary once the existence of labour power of different abilities and skills is recognized. In the face of heterogeneous labour power a theory of wage *differentials* must be developed, and it must be shown that such a theory remains consistent with the labour theory of value.

The second problem concerns the specific predictions which emerge, in the aggregate, from the postulate that wages tend to equality with the value of labour power. How far can this postulate be reconciled with actual long-run trends in real wages, and with the development of trade unions? Can Marx's "immiseration thesis" still be taken seriously?

Heterogeneous labour. The values of commodities are expressed in terms of units of embodied labour time. So long as labour is homogeneous, this is an entirely unambiguous measure. An hour of one man's labour is exactly the same as an hour of anyone else's. Now suppose that some men are skilled and others unskilled: what then? The labour of the skilled man must in some sense "count for" more than that of the unskilled. But how can this be reconciled with the labour theory of value? How can we determine the weights to be attached to different kinds of labour?

This requires the formulation of a theory of wage differentials. If a craftsman earns twice as much as a labourer, we might simply say that his labour is "worth" twice as much. But this begs the question. What determines this differential? Marx's answer is simple and direct:

"All labour of a higher or more complicated character than average labour is expenditure of labour-power of a more costly kind, labour-power whose production has cost more time and labour, and which therefore has a higher value, than simple or unskilled labour-power. This power being of a higher value, its consumption is labour of a higher class, labour that creates in equal times proportionately higher values than unskilled labour does" (Capital I, 197).

There is no circularity in this argument. In this passage, Marx

"was simply saying (a) that the value of the skilled labour power was higher because it had cost more labour to produce; and (b) that because it had cost more labour to produce, it was able to create a product of a higher value. Marx evidently regarded the labour expended on training the skilled labourer as being stored up, as it were, to be manifested when he actually begins to work" (Meek, 1973, p. 172).

All this is perfectly consistent with the labour theory of value[2], but there are two hidden assumptions involved. The first is that *all* skills can be acquired through training, and none is restricted to those possessing uncommon natural abilities (Schumpeter, 1954, pp. 593—6). The second is that workers are indifferent between different kinds of work. If either or both of these assumptions are false, the elasticity of supply of particular skills will be less than infinite: in the case of innate abilities, because the supply of those *able* to do certain types of work is limited by genetic factors; and in the second case because new recruits to a particular type of work are increasingly *unwilling* to perform it, and must be compensated by higher wages *over and above* the differential needed to offset any training costs (Wolfson, 1966, pp. 69–82). In either case the prices of different types of labour power seem to depend on "supply and demand" rather than on ratios of embodied labour[3], and the labour theory of value ceases to apply.

Consider first the problem posed by the existence of limited and variegated innate abilities. Sweezy (1946, p. 43) denies that any such problem exists; to compare the labour of men with different natural abilities, "it is only necessary to put them in the same line of production, where their relative effectiveness can be easily measured in purely physical terms". This is clearly wrong. *Which* line of production should be chosen for the experiment? What if, as is very likely, their relative effectiveness differs from one type of work to another?

Meek's (1973, p. 173) answer is much more satisfactory: he suggests that industries where such innate abilities are significant should be treated separately, as "specialist industries", "grouped together and dealt with in terms of the sort of analysis which Marx (and Ricardo) reserved for agriculture"[4]. The labour theory of value was always intended to apply only to those commodities which can be freely reproduced by human labour; as we have seen (above, p. 65), Marx praised Ricardo for having stressed this point. The number of exceptions which must be made because of the problem of innate abilities is unlikely to be large: sculptors and professional footballers are hardly typical of the modern worker. Once it is recognized that the labour theory of value was never intended to apply to such exceptional cases, a simple supply and demand theory of wages can be used to analyse them, without any inconsistency with the theory of value.

The second problem is potentially more serious. If it is accepted that the "disutility" of different types of labour plays a part in determining wage differentials, the door is open to explain prices in general in terms of utility theory (Wolfson, 1966, p. 55). There are three counterarguments which could be employed here. We could simply accept the validity of this point, but reformulate the labour theory of value in such a way as to allow demand to play some part in determining value (Bajt, 1971). Or we might treat it as a problem which relates only to the *individual* worker, but which disappears in the aggregate. I might be reluctant to empty dustbins, but there may be plenty of others who do not share my distaste; the elasticity of supply of dustmen would then be infinite *over the relevant range*.

Finally, we might take the position which Marx would probably have adopted in the face of such an argument: that the weight of the industrial reserve army is sufficient, in all normal circumstances, to ensure the suppression of individual preferences. Thus workers take jobs which they actively dislike (at the prevailing wage) in order to exist. Marx himself noted that the reduction of skilled to unskilled labour requires, *inter alia*, "indifference of the labourer to the nature of his labour", and "the elimination of all vocational prejudices among labourers" (*Capital* III, 196). And according to his theory of alienation, workers in capitalist society "shun work like the plague", as much because it entails subordination of the labourer to the capitalist as because of the intrinsic characteristics of specific jobs. Within very broad limits, then, men shun *all* types of work equally. Wolfson's argument is thus hardly the most serious objection which can be raised against Marx's theory of value.

Immiseration? It remains to be seen whether any subsistence theory of wages can be deemed at all relevant to the 1970s. On average, real wages are now more than four times as high as in the mid-1870s (Brown and Browne, 1968, p. 344). Whatever the defects of long-run wage series, no one any longer seriously disputes that the trend has been upwards, and that the pace of advance has been significant. Can we take at all seriously a theory which predicted that the working class would become, if not increasingly poor, at least no better off? Is the immiseration thesis at all credible?[5].

One answer is to suggest that Marx did not in fact predict increasing misery, at least in the conventional sense of constant or falling living standards for the mass of the population. Sowell (1960) argues that the "immiseration thesis" has been seriously misunderstood, and that many of the criticisms levelled against Marx on this score are irrelevant. He suggests that both the classical and the Marxian concepts of "real wages" referred to the *share* of wages in net output. On this interpretation, it is *relative* immiseration which Marx predicts. We have already seen that Marx rejected the assumption that "utility" is independent between individuals (above, pp. 31–2). He gives a very suggestive example to show that relative wellbeing is the crucial magnitude:

"A house may be large or small; as long as the surrounding houses are equally small it satisfies all social demands for a dwelling. But let a palace arise beside the little house, and it shrinks from a little house to a hut. The little house shows now that its owner has only very slight or no demands to make; and however high it may shoot up in the course of civilisation, if

the neighbouring palace grows to an equal or even greater extent, the occupant of the relatively small house will feel more and more uncomfortable, dissatisfied and cramped within its four walls" (SW I, 163).

Sowell argues that Marx's prediction of absolute immiseration was restricted to a section of the working class, the "pauper class" of the unemployed. But rising average living standards are, statistically at least, perfectly compatible with both a declining wage share and a growing volume of unemployment.

Sowell's argument is weak, both conceptually and empirically. If the industrial reserve army is rising, one would expect, in terms of Marx's own theory, that real wages would not rise above subsistence level. In any case, the evidence suggests that the wage share in net output is no lower today than it was a century ago, despite a sharp fall in the ratio of wage-earners to the total numbers employed; if wages and salaries are taken together, the "labour share" is now very much higher than it was a century ago (Feinstein, 1968). Nor, with the significant exception of the interwar years, is there the slightest evidence of a secular increase in the unemployment rate. This again suggests that something is wrong with Marx's theoretical analysis, which we discuss in Chapter 6.

It is possible that even a rigidly defined subsistence wage theory could be made consistent with a secular increase in living standards, as argued by Rosdolsky (1957—58). Increasing intensity of work, for example, would tend to exhaust the worker's labour power more rapidly, and would therefore require a higher real wage. This is true but almost certainly irrelevant: the traditional lumberjack requires a higher calorie intake than the modern circular saw operator!

Equally, if skill levels have risen over the last century—and this would be contrary to Marx's expectations—the socially necessary labour inputs needed to produce "average" labour power would have risen, so that real wages could remain at subsistence level and still show a significant increase. It is doubtful, though, whether such an argument could account for the magnitude of the increase in living standards over the last century.

One final possibility remains to be discussed. Might not the growth of trade unions be largely responsible for the long-run increase in real wages? Those modern neo-Ricardians who have interpreted Marx as postulating a bargaining power theory of wages are, in our view, wrong (see, for example, Nell, 1967). Marx's degree of freedom with respect to income distribution is severely constrained by his attempt to apply the labour theory of value to distribution itself. The value of labour power *must* therefore depend only on the quantity of labour needed to produce and reproduce it, so that a subsistence theory of wages is necessarily entailed.

Now it is possible to reconcile this with the neo-Ricardian argument in only one way. If trade unions have been able to increase the "historical and moral element" in the value of labour power, then real wages can increase *and* remain at the (growing) subsistence level.

There are two objections to this approach. First, it is difficult to see how it could be reconciled with the existence of the industrial reserve army. Second, it very easily degenerates into tautology. It is very difficult to avoid *defining* "subsistence" in terms of wages, thus explaining the value of labour power in terms of wages, rather than vice versa. This is a problem inherent in any subsistence wage theory which is not based on purely physiological needs, and it is clearly a danger in the case of Marx.

Marx's own attitude towards the narrowly economic prospects for trade unions has been the object of some misunderstanding. This issue is dealt with most thoroughly in *Wages, Price and Profit*, in which it is possible to find passages which, like the following, appear to support the neo-Ricardian argument:

"But as to profits, *there exists no law which determines their* minimum. *We cannot say what is the ultimate limit of their decrease. And why cannot we fix that limit? Because, although we can fix the* minimum *of* wages, *we cannot fix their* maximum. *We can only say that, the limits of the working-day being given, the* maximum *of profit corresponds to the* physical minimum of wages; *and that wages being given, the* maximum of profit *corresponds to such a prolongation of the working-day as is compatible with the physical forces of the labourer. The maximum of profit is, therefore, limited by the physical minimum of wages and the physical maximum of the working-day. It is evident that between the two limits of this* maximum rate of profit *an immense scale of variations is possible. The fixation of its actual degree is only settled by the continuous struggle between capital and labour, the capitalist constantly tending to reduce wages to their physical minimum, and to extend the working-day to its physical maximum, while the working man constantly presses in the opposite direction.*

The matter resolves itself into a question of the respective bargaining powers of the combatants" (*SW* II, 72−3).

Wrenched from its context, this appears to provide support for a bargaining power theory of wages in Marx. Seen in terms of the argument of *Wages, Price and Profit* as a whole, however, Marx's assessment of the economic role of trade unions is seen to be much more cautious.

In the first place, trade union activity is viewed as very largely *defensive*. "In 99 cases out of 100 their efforts at raising wages are only efforts at maintaining the given value of labour [power]" (*SW* II, 75).

They may therefore be able to prevent the permanent depression of wages *below* the value of labour power, which Marx saw as an otherwise chronic tendency in an early capitalism which lacked sufficient foresight to pay enough to reproduce its supplies of labour power for future generations. It might ensure that wage gains in years of prosperity offset losses in years of depression, so that on average wages were *maintained* in equality with the value of labour power (*ibid*, II, 69–70). More than this Marx did not expect. He saw the strike as a "test" of "the real state of demand and supply" in the labour market, and by implication as very little more (*ibid*, I, 45).[6].

Marx therefore argues that real wages, as defined by modern economists, are very little affected by union activity. But in the classical sense of real wages, as a *share* of net output, his position is rather different. For Marx, as we have seen, the only lower limit to the length of the working day is that which reduces unpaid labour, and thus surplus value and the rate of profit, to zero.

"As to the limitation of the working-day in England, as in all other countries, it has never been settled except by legislative interference. Without the working men's continuous pressure from without that interference would never have taken place" (SW II, p. 73).

The same argument is repeated in Chapter x of *Capital* I, and is supported by the recent research of Bienefeld (1972). A similar view may be imputed to Marx concerning the *intensity* of labour, which is also a major determinant of the rate of surplus value.

Thus the production of surplus value can be influenced by trade union pressures, even though the real wage cannot. Only in this sense are the modern neo-Ricardians correct to attribute to Marx a bargaining power theory of the rate of exploitation, and thus of income distribution. But this does not really rescue Marx from the false implications of the "immiseration thesis", however generously the latter is interpreted. The rate of exploitation is the ratio of surplus value (unpaid labour) to variable capital (paid labour). Even if the numerator can be influenced by bargaining power, Marx argues that the denominator cannot.

We must agree with Meek (1967, p. 124) that there is no way in which Marx's predictions can be reconciled with the actual course of real wages over the last century. Unless we are prepared to resort to a tautological *identification* of the real wage and the value of labour power, Marx's attempt to integrate the labour theory of value with the theory of wages must be judged a failure, and the theory of income distribution remains an open question.

Monopoly

The recognition of the existence of "non-competing groups" in the labour market raises much wider issues. Marx's development of the labour theory of value rests heavily (as does Ricardo's) on the postulate of free competition. Capital must be free to enter and leave industries at will, in search of higher rates of profit. If capital mobility is not free, equilibrium prices will not act as the limit towards which market prices tend. In the terms of the transformation problem, this means that commodities need no longer sell at their prices of production, since there is no longer any force compelling the equalization of rates of profit throughout the economy (*Capital* III, 196).

For the moment, however, we abstract from the problem of transforming values into prices. Assume for simplicity that organic compositions of capital are everywhere the same, so that under conditions of free competition all commodities would tend to sell at their values. It is clear that in the absence of free competition there is nothing which would enforce the law of value, since profit rates may differ between sectors permanently. The question of monopoly[7] thus raised is independent of the transformation problem, and would persist even in the absence of the latter.

For Marx a discussion of this problem is especially important, since he was probably the first economist to provide a convincing analysis of the pressures leading away from free competition:

"The battle of competition is fought by cheapening of commodities. The cheapening of commodities depends, ceteris paribus, on the productiveness of labour, and this again on the scale of production. Therefore the larger capitals beat the smaller . . . with capitalist production an altogether new force comes into play — the credit system, which in its first stages furtively creeps in as the humble assistant of accumulation, drawing into the hands of individual or associated capitalists, by invisible threads, the money resources which lie scattered, over the surface of society, in larger or smaller amounts; but it soon becomes a new and terrible weapon in the battle of competition and is finally transformed into an enormous social mechanism for the centralization of capitals.

Commensurately with the development of capitalist production and accumulation there develop the two most powerful levers of centralization — competition and credit" (*Capital* I, 626)[8].

This at least of Marx's economic predictions has been verified by history. Note that the forces leading to increased centralization are endogenous and structural, and do not depend on malice on the part of individual capitalists; Marx's account is thus quite different from that of Adam

Smith, for whom free competition breaks down only because of the propensity of capitalists to collude. Nothing of this sort is found in Marx's argument, where competitive struggle rather than collusion is the agent of centralization.

The crux of Marx's argument, then, is that competition under decreasing costs invariably leads to its own demise[9], which is accelerated by the growth of the modern credit system. But where does this leave the labour theory of value, which is enforced by competitive compulsion? We have seen that Marx treats "competition" as a surface phenomenon which distorts and mystifies the underlying reality. He therefore has very little to say about the implications of monopoly. What he does say is an extension of this basic position:

"If equalization of surplus-value into average profit meets with obstacles in the various spheres of production in the form of artificial or natural monopolies, and particularly monopoly in landed property, so that a monopoly price becomes possible, which rises above the price of production and above the value of the commodities affected by such a monopoly, then the limits imposed by the values of the commodities would not thereby be removed. The monopoly price of certain commodities would merely transfer a portion of the profit of the other commodity-producers to the commodities having the monopoly price. A local disturbance in the distribution of the surplus-value among the various spheres of production would indirectly take place, but it would leave the limit of this surplus-value itself unaltered. Should the commodity having the monopoly price enter into the necessary consumption of the labourer, it would increase the wage and thereby reduce the surplus-value, assuming the labourer receives the value of his labour-power as before. It could depress wages below the value of labour-power, but only to the extent that the former exceed the limit of their physical minimum. In this case the monopoly price would be paid by a deduction from real wages (i.e. the quantity of use-values received by the labourer for the same quantity of labour) and from the profit of the other capitalists. The limits within which the monopoly profit would affect the normal regulation of the prices of commodities would be firmly fixed and accurately calculable" (Capital III, 861).

Here Marx argues that the total amounts of value and surplus value which are produced remain exactly the same. The only result of the growth of monopoly is a *reallocation* of surplus value from those with less monopoly power to those with more. Monopolists sell their commodities at prices greater than their values (or, allowing for the transformation, at prices greater than the relevant prices of production), and capitalists in competitive industries are forced to sell below their values, a process which "always ends in the ruin of many small capitalists" (*Capital* I, 626), and speeds up centralization.

The great bulk of the gains made by monopolists are thus at the expense of their weaker fellow-capitalists. Part of the incidence might, however, fall on the workers if the real wage could be reduced due to the monopolization of *wage-goods* industries[10]. There is no question of prices exceeding their values *in aggregate*, nor, with the one exception which we have just noted, of aggregate profits increasing as monopolization progresses.

The impact of monopoly on income distribution is the crucial issue at stake. Kalecki's model of the share of wages in national income (Kalecki, 1954), in which the wage share falls directly as the *overall* degree of monopoly increases, has often been described as Marxian. Steindl (1952) also imputes a view similar to this to Marx himself. It is clear from what we have said that this is mistaken. Kalecki's model predicts a fall in the wage share *wherever* the increase in the degree of monopoly occurs, while on Marx's argument *only* the wage-goods industries are relevant. The incidence of growing monopoly power in departments I or III, Marx argues, will simply fall on less fortunate capitalists in competitive industries. Subject to this one qualification, Marx's position is that changes in market structure and in the intensity of competition do *not* affect the distribution of income.

In this sense we can agree with Sweezy when he claims that:

"*Qualitative-value relations are undisturbed by monopoly; quantitative-value relations are not. . . . even under monopolistic conditions we can continue to measure and compare commodities and aggregates of commodities in terms of labour-time units in spite of the fact that the precise quantitative relations implied in the law of value no longer hold*" (Sweezy, 1946, p. 55).

Unfortunately, the quantitative-value problem is also of no little significance. If, as experience suggests, wage-goods industries often do not operate under conditions of free competition, some theory of relative prices under monopoly is required for the analysis of income distribution. Marx supplies very little in the way of such a theory, except to hint that a supply and demand approach is all that can be expected:

"*When we refer to a monopoly price, we mean in general a price determined only by the purchasers' eagerness to buy and ability to pay, independent of the price determined by the general price of production, as well as by the value of the products*" (*Capital* III, 775).

Sweezy's position is equally agnostic: he denies that *any* general theory of monopoly price is possible, let alone a specifically Marxian theory (Sweezy 1946, pp. 272—4). It is not by accident that when he, in conjunction with Paul Baran, attempted to formulate a general theory of "monopoly capital", the resulting model was not based on the labour theory of value at all (Baran and Sweezy, 1968).

Meek rejects Marx's approach as "not capable of giving anything much more than a purely formal answer to the problem of monopoly price", and argues that "there are now many cases in which a part of the excess profits received by certain monopoly capitalists should properly be regarded as something like the old 'profit upon alienation' characteristic of the Mercantilist period" (Meek, 1973, p. 286; see also Dobb, 1973, p. 270). This is in effect a rejection of the relevance of the labour theory of value under conditions of monopoly.

In any case it is clear that the modern neo-Ricardian school is wrong to attribute to Marx the view that income distribution depends on the direct exercise of social power rather than on economic laws. Marx's position is that issues of distribution must be analysed in terms of the labour theory of value, and that the modifications which must be made to that theory on account of monopoly are relatively minor. We do not find this position entirely satisfactory[11]. Marxians least of all should be content with a theoretical apparatus which applies only under conditions of free competition. Marx's failure to elaborate a theory of monopoly price must be viewed as a major shortcoming.

Rent

Marx's theory of rent has come in for relatively little critical scrutiny. It has been customary for writers on the labour theory of value to make the same abstraction from landed property which Marx himself makes in Volumes I and II of *Capital*, and to ignore the analysis of rent which is undertaken in Volume III, Part VI[12]. Thus Samuelson complains that "in reading a thousand pages on the labour theory of value, I can remember but one author who comes close to emphasizing that land — and not merely capital — vitiates a labour theory of value and that no tricks with no-rent land can change this" (Samuelson, 1959a, p. 8)[13]. But it is possible to reject Samuelson's conclusion without denying the validity of his complaint. We must now ask whether Marx's theory of rent is either a necessary or a sufficient condition for an explanation of rent which is consistent with the labour theory of value.

It will be remembered that Marx also criticized Ricardo's "tricks with no-rent land". He developed instead a theory of absolute rent, paid even on marginal land, based on his analysis of the transformation of values into

140

prices. The existence of landed property, Marx argues, impedes the free entry of capital which is necessary to equalize rates of profit throughout the economy. In agriculture, "capital meets an alien force which it can but partially, or not at all, overcome, and which limits its investment in certain spheres, admitting it only under conditions which wholly or partly exclude that general equalization of surplus-value to an average profit" (*Capital* III, 761). "Surplus-profit" thus accrues in agriculture, which is paid to the landlords as rent.

Marx's theory of rent is fatally flawed. He seems to have interpreted Ricardo's denial of absolute rent as implying that there must exist in cultivation land on which no rent is paid (the extensive margin); and this is empirically false. But no such assertion is required. So long as the marginal unit of *capital-and-labour* yields no rent, there is a perfectly valid sense in which all rent is differential rent, and the value of corn is still determined solely by the embodied labour requirements at the margin.

Marx's apparent neglect of the *intensive* margin thus destroys his critique of Ricardian rent theory. His own theory is rather odd: it implies, for example, that the landlords have an interest in preventing the entry of capital into agriculture, which is surely the reverse of the truth. It suggests, moreover, that if the organic composition of capital in agriculture rises *above* the social average, absolute rent would become *negative*; it is not clear that this has any meaning at all.

Nor is Marx's analysis necessary to preserve the coherence of the labour theory of value. He accepted a Ricardian theory of differential rent, and this, in conjunction with the concept of the intensive margin, is all that is necessary. Land is scarce, non-reproducible and privately owned; like antiques and old masters, it will therefore command a price (though, of course, it has no value):

"It should be borne in mind in considering the various forms of manifestation of ground-rent ... that the price of things which have in themselves no value, i.e., are not the products of labour, such as land, or which at least cannot be reproduced by labour, such as antiques and works of art by certain masters, etc., may be determined by many fortuitous combinations. In order to sell a thing, nothing more is required than its capacity to be monopolized and alienated" (*Capital* III, 633).

In this passage, and in one referred to in our discussion of monopoly (above, p. 137), Marx considers landed property as one particularly important form of monopoly. Now the prices of monopolized commodities are determined by supply and demand, not by their values, and there is no reason why the price of land (and therefore the level of rent) should not be explained in exactly the same way. Rent is, then, simply a form of monopoly profit. (In orthodox theory the order of priority is reversed, and monopoly profit is misleadingly seen as a subdivision of rent.)

Thus we may admit all Samuelson's "objections" to the labour theory of value on this issue, without yielding at all on the fundamental question of the applicability of the theory under *competitive* conditions. It may be further objected that *all* industries use land. Only a few, however, are sufficiently land-using for this to be a serious practical problem. Marx's complex and rather confusing analysis of rent can thus be seen as redundant as well as inadequate.

Productive and unproductive labour

Marx's theory of productive and unproductive labour has incurred even less critical scrutiny than his theory of rent. Blaug's dismissal of the whole question is exceptional only in being made explicit: "Marx's distinction between productive and unproductive labour, therefore, stands or falls with the labour theory of value, and has no interest apart from it" (Blaug, 1968, p. 282). In fact, as we have seen and Robinson (1964, pp. 43—4) recognizes, the reverse is true. Without a coherent theory of productive and unproductive labour, the labour theory of value itself fails, since without such a distinction the crucial proposition that surplus value arises in production and not in exchange becomes meaningless, and Mercantilist fallacies cannot be avoided (see above, p. 72).

In principle, Marx's theory is simple and clear[14]. He applies the distinction specifically and solely to capitalism (*TSV* I, 152, 393—6), and points out that a quite different distinction might be called for in other types of society. Value judgments are entirely irrelevant, since "there is no question of moral or other standpoints in the case of either the one or the other kind of labour" (*ibid*, I, 171). The production of use value is a necessary condition for the performance of productive labour, but in this context use value means simply that there is a demand for whatever is produced: "the use value of a commodity in which the labour of a productive worker is embodied may be of the most futile kind" (*ibid*, I, 158).

The distinction has nothing at all to do with the production of material goods as opposed to (immaterial) services, and Adam Smith is severely criticized for suggesting that it has (*TSV* I, 171—4). Marx in fact adopts Smith's other, and quite incompatible, version of the distinction, in which

"he defines productive labour as labour which is directly exchanged with capital; that is, he defines it by the exchange through which the conditions of production of labour, and value in general, are first transformed into capital (and labour into wage-labour in its scientific meaning).

142

This also establishes what unproductive labour *is. It is labour which is not exchanged with capital, but* directly *with revenue, that is, with wages or profit. . . . These definitions are therefore not derived from the material characteristics of labour (neither from the nature of its product nor from the particular character of the labour as concrete labour), but from the definite social form, the social relations of production, within which the labour is realized. An actor, for example, or even a clown, according to this definition, is a productive labourer if he works in the service of a capitalist (an entrepreneur) to whom he returns more labour than he receives from him in the form of wages; while a jobbing tailor who comes to the capitalist's house and patches his trousers for him, producing a mere use-value for him, is an unproductive labourer. The former's labour is exchanged with capital, the latter's with revenue. The former's labour produces a surplus-value; in the latter, revenue is consumed"* (ibid, I, 157).

Productive labour produces surplus value, unproductive labour does not. The distinction is as simple as that. Labour employed by the capitalist's variable capital, in the pursuit of profit, is productive. Labour employed by the capitalist's revenue (that is, his consumption expenditure) is unproductive. The *same* type of work is productive or unproductive, depending on the context in which it is performed. Marx's tailor would be a productive labourer if employed by a capitalist in a factory; his clown would be an unproductive labourer if giving a private performance for a wealthy patron. It may in fact be true that most productive labour is employed in the production of material goods, and most unproductive labour in supplying immaterial personal services; but this is wholly irrelevant to the formal distinction which Marx makes.

All this is crystal clear. But Marx has — indeed, must have — another criterion for distinguishing between productive and unproductive labour, which must *also* be used. Productive labour, as we have seen, is that responsible for the creation of surplus value. Now it is a cardinal feature of Marx's analysis that surplus value arises in production, and not in exchange (above pp. 68—72). For consistency with his theory of surplus value, then, Marx's distinction between productive and unproductive labour must represent a division of activities between "production" and "exchange".

This is where the difficulty arises. Marx deals with this question in *Capital* II, ch. vi, where he discusses the division between production and circulation.

"The general law is that all costs of circulation which arise only from changes in the forms of commodities do not add to their value. *They are merely expenses incurred in the realization of the value or its conversion from one form to another"* (Capital II, 152).

Thus transportation is a productive activity, but book-keeping is not; Marx is unclear as to the status of labour employed in the storage of goods (*ibid*, II, 139—52).

His argument here seems to be based on a classification of activities according as they are necessary to *all* production, or only to *commodity* production. The Incas, as Marx observes, required transportation "although the social product neither circulated as a commodity nor was distributed by means of barter" (*Capital* II, 152). This sector is therefore productive, while activities such as commerce and retailing, which the Incas did not need, are unproductive. The question is left in a very unsatisfactory state, and no precise criteria are given for distinguishing between "changes in the forms of commodities" and production *per se*.

If Marx can be convicted of vagueness on this point, it is nevertheless true that the distinction between the employment of labour to produce surplus value, on the one hand, and to "realize" it by converting commodities into money on the other, remains of fundamental importance to his theory of value. This distinction is based neither on a metaphysical obsession with material production, nor on arbitrary value judgments. There is no need to reject the labour theory of value on this score.

5.3 The Transformation Problem

In Chapter 4 we saw that Marx attacked the classical identification of values with (equilibrium) prices, and surplus value with profit. Above all, he argued, this error served to mystify the origins of profit. The analysis of the transformation from values into prices is thus central to Marx's economic theory[15]. He claimed to have shown that nothing more was involved than a redistribution of surplus value between capitalists operating with different organic compositions of capital. The total *mass* of profit, and also the average *rate* of profit on capital employed, could be completely and consistently explained in terms of the labour theory of value. In this sense, Marx observed, the theory of value has *logical* priority over his theory of price, so that prices are inexplicable without a theory of value. Moreover, it has *historical* priority too: the transformation problem arises only when capitalism is sufficiently well developed for competition, and the resulting mobility of capital, actually to give rise to a tendency for the equalization of the rate of profit in different sectors of the economy. In earlier stages of capitalism, and even more in pre-capitalist societies, the problem is wholly irrelevant[16].

The essence of the problem, for Marx, is to prove that a coherent theory of prices can *and must* be derived from the labour theory of value. His most elaborate numerical example has been analysed in Chapter 4.

Table 4.1 (p. 107) appears to provide a complete and convincing defence of Marx's arguments. The sum of prices equals the sum of values, and the sum of profits equals the sum of surplus values. As a result, total capital remains unchanged by the transformation[17]. Since both numerator and denominator are the same, the *rate* of profit is also identical in both the value and the price systems.

Unfortunately, the position is not as simple as this. In Table 4.1 constant and variable capital are not expressed in terms of prices at all; they have not been transformed, but left exactly as they are. But means of production and means of subsistence are produced by some, at least, of Marx's five industries in this example. And if the prices of individual commodities, seen as *outputs*, differ from their values, then the same will be true when these same commodities are viewed as *inputs*. Column 9 of Table 4.1, which purports to show "cost-prices", remains in value terms. Marx recognized the need to transform input as well as output values into prices of production (*Capital* III, 161), but was unable to extend his analysis to allow him to do so. He thus completed only *half* the process of transformation.

A little manipulation of Table 4.1 will demonstrate just how serious this problem is. Following Bortkiewicz (1907), we made two minor alterations in Marx's original figures. These alterations allow us to aggregate the five industries of Table 4.1 into the three departments used extensively by Marx in his analysis of accumulation. Department I produces means of production, department II wage-goods (bought exclusively by workers), and department III luxuries (bought solely by capitalists for their personal consumption). Now assume that industries III and IV produce means of production; industries I and V produce wage-goods; and industry II produces luxuries. These three groupings thus constitute departments I, II and III respectively.

We can thus see that, in terms of *values*,

(a) the output of department I   = 202 = used-up constant capital
(b) the output of department II = 110 = total wages
(c) the output of department III = 110 = total surplus value.

The demand and supply for each type of commodity balance exactly[18]. But in terms of *prices* this is not true, since

(a) the output of department I   = 191 ≠ used-up constant capital
                                              (= 202)
(b) the output of department II = 129 ≠ total wages (= 110)
(c) the output of department III = 102 ≠ total profits (= 110).

The prices of production calculated by Marx cannot therefore be *equilibrium* prices, and his failure to transform inputs as well as outputs appears fatal to his treatment of the transformation problem.

The most famous way out of this dilemma was suggested nearly seventy years ago by Bortkiewicz (1907). If we assume for convenience that the conditions for simple reproduction are satisfied, and denoting the total value of output in each department as a_1, a_2 and a_3 respectively, we can write the "supply and demand" equations for each department, in terms of values, as:

Supply   *Demand*

Department I $c_1 + v_1 + s_1 = c_1 + c_2 + c_3 = a_1$ [5.1]

Department II $c_2 + v_2 + s_2 = v_1 + v_2 + v_3 = a_2$ [5.2]

Department III $c_3 + v_3 + s_3 = s_1 + s_2 + s_3 = a_3$ [5.3]

Equation [5.1], for example, shows that the value of the output of department I is equal to the value of the constant capital used by all three sectors. Equation [5.2] shows that the value of the output of department II equals the value of the variable capital used by all three. Equation [5.3] shows that the value of the luxuries produced by department III is equal to the total surplus value produced in all three departments.

Now denote the ratios of price to value in departments I, II and III respectively by x, y and z, and the rate of profit by r. Equations [5.1], [5.2] and [5.3] can then be written, in terms of prices, as follows:

Supply   *Demand*

Department I $(c_1x + v_1y)(1 + r) = (c_1 + c_2 + c_3)x = a_1x$ [5.1]'

Department II $(c_2x + v_2y)(1 + r) = (v_1 + v_2 + v_3)y = a_2y$ [5.2]'

Department III $(c_3x + v_3y)(1 + r) = (s_1 + s_2 + s_3)z = a_3z.$ [5.3]'

Here the lefthand side of each equation gives the *prices* of constant and variable capital used in each department, multiplied by one plus the rate of profit. The righthand side, reading down from equation [5.1]' to equation [5.3]', gives the prices of the total constant and variable capital used, and the luxuries consumed. We thus have three equations and four unknowns (x, y, z and r). Bortkiewicz's procedure is to determine the rate of profit and prices by putting $z = 1$, so that x and y express the prices of means of production and wage-goods, in terms of luxuries. Department III thus acts as the numeraire. Equations [5.1]', [5.2]' and [5.3]' can now be solved simultaneously for x, y and r; the solution is demonstrated in Appendix 1 (section 5.8, pp. 166–7).

The implications of Bortkiewicz's solution can best be seen by using a very simple numerical example. The value system is as follows:

Case 1

Department I $\quad 5c_1 + 2v_1 + 2s_1 = 5c_1 + 1c_2 + 3c_3$ (=9)

Department II $\quad 1c_2 + 4v_2 + 4s_2 = 2v_1 + 4v_2 + 3v_3$ (=9)

Department III $\quad 3c_3 + 3v_3 + 3s_3 = 2s_1 + 4s_2 + 3s_3$ (=9)

Using the formulae given in Appendix 1, we find that $x = \frac{4}{3}$, $y = \frac{2}{3}$ and $r = 50$ per cent. The price of production of department I, which has an organic composition of capital higher than the average (which is unity), is greater than its value; x is therefore greater than unity. The reverse is true for department II, where the organic composition is less than the average. Substituting these values into equations [5.1]´, [5.2]´ and [5.3]´, we find that both Marx's conditions for successful transformation are satisfied. The sum of values equals the sum of prices (= 27), and the sum of the surplus values equals the sum of the profits (= 9). Note also that the rate of profit, at 50 per cent, is the same in both the value and the price systems, since the value of the total capital equals its price (= 18).

This, however, is a *special case*. Prices have been expressed in terms of the luxury commodity, produced by department III, and our figures were carefully chosen so that the organic composition in this department (equal to unity) is the same as that of all three departments taken together. If the organic composition in this department is not equal to the average, Bortkiewicz's procedure does *not* give a satisfactory solution.

Suppose that we transpose two rows in the value system, to give:

Case 2

Department I $\quad 3c_1 + 3v_1 + 3s_1 = 3c_1 + 1c_2 + 5c_3$ (=9)

Department II $\quad 1c_2 + 4v_2 + 4s_2 = 3v_1 + 4v_2 + 2v_3$ (=9)

Department III $\quad 5c_3 + 2v_3 + 2s_3 = 3s_1 + 4s_2 + 2s_3$ (=9)

Department I now has the average organic composition, and that in department III is above average. Using the same formulae, we find that (approximately) $x = 0.80$, $y = 0.61$ and $r = 0.70$. The sum of surplus value remains equal to the sum of profits (=9), since z is still equal to unity. But the sum of prices (=21.66 approximately) is now less than the sum of the values, and the rate of profit is higher than in the value system.

It is easy to see why this has happened. Since it has an above-average organic composition, department III must also have an above-average price: value ratio; z is thus greater than both x and y. But, since we continue to take the output of department III as our numeraire, $z = 1$, and x and y must both be less than unity[19]. So while the price of the output of department III remains equal to its value, the prices of the outputs of *both* the other departments are lower than their values. Hence the inequality between the sum of the prices and the sum of the values. But departments I and II produce the capital — constant and variable — used by each other and by department III. The combined value of the outputs of I and II is thus the value of the total capital[20], and this is the donominator in the expression for the rate of profit. The numerator is, as we have seen, the same in terms both of prices and of values, since $z = 1$. So, given that the prices of both I and II are less than their values, the rate of profit must be higher in the price system than in the value system.

We could equally well have transposed the rows in a different way, to give department III a below-average organic composition, as in

Case 3

Department I $5c_1 + 2v_1 + 2s_1 = 5c_1 + 3c_2 + 1c_3$ (=9)

Department II $3c_2 + 3v_2 + 3s_2 = 2v_1 + 3v_2 + 4v_3$ (=9)

Department III $1c_3 + 4v_3 + 4s_3 = 2s_1 + 3s_2 + 4s_3$ (=9)

Using the formulae in Appendix 1 (section 5.8), we find (again approximately) that $x = 1.55$, $y = 1.275$ and $r = 0.35$. Again, since we put $z = 1$, the sum of profits equals the sum of the surplus values (=9). But this time the sum of prices is *greater* than the sum of values, and the rate of profit *lower* in the price than in the value system. The reasons for this are analogous to, in fact a mirror image of, those which explained why the opposite results were obtained in case 2. Once again, it will not help if we take as numeraire department II, which has the average organic composition[21].

This is not merely a quirk of arithmetic. It is inherent in Bortkiewicz's procedure that Marx's conditions for successful transformation *cannot* be met unless *both* (a) the organic composition of capital in department III is equal to the social average; *and* (b) the prices of the outputs of departments I and II are expressed in terms of that of department III (that is, $z = 1$). If these two conditions are not met, then either (a) if another department is used as numeraire, so that $z \neq 1$, the sum of profits will not equal the sum of surplus values; or (b) if the organic composition of capital in department III is not equal to the average, the sum of prices will not be equal to the sum of values; or (c) both. In any of these cases there will almost certainly be a discrepancy between the rate of profit in the value system and that in the price system. Formal proofs of these statements are given by Seton (1957), who is responsible for the first, and quite possibly the last, major development of the Bortkiewicz procedure for transformation, and uses more sophisticated mathematical techniques. Seton also provides a formal proof of Marx's argument that price exceeds value in sectors with above-average organic compositions, and vice versa[22].

Seton discusses the question of the "invariance postulates" required to convert relative into absolute prices. As we have seen, Marx has two such postulates: the equality of total prices and total values, and the equality of total profits and total surplus values[23]. Seton's discussion of these postulates is typical of many mathematical treatments of the transformation problem:

"No doubt the three invariance postulates ... do not exhaust all the possibilities. There may be other aggregates or relationships with perfectly reasonable claims to invariance whose candidacy has not so far been pressed. But the point which concerns us here is that the principle of equal profitability ... in conjunction with any one invariance postulate will completely determine all prices ... and thereby solve the transformation problem. However, there does not seem to be an objective basis for choosing any particular invariance postulate in preference to all the others, and to that extent the transformation problem may be said to fall short of complete determinacy" (Seton, 1957, p. 153; original stress omitted).

From a purely *mathematical* viewpoint this is certainly correct. Our three equations, [5.1]′, [5.2]′ and [5.3]′, will give solutions for the rate of profit and *relative* prices, which are then (given certain assumptions) uniquely determined[24]. All that we are doing in selecting one of Marx's invariance conditions (for example, putting $z = 1$), is to determine *absolute* prices. But, mathematically at least, any method of doing this is as good as any other, and it does not matter if aggregate prices come to diverge from aggregate values in the process. It is *relative* prices which matter, and once this is settled the rest is unimportant. One of Marx's invariance postulates, or perhaps both if a suitable alternative can be found, is redundant and can be dropped.

If we treat the analysis of transformation merely as a method for deriving relative prices, this would be perfectly acceptable. But we have already suggested that Marx intended it to be much more than this. He claimed to have shown, not merely that a coherent theory of relative prices *can* be derived from the labour theory of value, but also that such a theory can *only* be derived from the labour theory. Above all, it seems clear to us that Marx argued that the rate of profit was determined in the value system, the analysis of which was thus a necessary condition for the analysis of relative prices[25].

This is why *both* invariance conditions must apply. Otherwise, as we have seen in our numerical examples, the rate of profit given in the value system will differ from that found in the price system, and the most important economic ratio of all will be influenced by "competition". The satisfaction of both invariance conditions is therefore necessary if the labour theory of value is to do what Marx expected of it. But we have seen that it is only in the special case (case 1 above) that this is possible. It thus appears that the coherence of the labour theory of value depends on an accident of history: there is no conceivable *a priori* reason why the organic composition of capital in department III should equal the economy-wide average.

It is only quite recently that a way out of this dilemma has appeared, ironically enough through the work of a neo-Ricardian (Sraffa, 1960). In the next section we show that Sraffa's analysis of prices and distribution makes possible a logically consistent solution to the transformation problem which satisfies, *in general,* Marx's very demanding criteria.

5.4 The neo-Ricardian solution

In the course of the famous "Cambridge controversies", summarized by Harcourt (1972), it became clear that the neoclassical theory[26] of capital, prices and distribution was fatally flawed. It transpired that the rate of profit is *not* in general equal to the "marginal product of capital", and that the neoclassical theory of distribution is valid only in the special case where the "capital–labour ratio" is identical in all sectors of the economy (Garegnani, 1970). This special case is itself equivalent to that of equal organic compositions of capital in all industries, where the Marxian labour theory of value applies without the complications of transformation!

These conclusions reopened the search, which Ricardo had begun, for an "invariable measure of value", a measuring rod which would itself remain unchanged as alterations took place in the distribution of income between wages and profits. The ideal numeraire would be the output of a "borderline industry" (Sraffa, 1960, pp. 13–16) which, as r changes, is neither in surplus nor in deficit. If such a borderline industry could be found, we would have an unambiguous measure of changes in the property share in net output, without running into the valuation problems which wrecked neoclassical theory.

In his analysis of the transformation of values into prices of production, Marx defined the borderline industry as that which possessed the average ratio of dead to living labour, the social average organic composition of capital. Whatever the rate of profit, he claimed, such an industry would always sell its output at a price equal to its value. Using the output of this industry as the numeraire, it should therefore be possible to measure economic magnitudes in terms of labour values.

We have already seen that Marx's analysis, through its failure to transform inputs as well as outputs, was seriously incomplete[27]. The implications of this defect can be seen very clearly if we consider the criterion which must be satisfied by the borderline industry: that is, invariance of price in the face of changes in distribution without incurring either a surplus or a deficit in receipts over payments. Now an industry with an average organic composition of capital will nevertheless almost certainly use *inputs* which are themselves produced by industries with above- or below-average organic compositions. Except in the most exceptional circumstances, then, the input prices will, in aggregate, alter with a change in distribution[28], and this will result in a deviation of the *using* industry's price of production from its value. Marx's proposed numeraire simply does not work.

The criteria for the borderline industry are not, however, wholly dissimilar from those suggested by Marx. It must use the required or "balancing" ratio of labour to means of production, and this ratio must also *recur* "in all the successive layers of the industry's means of production without limit" (Sraffa, 1960, p. 16). Our problem is to find this critical balancing ratio between means of production and labour which leaves unchanged the price of the output of the borderline industry as distribution changes.

To explain Sraffa's solution to this problem, we write gross output as gp; means of production as mp; and net output as np, so that

$$gp = mp + np. \qquad [5.4]$$

It follows from Sraffa's definition of the borderline industry that the price of both gp and of mp in this industry will be invariant with respect to changes in r. Inevitably, therefore, np will also be unaffected by changes in distribution, and so also will be np/mp, the ratio of net output : means of production. One characteristic of the borderline industry, then, is that the ratio np/mp remains the same, whatever changes may occur in the rate of profit.

Now Sraffa, who rejects the validity of a subsistence wage theory, defines wages as a share in net output, rather than as an input required to produce labour power. If wages are zero, all the net output accrues to the capitalists as profits. In this case the ratio np/mp equals the ratio of total profits : means of production, and represents the maximum possible rate of profit. That is,

$$r_{max} = R = \frac{np}{mp} \qquad [5.5]$$

In practice, of course, workers cannot "live on air", so that the actual rate of profit will be lower than this maximum figure. But we have established that in the borderline industry the maximum rate of profit is independent of the *actual* rate of profit, and hence also *independent of relative prices*. If we can find an industry of which this is true, we have found our borderline industry.

Consider first Ricardo's simple corn model, in which the only commodity used as a means of production is corn (as seed), and in which both gross and net outputs consist entirely of corn. Here both terms in the ratio np/mp ($= R$) are simply quantities of corn. No change in the price of corn relatively to other commodities can possibly affect this ratio. The corn industry is thus our borderline industry, and corn can be used as an invariable measure of value.

Once we know R, and given the wage share in net output, we can easily find the actual rate of profit. Since we have defined w as the wage share in net output, the profit share is simply $(1 - w)$, so that total profits are $np(1 - w)$. The rate of profit is thus

$$r = \frac{\text{total profits}}{mp} = \frac{np(1 - w)}{mp} = R(1 - w) \qquad [5.6]$$

Now, ignoring social influences on work intensity, R depends on the technical coefficients of production; like the latter, therefore, it is constant. When all magnitudes are measured in terms of corn, the relation between w and r is the simple linear one given by equation (5.6).

These results will continue to apply in a multisector economy, as long as two conditions are satisfied. It must remain true, firstly, that corn is the only input (other than labour) into the corn industry. Secondly, the net output of all other commodities must be zero, so that the net output of the economy as a whole continues to consist entirely of corn. Both wages and profits are paid in corn, and the formula $r = R(1 - w)$ is still valid. Given w, we need to know only the technical conditions of production (which determine R), in order to find the *economy-wide* rate of profit. Changes in relative prices will not affect r, which depends—given w—solely on corn technology; they simply bring the rate of profit in other industries into line with that already established in the corn industry. And corn remains an ideal "invariable measure of value" in terms of which to measure changes in income distribution.

Neither of these two conditions is likely to be found in reality[29]. In modern agriculture tractors (and a great many other commodities) are used as inputs. The net output of the economy consists of a whole range of different commodities, not merely of corn. In general, where there are two or more industries, both R and r are ratios of two sets of heterogeneous commodities, and will change as the relative prices of these commodities alter[30].

But we might be able to find a group of industries in which R is determined in this way; in which, that is, the maximum possible rate of profit is given by a ratio of physical quantities of net output to physical quantities of the same commodities used as means of production, and which does not alter with changes in relative prices. The composite commodity represented by the net output of such a group of industries could, by an argument exactly analogous to that of the simple corn model, be used as an invariable measure of the values of all other commodities.

Sraffa (1960, p. 19) gives an example of a group of industries which, apart from labour, use only iron, coal and wheat to produce iron, coal and wheat. We can write the technical relations between inputs and outputs as in system I:

System 1

90 tons iron + 120 tons coal + 60 qr wheat + 3/16 labour *produce* 180 tons iron
50 tons iron + 125 tons coal +150 qr wheat + 5/16 labour *produce* 450 tons coal
40 tons iron + 40 tons coal +200 qr wheat + 8/16 labour *produce* 480 qr wheat
———
180   285   410   1

To produce one ton of iron, for example, requires inputs of $90/180 = \frac{1}{2}$ ton of iron; $120/180 = \frac{2}{3}$ tons of coal; $60/180 = \frac{1}{3}$ qr of wheat; and $\frac{3}{16}/180 = 1/960$ units of labour[31].

It is easy to see that system 1 provides no solution to our problem. Adding the columns, we find that the total quantities of means of production used are 180 tons of iron, 285 tons of coal, and 410 qr of wheat. Net output therefore consists of *zero* tons of iron, 165 tons of coal, and 70 qr of wheat. If wages are zero, this is all paid to the capitalists, and

$$R = \frac{165 \text{ coal} + 70 \text{ wheat}}{180 \text{ iron} + 285 \text{ coal} + 410 \text{ wheat}}$$

This cannot be reduced to a fraction without knowledge of the relative prices of these three commodities. Thus R is equal to

$$\frac{165 \times p_{coal} + 70 \times p_{wheat}}{180 \times p_{iron} + 285 \times p_{coal} + 410 \times p_{wheat}}$$

The net output of this composite industry cannot, therefore, be used as an invariable measure of value, since it itself depends on relative prices.

Now let us suppose that we are dealing with a slightly different system:

System 1^a

90 tons iron + 120 tons coal +   60 qr wheat +   3/16 labour *produce* 180 tons iron
30 tons iron +   75 tons coal +   90 qr wheat +   3/16 labour *produce* 270 tons coal
30 tons iron +   30 tons coal + 150 qr wheat +   6/16 labour *produce* 360 qr wheat
───   ───   ───   ─────
150   225   300   12/16

Here the net output consists of 30 tons of iron, plus 45 tons of coal, plus 60 qr of wheat. R is now equal to

$$\frac{30 \text{ tons iron} + 45 \text{ tons coal} + 60 \text{ qr wheat}}{150 \text{ tons iron} + 225 \text{ tons coal} + 300 \text{ qr wheat}}$$

It can be seen that $R = 0.2$, *whatever* the relative prices of the three commodities. Nor is it too difficult to see why this should be so. The system has been chosen in such a way that "the various commodities are represented among its aggregate means of production *in the same proportions* as they are among its products" (Sraffa, 1960, p. 19). They thus appear in this same proportion in the net output; a ratio, that is, of $1 : 1\frac{1}{2} : 2$.

Two conclusions follow from this. First, for reasons which parallel those operating in the case of the corn model, this value of R gives the maximum rate of profit for the economy as a whole[32]. Second, the relationship between the wage and the rate of profit — shown by equation [5.6], where $r = R (1 - w)$ — still holds, so long as we measure wages in terms of the net output of this composite industry[33].

The solution to the problem of the ideal numeraire, or invariable measure of value, is now quite clear. We have to construct a composite industry[34] which meets the conditions laid down above. Sraffa has shown that there exists a unique set of multipliers[35] which can be applied to the industries of any actual economic system to produce the required composite industry. System 1^a was actually built up in this way: it was derived from system 1 by taking the whole of the iron industry (that is, a multiplier of unity), $\frac{3}{5}$ of the coal industry, and $\frac{3}{4}$ of the wheat industry. The procedure for calculating these multipliers is demonstrated in Appendix 2 (section 5.9, pp. 168–71)[36].

Thus the answer to a famous Ricardian problem has been found by an essentially Ricardian analysis. What relevance has this to the Marxian *labour* theory of value? Two immediate similarities spring to mind. The first concerns the very limited role played by demand; the second concerns the peculiar position of "non-basic", or luxury industries.

We deal first with the role of demand. Sraffa derives a fully determinate set of prices from only two pieces of information. The first consists of the technical input coefficients of production, and the second is *either* the wage *or* the rate of profit. We shall say more about Sraffa's treatment of distribution in section 5.6. For the moment it suffices to observe that it does *not* reflect supply and demand conditions in the markets for "factors of production". Thus in Sraffa's system demand plays no part in the *determination* of long-run equilibrium prices. For Sraffa, as for Marx[37], "supply and demand" merely ensure that actual market prices tend towards those long-run equilibrium prices (or "prices of production") because of the equalization of the rate of profit brought about by competition[38].

There is however an important qualification which must be made to this statement. Sraffa makes it clear that his analysis deals with an economy in which nothing changes, so that production goes on at exactly the same level from year to year (Sraffa, 1960, p.v). Now "the exclusion of change is crucial. In an actual economic system, in which change is occurring, it would not be possible, in the absence of constant returns to scale, to determine prices independently of the level and composition of output" (Harcourt, 1972, p. 195). Thus, although Sraffa warns against attributing to him an assumption of constant returns, such an assumption must in fact be made if his analysis is to be applied to actual economies.

Thus it is only if the technical input coefficients are constant with respect to changes in output that information about demand is not necessary in order to determine relative prices. If they do vary with output (that is, if either increasing or diminishing returns to scale prevail) then it is impossible to determine relative prices without some knowledge of demand. This is not a new discovery. It has long been known that Marx's labour theory of value can dispense with demand functions only on this condition[39]. If, however, input coefficients *are* constant, demand plays no part in determining long-run equilibrium *prices*, or labour values; it merely determines the *outputs* of the various commodities.

A problem is apparent, however, if we remember Marx's analysis of the development of monopoly. We saw above (p. 136) that, in Marx's words, "the cheapness of commodities depends, *ceteris paribus*, on the productiveness of labour, and this again on the scale of production. Therefore the larger capitals beat the smaller . . ." (*Capital* I, 626). Marx fully recognized the colossal importance of economies of scale in modern industry. But, as a result, the input coefficients depend on the level of output in each industry, and thus on demand. It seems, therefore, that Marx's defence of the labour theory of value is inconsistent with his entirely realistic appraisal of the implications of capitalist development[40].

This is part of the *general* problem raised by monopoly. The latter applies with equal force to Sraffa, whose analysis rests on the assumption, applicable only to free competition, that an equal rate of profit is paid in all industries. Thus the neo-Ricardian as much as the Marxian theory of value is strictly valid only in free competition. As both Marx and Ricardo realized, the equilibrium prices of commodities produced by monopolists are invariably dependent on demand.

The second obvious similarity between Sraffa and Marx lies in the fact that not all industries can play a part in the composite — or, in Sraffa's term, "Standard" — industry. Only those commodities which are used, directly or indirectly, as a means of production in *all* industries enter into the Standard system. These Sraffa terms "basics". "Non-Basics", on the other hand,

"have no part in the determination of the system. Their role is purely passive. If an invention were to reduce by half the quantity of each of the means of production which are required to produce a unit of a 'luxury' commodity of this type, the commodity itself would be halved in price, but there would be no further consequences; the price relations of the other products and the rate of profits would remain unaffected. But if such a change occurred in the production of a commodity of the opposite type, which does enter the means of production, all prices would be affected and the rate of profits would be changed. This can be seen if we eliminate from the system the equation representing the production of a 'luxury' good. Since by the same act we eliminate an unknown (the price of that good) which appears only in that equation, the remaining equations will still form a determinate system which will be satisfied by the solutions of the larger system. On the other hand, if we eliminated one of the other, non-luxury, equations, the number of unknowns would not thereby be diminished since the commodity in question appears among the means of production in the other equations and the system would become indeterminate" (Sraffa, 1960, pp. 7–8).

There is a close parallel here with the role of department III in Bortkiewicz's analysis of the transformation of values into prices. The "conditions of production" — technical input coefficients — of department III do not appear in the formula for the rate of profit, as may be seen from equation [A11] of Appendix 1 (p. 167); the reasoning involved is exactly the same[41].

We can go further than these suggestive parallels between the Sraffian and Marxian analyses. It has been shown, firstly, that Sraffa's analysis can be translated into that of Marx, and secondly, that Sraffa's derivation of the Standard system provides a complete solution to the Marxian transformation problem (Meek 1967, pp. 161–78; Medio, 1972).

Consider Sraffa's fundamental equation (equation [5.6] above), which shows that $r = R(1 - w)$. The maximum rate of profit (R) depends solely[42] on the technical relationships between inputs and outputs. In the corn model, to take a very simple example, if $mp = \frac{1}{2}$, $gp = 1$ and $np = \frac{1}{2}$, so that half a ton of corn is needed to produce one ton of corn at harvest, R is equal to $(1 - \frac{1}{2})/\frac{1}{2} = 1$. But this ratio is also equal to the labour embodied in the net output of the Standard system, divided by the labour embodied in its means of production.

In Marx's terminology, but retaining Sraffa's treatment of the wage as part of net output, we have net output equal to $(v + s)$, and the means of production equal to constant capital, c. Thus $R = (v + s)/c$. Now Sraffa's expression $(1 - w)$ is simply the proportion of the net output of the Standard system which goes to profits, which is $1 - (v/v + s)$, where $(v/v + s)$ is the wage share in net output. We can thus write, for the rate of profit,

$$r = R(1 - w) = \frac{v + s}{c} \cdot \left[1 - \frac{v}{v + s} \right] \qquad [5.6a]$$

$$= \frac{v + s}{c} - \frac{v(v + s)}{c(v + s)} = \frac{v + s}{c} - \frac{v}{c} = \frac{s}{c}$$

Thus, remembering again that Sraffa includes only constant capital in the denominator of the fraction, his definition of the rate of profit is identical with the definition which is given by Marx in terms of labour values.

This suggests that there must be some relationship between Sraffa's Standard system and Marx's abortive search for an industry with the social average organic composition of capital. In fact this relationship is a very close one, for, as Meek has pointed out, "Sraffa's 'standard' industry, seen from this point of view, is essentially an attempt to *define* 'average conditions of production' in such a way as to achieve the identical result which Marx was seeking" (Meek, 1967, p. 178). Instead, that is, of looking for *one* industry or department with the "average organic composition", Marx could have constructed a composite industry displaying the characteristics of Sraffa's standard industry, and used *this* as his numeraire. If he had done so, as equation [5.6a] makes clear, the rate of profit in the price system would be identical with the rate of profit in the value system, and Marx's claims about the logical priority of the value system would have been better substantiated. Sraffa, then, has produced an apparatus for transformation which does, *in general* and not merely in exceptional cases, satisfy Marx's two invariance conditions. Even the mathematical procedures used to obtain a borderline industry to play this role for Marx are equivalent to those used by Sraffa (see Medio, 1972).

5.5 The problem of fixed capital

Part I of Sraffa (1960), which we have outlined in the previous section and in Appendix 2, (section 5.9, pp. 168—71), assumes that there are no joint products or alternative processes in the system. Thus, in systems I and I^a, there is only *one* way in which coal (for example) can be produced, and coal is the *only* product of the "coal industry". These assumptions provide a sufficient condition for the number of equations in the system to equal the number of unknowns (given w or r), so that a unique economically meaningful solution can be found to equations [A15] and [A16] in Appendix 2.

In Part II of his book, Sraffa shows that joint products and alternative processes can be incorporated into his analysis, so long as the total number of processes used equals the number of commodities produced. This leads to certain complications, notably in the definition of basic and non-basic industries (*ibid*, pp. 49—55). It may also result in some of the q-multipliers of equation [A18] in Appendix 2 becoming negative, so that the Standard system is now a purely abstract concept, and can no longer be regarded as "a conceivable rearrangement of the actual processes" (*ibid*, p. 48). Moreover, some prices might become negative: "and this being unaccept-able, those among the methods of production that gave rise to such a result would be discarded to make room for others which in the new situation were consistent with positive prices" (*ibid*, p. 59). This might be treated as analogous to the case cited by Marx in which a commodity with a zero (and, *a fortiori*, a negative) use-value possesses zero value. As such, it could be assimilated into Marx's requirement that only socially necessary labour time "counts" in the determination of value (Morishima, 1973, pp. 186—7).

If the number of processes (equations) is not equal to the number of commodities produced (the prices of which are the unknowns) there are further complications, for Sraffa's system will be either over- or under-determined. In particular, if there are more processes than products the system is over-determined. And an identical problem will arise for the labour theory of value. Morishima has shown that, since there is no unique solution, a single commodity produced (at a switchpoint between two techniques) by two processes may have *more than one* labour value, even though in competition all units of the commodity, by whichever process they have been produced, will sell at the same price of production.

This point may be illustrated by a simple example (Morishima, 1973, pp. 189—90). Assume that tractors and labour are used to produce tractors, and that there are two processes available:

Process 1: $\frac{1}{4}$ tractor + $\frac{1}{2}$ labour *produce* 1 tractor

Process 2: $\frac{1}{2}$ tractor + $\frac{1}{4}$ labour *produce* 1 tractor.

Writing λ for the value of a tractor, measured in labour units, we may summarize process 1 as follows:

$$\frac{1}{4} \lambda + \frac{1}{2} = \lambda \qquad\qquad [5.7]$$

which is easily solved to give $\lambda = \frac{2}{3}$. This is the labour value of a tractor produced by process 1. Similarly, for process 2:

$$\frac{1}{2} \lambda + \frac{1}{4} = \lambda \qquad\qquad [5.8]$$

which gives a solution where $\lambda = \frac{1}{2}$.

Capitalists will choose the most profitable method open to them, that is, the process which minimizes the cost of producing tractors. This in turn will depend on income distribution: some levels of the rate of profit relative to the wage will encourage the use of one process, some the use of the other process. If distribution is such that two processes are *equally* profitable, capitalists will be indifferent as to which they use, and the total output of tractors will be produced by some (arbitrary) combination of the two processes. Such a situation occurs in Morishima's example when the rate of profit equals $\frac{1}{3}$; this is demonstrated in Appendix 3 (section 5.10, pp. 170–1). In this case the labour value of a tractor will alter with changes in the proportions in which the two processes are used, and there is no unique labour value for tractors[43].

The implications are very damaging for the labour theory of value, much less so for the neo-Ricardian approach. Every tractor will, of course, sell at the same price of production, since we have assumed competitive capitalism with free mobility of capital and commodities. But to one price there corresponds two (or more) labour values[44]. In what sense, then, can values be said to determine prices, or even to be in a certain definite relationship to prices? In this situation the labour theory of value does not appear very meaningful.

This does *not* appear to be a serious problem for the neo-Ricardian analysis. In the latter, it is argued that (given the distribution of income) technology determines long-run equilibrium prices. This remains unambiguous even if more than one set of technical input coefficients is used to produce a single commodity which sells at a single price. The labour theory of value, on the other hand, is based on a reduction of the vector of input coefficients to a *single quantity*, embodied labour. In the case under discussion, it is evident that this cannot be done. Thus the neo-Ricardian approach is superior to the labour theory of value in its ability to cope with this problem.

The labour theory of value, then, cannot easily handle cases of joint production or multiple processes unless, by some accident, the number of products equals the number of processes. On its own, this might not be too serious a limitation. But Morishima (1973, pp. 174—5) has claimed that such an inequality is *generally* found in any economy which uses fixed capital. And Marx's economics without fixed capital would be Hamlet without the Prince, as we shall see when we come to discuss his theory of economic development in Chapter 6.

Let us see how Morishima comes to make this claim. In Sraffa's words, "the interest of Joint Production does not lie so much in the familiar examples of wool and mutton, or wheat and straw, as in its being the genus of which Fixed Capital is the leading species" (Sraffa, 1960, p. 63). A process which uses fixed capital—say a machine—in effect produces *two* commodities: the final product, *and* a machine which is older by the length of the production process than it was when production began. By itself this need not cause any great difficulty, Sraffa suggests: it also provides a second process, since the older machine can be used next year to produce the same final product. Sraffa concludes that, even if fixed capital is used, the number of processes will remain equal to the number of products[45].

It appears, however, that this is in general *not* true. Consider an economy in which there are fifty different types of machine, each of which lives for two production periods (years). Each type of machine is specific to the production of a single final product. We may write the production equations for this system as follows:

Process

  1. new machine 1 + labour *produce* wheat + old machine 1
  2. old machine   1 + labour *produce* wheat
  3. new machine 2 + labour *produce* new machine 1 + old machine 2
  4. old machine   2 + labour *produce* new machine 1

. . . .

  99. new machine 50 + labour *produce* new machine 49 + old machine 50
100. old machine 50 + labour *produce* new machine 49

Here we have 100 processes, and also 100 products (wheat; old and new machines 1—49; and old machine 50).

But the system is clearly incomplete, for there is no process which produces new machine 50. It is no use to assume that this is done by a further machine, 51, since this simply pushes the problem one stage further back; we would then need an extra process to produce machine 51 itself. Nor will it help if machine 50 is used to produce itself, for this will add *two* further processes:

101. new machine 50 + labour *produce* new machine 50 + old machine 50
102. old machine 50 + labour *produce* new machine 50.

These two extra processes add only one new product (new machine 50)
The number of processes is now 102, which exceeds the number of
products (101), and our problem remains.

There are at least two possible ways of escaping from this problem. We
might, firstly, assume that the production of new machine 50 requires
only labour, giving just *one* extra process:

101. labour *produces* new machine 50.

But there is no clear *a priori* reason why it should be possible to produce
any one machine in this way. Secondly, it might be assumed that one of
our 102 processes would be less efficient than the others, therefore
unprofitable, and hence not be used. Again, there is no obvious reason
why *exactly* one process should be rejected in this way. If more than one
process proved unprofitable, we would end up with *fewer* processes than
products. We are forced to conclude that the analysis in Part II of Sraffa
(1960), which assumes that the number of processes is equal to the
number of processes, is a special case. In the general case, the validity of
the labour theory of value is seriously shaken.

5.6 An assessment of the labour theory of value

In assessing Marx's theory of value we must first be clear as to exactly
what purpose he intended it to serve. We raised this question in our
discussion of Ricardo (above pp. 79—80), and suggested that in some ways
Marx's view of the role of the labour theory was very close to that of
classical political economy. On this interpretation, the theory was *not*
intended as an ethical attack on property incomes, based on notions of
social justice or "natural law". Moreover, the labour theory of value
cannot be seen as necessary to demonstrate the *existence* of surplus value:
this can be done far more simply. Property incomes can be observed, *as a
fact*, in any capitalist economy. They can be *explained*, however, in
different ways. One explanation, favoured by neoclassical economists, is in
terms of the "productive contributions" of non-labour "factors of
production", notably "capital" and land.

Marx of course was a vigorous opponent of such explanations, which he
regarded as a form of mystification or fetishism (above p. 39f). Profit and
rent, he pointed out, are paid to *people* (or more accurately to social
classes), not to things. It is therefore to the structure of society, and not
to the physical properties of objects, that we must look for the origin of
property incomes. Profit and rent, that is, are categories of income

accruing to specific social classes, and their *existence* must therefore be explained in terms of the relations of property ownership and non-ownership. Even if, in (disputed) modern terminology, "capital" has a "marginal productivity" which can be rigorously quantified, this is irrelevant to the question of the existence of profit. Profit exists because the means of production are monopolized by a specific minority class, not because they are *useful* in the production of material wealth. (That they are useful Marx certainly did not deny.) The means of production only become "capital" when they are *owned* in this way (above pp. 37–8).

Marx's solution to the problem of the existence of property incomes, which we have termed the "qualitative" problem of distribution (above pp. 114–5), is thus in principle independent of *any* theory of value. It is true that the existence of surplus value, and its origins in the performance of surplus labour, may be most clearly *exposed* in terms of the labour theory of value, for the same reason that, for example, the existence of exploitation is more blatantly obvious in a non-market feudal economy than in capitalist societies. But adherence to the labour theory of value is in no sense a necessary condition for a coherent theory of exploitation, which rests more directly on the class relations of society. Once again this is an *analysis* of a class society, and does not entail an ethical condemnation of it: an exploitation theory could be held, without any inconsistency, by a *supporter* of capitalism (as in effect it was by Ricardo, for example).

It is thus misleading to argue that Marx's "claim is that the theory of *value* is precisely what accounts for exploitation" (Robinson, 1964, p. 36). Even if Marx had made such a claim, which is doubtful, he would have been wrong to do so. Meek's assessment is much nearer the mark:

"Historically, at any rate, so far from the existence of surplus value being derived from the labour theory, the labour theory was in fact evolved precisely in order to explain the manifest existence of surplus value in the real world. The emergence of a value-difference between input and output which eventually resolved itself into rent and profit and which was not significantly attributable to any expenditure of productive effort on the part of its recipients, was regarded by the Classical economists as a simple fact. One of the main tasks which the labour theory of value was asked to perform was that of accounting for the origin and persistence of this surplus value and measuring its extent" (Meek, 1973, pp. 126–7).

It will be clear from what we have said that, although this is quite true, the labour theory of value is not *necessary* for "accounting for the origin and persistence" of surplus value, but only (if at all) for "measuring its extent".

It is important to get this point into perspective. Marx's use of the labour theory of value in the context of his theory of exploitation is not a "confusion", as has been alleged (Robinson, 1965, p. 176); see the perceptive criticism by Bose, (1971, p. 301). The *quantitative* problem of distribution remains: we have to measure surplus value, its size and rate of change. This is no trivial problem. As we have seen above (p. 80) in relation to classical political economy, and will see in Chapter 6 in the context of Marx's macro-economic theory, it was the way in which both Ricardo and Marx set about the analysis of the long-run economic development of capitalism.

This, then, is the second stage of the problem of income distribution, and here *some* principle of valuation is very clearly necessary. Marx, as Morishima (1973, p. 10) observes, used the labour theory of value as an aggregation device to derive the three departments used in his analysis of the transformation of values into prices, and the two departments of his theory of reproduction and accumulation. On this view, the labour theory of value is a rather technical tool of analysis, which is useful as soon as we leave the simple one-sector world of Ricardo's corn model and have to measure output, surplus, and so on, in terms of values rather than as physical quantities of a single homogeneous commodity.

It might therefore be argued that the labour theory of value *is* necessary to a usable theory of exploitation in which quantifiable predictions can be made about the development of capitalist economies. At the end of this section, however, we argue that this is not in fact so, and that a neo-Ricardian theory of value is a more direct and more acceptable substitute for it in this role.

First, however, we must refute a common methodological attack on the labour theory of value. Following Böhm-Bawerk (1896), Wolfson (1966, p. 46) argues that "we can observe prices . . . but we do not and cannot observe values. Why not simply jettison the concept [of value] as a metaphysical philosophers' stone?" Blaug (1968, p. 239) argues that Marx's concept of value "is not a ratio at which products exchange but purely an abstraction that is posited and not observed". Furthermore, "the rate of surplus-value is not observable in the market; no-one acts in response to it; workers are interested in maximizing wages and capitalists are motivated by the rate of profit. Marx . . . presumes the existence of a purely fictitious ratio s/v" (*ibid*, p. 237).

Robinson (1964, p. 47) is even more forthright: "*Value* will not help. It has no operational content. It is just a word." She argues that value is a meaningless metaphysical concept. In the same chapter as that from which we have just quoted, she uses the terms "metaphysics" or "metaphysical" no less than eight times in four pages in the course of her attack on the labour theory of value (*ibid*, pp. 38—41).

These are expressions of the extreme positivist view that all meaningful concepts must refer to entities which are *directly* observable. If valid this view would destroy, not merely Marx's theory of value, but scientific enquiry in general. All sciences, natural and social, use and must use such concepts in order to explain observable phenomena. As examples, consider the use of *molecules* in chemistry, *electrons* in physics, *role* in sociology, *ego* in psychology, or, for that matter, *utility* in neoclassical economics (Ryan, 1970)[46].

Sophisticated positivists do not take such an untenable position as this. They argue instead that "non-observable" concepts like value — and the other examples which we have just given — can be validly used so long as they can be translated into concepts which refer to entities which are themselves *directly* observable. Now it has recently been pointed out that precisely such a translation is possible for Marx's concept of value: "the accounting in terms of value is observable, since it is no more than the calculation in terms of employment" (Morishima, 1973, p. 20)[47]. Statements about values, that is, can be reformulated as statements which refer to the quantities of labour employed in different industries; and employment is certainly directly observable. It should be noted, however, that this sophisticated positivist argument is not without its own problems, and that many philosophers of science adhere to a "realist" position in which valid scientific concepts *can* be formulated which are not translatable in this way (Keat and Urry, 1974). *In either case*, the Blaug—Robinson—Wolfson methodological attack on the labour theory of value is misconceived.

This mistake may be due in part to a confusion about Marx's distinction between "appearance" and "reality" (above pp. 39—45). When Marx says that "reality" is unobservable he does not mean it in an epistemological sense, but in a *sociological* sense. The underlying causal importance of the social relations of capitalism, he argues, is rarely observed by its economic actors. Capitalists, in particular, observe only prices and profits, not values and surplus values. This is because they have no reason to be analysts of capitalism as a whole. Their perspective is not only narrow, and restricted to superficial phenomena, it is also false and misleading: in a word, ideological. Marx argues that it is only by going beyond and beneath appearances that reality can be uncovered, so that value and surplus value, for example, can be seen as the determinants of prices and profits. *In this sense* the concept of value in Marx is certainly and necessarily "non-observable", but in social practice, not in principle; to economic agents, not to scientific investigators.

It is important, though, that theoretical deductions involving such concepts must be logically coherent; and that the propositions finally arrived at must be capable of falsification. This suggests an alternative methodological criticism of the labour theory of value: that it is *tautological*, that is, true by definition, and hence irrelevant to empirical reality. Can Marx perhaps be criticized on this score?[48].

Marx was often very dogmatic in his defence of the labour theory of value, and occasionally suggested that it was in some way above criticism and beyond falsification[49]. But this is not typical. The very nature of the logical-historical method clearly requires that economic theory be related very closely to reality. Marx's analysis of the transformation of values into prices of production, for example, hinges on the empirical observation that in competitive capitalism the rate of profit tends to equality throughout the economy, while organic compositions of capital differ between industries. Simple untransformed values would therefore give a *false* picture of long-run equilibrium exchange ratios, and must be transformed into prices of production. The whole procedure shows that Marx was aware that falsification tests are applicable to the labour theory of value.

There are thus no grounds for these methodological criticisms of the labour theory of value, and it is noticeable that the onslaught recently mounted on the theory by Samuelson (1970, 1971, 1972, 1973), does not hinge on this line of attack. Samuelson's 1971 article is equally remarkable for the author's evident unwillingness to support a neoclassical theory of distribution in place of "Marxian exploitation". Samuelson makes many references to the "competitive rate of profit", but nowhere does he present a *theory* of profit, presumably because he hasn't got one. Eventually he declared his 1971 article to be Sraffian in approach (Samuelson, 1973, p. 64), which, as we shall shortly see, commits him to no theory of distribution whatsoever. It is Samuelson's confrontation of Marx with Sraffa, however, which forms the crux of an important but, in his hands, opaque and unnecessarily complex argument.

We have seen that a complete and rigorous solution to Marx's transformation problem is possible in terms of Sraffa's Standard system (above pp. 149–56). What is more, Meek (1973, pp. xxvi–xliii) has shown that Sraffa's analysis can be presented in terms of Marx's logical-historical method[50]. Now Samuelson's fundamental argument is that such a presentation is superfluous: all the crucial problems in the theory of value can be settled, as they are by Sraffa, *directly* in terms of physical input coefficients. A *labour* theory of value, then, is (in the words of an earlier article) merely a "complicating detour" (Samuelson, 1957, p. 892). Instead of going, via a fairly complicated argument, from technical coefficients to labour values, Sraffa misses out the intermediate stages. His analysis is simpler, more direct and more elegant than Marx's. (It is also, as we saw in 5.5, better able to deal with the problem of fixed capital.) Since the results are the same in both cases, what need is there for a labour theory of value?[51]

The only answer to this question concerns the treatment of income distribution in the two analyses. Marx integrates the theory of value with the theory of income distribution, through his treatment of labour power as a commodity, the value of which depends (like that of any other commodity) on the quantity of socially necessary labour needed to produce it. Distribution is thus determined[52] by economic laws. Although these laws are specific to, and dependent on, the class relations of capitalist society, they are nevertheless economic laws; distribution is determined *endogenously*.

Sraffa's treatment of distribution is quite different. His system operates with one degree of freedom. Given distribution, relative prices are fully determined; but distribution itself is left undetermined by the production equations of the system. The rate of profit "is accordingly susceptible of being determined from outside the system, and in particular by the level of the money rates of interest" (Sraffa 1960, p. 33). It is the principle of exogenous determination which is important here, rather than Sraffa's implausible suggestion that interest rates determine the rate of profit. Other and more convincing explanations of relative shares are easily found, in terms, for example, of relative class bargaining power, the degree of monopoly, or the rate of accumulation. But is not Sraffa's procedure incompatible with a theory of exploitation, and does this not provide grounds for a continued adherence to the labour theory of value?

These questions must be answered in the negative. In the first part of this section it was shown that the qualitative distribution problem, concerning the *existence* of surplus value, can be solved without reference to any theory of value. It is thus only with respect to the quantitative distribution problem, involving the explanation and measurement of the *size* of surplus value, that a theory of value becomes relevant. Marx solves this second stage of the problem in terms of the industrial reserve army, which fixes the long-run equilibrium wage at the value of labour power, defined as the subsistence requirements of the worker and his family. A Sraffian formulation of Marx's argument would involve simple the definition of a fixed "wage-goods bundle", or vector of input coefficients required to produce and reproduce labour power. This has been done, for the labour theory of value, by Morishima (1973, p. 47). Sraffa drew back from postulating a subsistence wage, because of his doubts — which seem to us to be well founded — about the relevance of the subsistence wage in modern capitalism[53]. But it could easily be done: the advantage of Sraffa's system in this respect is its flexibility. So long as the mechanism of

166

the industrial reserve army was used to determine the equilibrium wage level, it is difficult to see that anything central to Marx's theory of distribution would be lost by doing so.

5.7 Conclusion

Traditional neoclassical criticism of the labour theory of value has not been very successful. Most of the objections raised in section 5.2 are not very damaging, and, as we have seen in 5.4, the transformation problem can be fully solved by the use of a Sraffian numeraire. The methodological criticisms discussed in 5.6 are particularly unconvincing.

Certain restrictions must however be made on the applicability of the theory. Most important is its inability to deal with economic systems in which the number of processes differs from the number of products, and especially with the existence of fixed capital. Moreover the labour theory of value rests on the assumption of free competition, and very little can be said about a "world of monopolies"[54]. Neo-Ricardian theory is formally equivalent to the labour theory of value in pure circulating capital models, and superior in the case of fixed capital. It is also simpler and more direct. On these grounds we must conclude that the labour theory of value is no longer necessary for the quantitative analysis of capitalist economic development.

It is important, however, to recognize that rejection of the *quantitative* labour theory of value is not inconsistent with the *qualitative* insights which it yields. Value and distribution still depend on the interaction of objective technical and social relations, and Marx's general analysis of capitalist commodity production (outlined in Chapter 2) is no less valid. Indeed, as Meek (1973) has shown, the application of Marx's economic method enriches Sraffa's analysis by allowing its formulation in terms of the logical-historical method. Sraffa is not a "vulgar economist", and a neo-Ricardian theory of value is not subject to commodity fetishism. None of our conclusions offers the slightest comfort to neoclassical theory[55].

5.8 Appendix 1

We start with the three equations on p. 145:

$$(c_1 x + v_1 y)(1 + r) = (c_1 + c_2 + c_3)x = a_1 x \qquad [5.1]'$$

$$(c_2 x + v_2 y)(1 + r) = (v_1 + v_2 + v_3)y = a_2 y \qquad [5.2]'$$

$$(c_3 x + v_3 y)(1 + r) = (s_1 + s_2 + s_3)z = a_3 z \qquad [5.3]'$$

These can be simplified by writing

$$f_1 = v_1/c_1; \quad f_2 = v_2/c_2; \quad f_3 = v_3/c_3 \qquad [A1]$$

$$g_1 = \frac{c_1 + v_1 + s_1}{c_1} \; ; \quad g_2 = \frac{c_2 + v_2 + s_2}{c_2} \; ; \quad g_3 = \frac{c_3 + v_3 + s_3}{c_3} \qquad \text{[A2]}$$

Substituting [A1] and [A2] into [5.1]$'$, [5.2]$'$ and [5.3]$'$, we obtain

$$(x + f_1 y)(1 + r) = g_1 x \qquad \text{[A3]}$$

$$(x + f_2 y)(1 + r) = g_2 y \qquad \text{[A4]}$$

$$(x + f_3 y)(1 + r) = g_3 z \qquad \text{[A5]}$$

Now since $z = 1$, we have

$$(x + f_3 y)(1 + r) = g_3 \qquad \text{[A6]}$$

From [A3], we find that

$$x = \frac{f_1 y (1 + r)}{g_1 - (1 + r)} . \qquad \text{[A7]}$$

From [A4] we find that

$$x = \frac{y[g_2 - f_2(1 + r)]}{(1 + r)} . \qquad \text{[A8]}$$

And from [A6] we find that

$$x = \frac{g_3 - f_3(1 + r)y}{(1 + r)} . \qquad \text{[A9]}$$

Equating [A7] and [A8], we obtain

$$(f_2 - f_1)(1 + r)^2 - (g_2 + g_1 f_2)(1 + r) + g_1 g_2 = 0. \qquad \text{[A10]}$$

Using the rule for the solution of quadratic equations, we find that

$$(1 + r) = \frac{(g_2 + g_1 f_2) \pm \sqrt{(g_2 + g_1 f_2)^2 - 4 g_1 g_2 (f_2 - f_1)}}{2(f_2 - f_1)} \qquad \text{[A11]}$$

Note that neither g_3 nor f_3 appears in equation [A11]. The rate of profit is thus wholly independent of the organic composition of capital in department III.

Now equate equations [A8] and [A9] to obtain

$$y = \frac{g_3}{g_2 + (f_3 - f_2)(1 + r)} . \qquad \text{[A12]}$$

We can now find x by substituting the values of $(1 + r)$ and y, which we have obtained from equations [A11] and [A12] respectively, into equation [A7].

5.9 Appendix 2

Sraffa analyses a system with k commodities, all of which are basics. Annual gross outputs are $A, B, \ldots K$. The quantity of each commodity used to produce commodity A is denoted as $A_a, B_a, \ldots K_a$; that used to produce commodity B is denoted as $A_b, B_b, \ldots K_b$, and so on. The input coefficients, showing the quantity of each input needed to produce one unit of A, are thus $A_a/A, B_a/A, \ldots K_a/A$; and similarly for commodities $B, C, \ldots K$. Inputs of labour into each industry are denoted as $L_a, L_b, \ldots L_k$, the sum of which Sraffa makes equal to unity. Thus the labour input coefficients are $L_a/A, L_b/B, \ldots L_k/K$.

Assume that the system is in a "self-replacing state", so that the *net* output of each commodity is non-negative; that is

$$A_a + A_b + \ldots + A_k \leqslant A$$
$$B_a + B_b + \ldots + B_k \leqslant B$$
$$\cdot \quad \cdot \quad \cdot \quad \cdot \quad \cdot$$
$$K_a + K_b + \ldots + K_k \leqslant K \tag{A13}$$

The net output of each industry is thus

$$[A - (A_a + A_b + \ldots + A_k)]$$
$$[B - (B_a + B_b + \ldots + B_k)]$$
$$\cdot \quad \cdot \quad \cdot \quad \cdot \quad \cdot \quad \cdot \quad \cdot$$
$$[K - (K_a + K_b + \ldots + K_k)] \tag{A14}$$

The commodity prices are $p_a, p_b, \ldots p_k$.
Sraffa's production equations are

$$(A_a p_a + B_a p_b + \ldots + K_a p_k)(1 + r) + L_a w = A p_a$$
$$(A_b p_a + B_b p_b + \ldots + K_b p_k)(1 + r) + L_b w = B p_b$$
$$\cdot \quad \cdot \quad \cdot \quad \cdot \quad \cdot \quad \cdot \quad \cdot \quad \cdot$$
$$(A_k p_a + B_k p_b + \ldots + K_k p_k)(1 + r) + L_k w = K p_k \tag{A15}$$

He defines net output as equal to unity, so that

$$[A - (A_a + A_b + \ldots + A_k)] p_a + [B - (B_a + B_b + \ldots + B_k)] p_b + \ldots +$$
$$[K - (K_a + K_b + \ldots + K_k)] p_k = 1 \tag{A16}$$

Equations [A15] and [A16] together give $k + 1$ equations; the k prices, the wage (w) and the rate of profit (r) give $k + 2$ unknowns. Thus "the system can move with one degree of freedom" (Sraffa, 1960, p. 11).

To construct the Standard commodity, Sraffa needs a set of multipliers $(q_a, q_b, \ldots q_k)$ to apply to equations [A15] in such a way that

$$\frac{A}{A_a + {}^{1}\!A_b + \ldots + A_k} = \frac{B}{B_a + B_b + \ldots + B_k} = \ldots$$

$$= \frac{K}{K_a + K_b + \ldots + K_k} = 1 + R \qquad [A17]$$

He thus writes the q-system as follows

$$(A_a q_a + A_b q_b + \ldots + A_k q_k)(1 + R) = A q_a$$
$$(B_a q_a + B_b q_b + \ldots + B_k q_k)(1 + R) = B q_b$$

$$\cdot \quad \cdot \quad \cdot \quad \cdot \quad \cdot \quad \cdot \quad \cdot \quad \cdot \quad \cdot \quad \cdot$$

$$(K_a q_a + K_b q_b + \ldots + K_k q_k)(1 + R) = K q_k \qquad [A18]$$

He defines the units in which the multipliers are to be expressed by stipulating that

$$L_a q_a + L_b q_b + \ldots + L_k q_k = 1. \qquad [A19]$$

Equations [A18] and [A19] together give $k + 1$ equations, which can be solved for the $k + 1$ unknowns (the multipliers q_a, q_b, $\ldots q_k$, and R). Sraffa denotes the multipliers so found as q'_a, q'_b, $\ldots q'_k$, and applies these to the actual system of production equations [A15] to find the Standard system:

$$q'_a \left[(A_a p_a + B_a p_b + \ldots + K_a p_k)(1 + r) + L_a w\right] = q'_a A p_a$$
$$q'_b \left[(A_b p_a + B_b p_b \ldots + K_b p_k)(1 + r) + L_b w\right] = q'_b B p_b$$

$$\cdot \quad \cdot \quad \cdot \quad \cdot \quad \cdot \quad \cdot \quad \cdot \quad \cdot \quad \cdot \quad \cdot \quad \cdot \quad \cdot$$

$$q'_k \left[(A_k p_a + B_k p_b + \ldots + K_k p_k)(1 + r) + L_k w\right] = q'_k K p_k \qquad [A20]$$

The Standard net income, which is used as Sraffa's numeraire, is found by applying these multipliers to equation [A16], to give

$$[q'_a A - (q'_a A_a + q'_b A_b + \ldots + q'_k A_k)] p_a$$
$$+ [q'_b B - (q'_a B_a + q'_b B_b + \ldots + q'_k B_k)] p_b + \ldots$$
$$+ [q'_k K - (q'_a K_a + q'_b K_b + \ldots + q'_k K_k)] p_k = 1. \qquad [A21]$$

This may be illustrated in terms of the numerical example which we used in the text. System I (above, p. 152) can be written as follows, where A denotes iron, B coal, and C wheat:

$$(90p_a + 120p_b + 60p_c)(1 + r) + 3/16w = 180p_a$$
$$(50p_a + 125p_b + 150p_c)(1 + r) + 5/16w = 450p_b$$
$$(40p_a + 40p_b + 200p_c)(1 + r) + 8/16w = 480p_c$$

(In the iron industry, for example, $A_a = 90$;

$B_a = 120$; $C_a = 60$; $L_a = 3/16$; and $A = 180$.)

Its net output can be written, using equation [A16], as

$165p_b + 70p_c = 1$.

Substituting these values of A_a, and so on, into equations [A18] and [A19], we find that the relevant multipliers are $q'_a = 1$, $q'_b = 0.6$, and $q'_c = 0.75$. These are then applied, using [A20], to obtain system I^a. System I^a must be scaled up by a factor of $16 : 12 (= 4 : 3)$ in order to satisfy equation [A19], thus giving

$(120p_a + 160p_b + 80p_c)(1 + r) + 1/4w = 240p_a$

$(40p_a + 100p_b + 120p_c)(1 + r) + 1/4w = 360p_b$

$(40p_a + 40p_b + 200p_c)(1 + r) + 1/2w = 480p_c$

(Note that $R = 0.2$, exactly as in system I^a.) Using equation [A21], net income is defined as

$40p_a + 60p_b + 80p_c = 1$.

Given r we can find p_a, p_b, p_c and w. (If, for example, $r = R = 0.2$, then $w = 0$, and it can be checked that $p_a = 11/920$; $p_b = 4/920$; and $p_c = 3/920$.)

5.10 Appendix 3

Write p as the price of tractors; w as the wage rate; and r as the rate of profit. For the two processes to be equally profitable, there must be some set of values for p, w and r such that the equations

$$(\tfrac{1}{4}p + \tfrac{1}{2}w)(1 + r) = p \qquad \text{[A22]}$$

and

$$(\tfrac{1}{2}p + \tfrac{1}{4}w)(1 + r) = p \qquad \text{[A23]}$$

are simultaneously solved. These equations simply show that the "cost of production" of a tractor (including profits at the prevailing rate on total capital employed) must equal its price. Dividing both sides by w, we may rewrite these equations as

$$\left(\frac{1}{4}\frac{p}{w} + \frac{1}{2}\right)(1 + r) = \frac{p}{w} \qquad \text{[A24]}$$

$$\left(\frac{1}{2}\frac{p}{w} + \frac{1}{4}\right)(1 + r) = \frac{p}{w} \qquad \text{[A25]}$$

from which it is easily found that the required solution is $r = \frac{1}{3}$, $p/w = 1$. Thus the two processes are equally profitable when the price of tractors in terms of labour (p/w) equals unity, that is, when $r = \frac{1}{3}$.

Notes

1. See, for example, *Capital* I, 191, 205, 234, 263, 517, 596—8. An incisive criticism of the abstinence theory is given by Dobb (1940, pp. 127—84).

2. A very similar argument is found in *The Wealth of Nations* (Smith, 1776, pp. 112—13) and has been revived as an explanation of wage differentials in modern theories of "human capital".

3. A shift in demand, for example, would then affect wage differentials, and commodity prices, quite irrespective of any change in the labour time required to produce different types of labour power. This is a subclass of the *general* problem concerning the role of demand in the labour theory of value, which we consider above (pp. 153—5).

4. We suggest later that agriculture is part of the general category of monopoly, and that industries requiring scarce innate skills can be treated in a similar way, except that in such industries "excess profits" accrue to workers rather than to capitalists. In any case, the labour theory of value still sets a floor below which wages in these industries cannot, in the long run, fall.

5. Our discussion of this question is restricted to its *economic* content, narrowly defined. The syndrome of "non-economic" work deprivations which Marx analysed in terms of his theory of alienation is clearly of great importance, and we do not wish to suggest that immiseration in this sense has declined. The point which must be stressed, however, is that Marx's immiseration thesis also has *economic* implications, in the narrow sense, and that these are necessarily entailed by the labour theory of value. It is therefore these implications which we discuss here.

6. At least in economic terms; politically, strikes are much more important, and it can be argued that Marx's interest in trade unions was a largely political one. His concept of the economic role of strikes, quoted above, would satisfy the most fanatical neoclassical adherent to the view

172

that unions merely reflect labour market pressures, and have no effects on real wages independently of these pressures. It must be noted however, that Marx did not always take this position: "every combination of employed and unemployed disturbs the 'harmonious' action of this law" of wages (*Capital* I, 640).

7.   By "monopoly" we mean all market structures in which entry is impeded to any significant degree, so that unequal profit rates prevail. Most forms of oligopoly, for example, are relevant in this context.

8.   By "centralization" Marx means what is today termed industrial concentration; "concentration" in Marx refers to increasing enterprise *size*.

9.   Orthodox economic theory finally discovered this in the famous "costs controversy" of the 1920s; the classic reference is Sraffa (1926). A lot of ink might have been spared if the participants had realized that Marx had anticipated the whole question half a century earlier. We return above (pp. 153—5) to this question, which is relevant to our discussion of the role of demand in the labour theory of value.

10.   It might be thought that *monopsony* in the labour market was equally relevant, and that a significant role might be attributed to trade unions in resisting these pressures (Sweezy, 1946, pp. 272—4). Marx's discussion, however, is conducted solely in terms of product market competition.

11.   Neoclassical critics of Marx have been strangely silent on this issue. This may be because their own macro-economic models — and to a very great extent their micro-economic models too — usually have *nothing* to say about any market structure other than "pure competition".

12.   This neglect is apparent, for example, in Sweezy (1946); it is explicit in Meek (1973, p. 178n. 1).

13.   The author referred to here is Robbins (1958).

14.   It is developed at length in *TSV* I, ch. iv (esp. pp. 152—76), and in the brilliant Addendum 12 to *TSV* I, 389—413. A lucid account is given by Gough (1972), on which we have drawn heavily, while continuing to doubt the degree of coherence which Gough imputes to Marx's treatment of the problem.

15.   It is now rather old-fashioned, as well as wholly wrong, to claim that the analysis of prices in *Capital* III contradicts that of values in *Capital* I, or that Marx's analysis of transformation was an afterthought tacked on in response to an error in the labour theory of value (see, for example, Böhm-Bawerk, 1896). Many authors have recognized that Marx had seen the existence of the problem as early as 1862 (Letter to Engels, 2 August 1862, *SC* pp. 128–33). In fact the first glimpse of Marx's subsequent analysis is found in the *Grundrisse* (pp. 435–6), in a passage written in December 1857 or January 1858. This analysis permeates Marx's critique of classical economics in *Theories of Surplus Value*, which was written before the publication of *Capital* I. A very large part of Marx's economic theory is thus *based* on, and inexplicable without, his analysis of transformation. The fallacy, however, refuses to die: "In Volume III of *Capital*, Marx faced up to the contradiction" (Samuelson, 1971, p. 413).

16.   This point has given rise to so much misunderstanding that it is useful to amplify an earlier comment. Marx does *not* assume that no means of production are used in simple commodity production, or that in the early stages of capitalism organic compositions are everywhere equal. He does not need to do so. All he asserts is that in simple commodity production the relationship between capitalists and workers is absent, and the concept of a rate of profit on capital therefore does not apply; and that in early capitalism free competition and economic rationality are insufficiently developed to allow the equalization of the rate of profit. Meek (1973) dispels these confusions very clearly; see also above, pp. 108–9.

17.   The value of total capital equals total value produced, minus total surplus value. The price of total capital equals the price of total output, minus total profits. Thus, assuming that both variable and constant capital turn over exactly once a year, total capital is identical in both value and price terms.

18.   As we shall see in Chapter 6, these are the equilibrium conditions for simple reproduction, in which all profits are consumed by the capitalists and net investment is zero.

19.,   It would not help if we were to take department I, which now has the average organic composition, as our numeraire, and put $x = 1$ instead of z. The *ratio* $x : y : z$ will not be changed, and must remain at $0.80 : 0.61 : 1.00$. If we put $x = 1$, we simply raise y and z by a factor of 1.2 ($\approx 1/0.8$). Now *neither* will the sum of profits be equal to the sum of surplus value, *nor* will the total prices equal total values.

20. But only under the assumption that both constant and variable capital turn over exactly once a year can we identify the capital *used up* in the year with the total capital *employed* in the year; the latter concept is the relevant one when we are discussing the rate of profit. Some of the complications made necessary by this distinction have already been hinted at in our discussion of Table 4.1: worse is yet to come (see above, pp. 157—60).

21. This involves putting $y = 1$, and therefore scaling down x and z by a factor of $1/1.275$ (=0.78 approximately). The sum of profits is now obviously less than the sum of surplus values, since $z = 0.78$ rather than unity.

22. It should be noted that Seton's π is defined as the "ratio of profit to total value of output", and his cost ratio ρ as $1\text{-}\pi$ (Seton, 1957, p. 151). Marx's definition of the rate of profit (r), which is more commonly used in the literature, is equal to $\pi/1\text{-}\pi = 1\text{-}\rho/\rho$. Thus in Seton's arithmetic example (*ibid.*, p. 156 n. 3), where $\pi = 25$ per cent, the Marxian $r = 33\frac{1}{3}$ per cent.

23. "In the traditional three-sector analysis and *under conditions of simple reproduction*, the postulate [that the sum of surplus values equals the sum of profits] is equivalent to the Bortkiewicz postulate [$z = 1$], since the 'surplus' will then consist exclusively of department III products, i.e. luxuries for capitalists' consumption" (Seton, 1957, p. 153 n. 2; stress in original). More generally, these two postulates are *alternatives*, so that there are three, rather than two, possible invariance conditions.

24. That is, there is one, and only one, solution to the three equations which gives non-negative prices and a non-negative rate of profit. The most important assumption which must be made requires that there be no joint production or alternative processes (see above, pp. 157—60).

25. Laibman (1973—74) suggests that invariance of the *rate of exploitation*, rather than the rate of profit, is the most appropriate criterion. His argument is quite convincing, but it does not appear consistent with *Marx's* intentions, with which we are concerned here.

26. Neoclassical theory "comes in three handy sizes" (Harcourt, 1974, p. 1). The first uses the "aggregate production function" to explain income distribution in terms of the "marginal productivities" of capital and labour, and it is this version which was most comprehensively demolished in the course of the Cambridge controversies. The second

variety, framed in terms of the "rate of return on investment" (Solow, 1963), is equally defective (Pasinetti, 1969). The third version is general equilibrium theory, which claims to avoid the defects of the first two. General equilibrium theory may be able to provide a coherent alternative to Marxian and neo-Ricardian theories of value, and our subsequent comments on neoclassical theory should be taken as referring only to its first two versions.

27.   A further problem must be mentioned. Only if this industry represented *department III* could Marx's invariance conditions hold (see above, pp. 146–8). This is unnecessarily restrictive; it is also seriously misleading, as we shall see below in connection with Sraffa's important distinction between "basic" and "non-basic" industries.

28.   Suppose that the rate of exploitation rises. This will not affect labour values, since the quantity of labour required to produce a unit of each commodity is the same as before. It will, however, raise the rate of profit, and hence change the relative prices of the inputs.

29.   Moreover, if both the wage and the rate of profit are positive, some (non-corn) prices would be *negative*; such a case would thus have little economic significance.

30.   This can be shown very simply. Suppose that net output does consist entirely of corn, but that the corn industry uses as inputs tractors as well as seed corn; then

$$R = \frac{\text{net output of corn} \cdot p_{corn}}{\text{tractor inputs} \cdot p_{tractors} + \text{seed-corn inputs} \cdot p_{corn}},$$

and this will clearly not be unaffected by changes in the relative price of corn and tractors.

31.   For convenience, Sraffa defines the total quantity of labour employed as equal to unity.

32.   The rate of profit in this composite industry may be lower than R, depending on w. But there is no way in which it could be higher. It follows, then, given that the actual rate of profit must be the same in *all* industries, that relative prices of other commodities can never be such as to make the rate of profit in other industries (which is a ratio of two *price*-expressions) higher than R. The maximum rate of profit in the *composite* industry is therefore the highest possible rate of profit for the economy *as a whole*.

33. Workers will presumably consume mainly wheat, some coal, and very little iron. But we can still measure the value of their wages in terms of the proportion of the net output of the borderline industry which they could buy.

34. A *composite* industry will almost certainly be needed, as it is extremely unlikely that any single industry will fit the bill. As Sraffa initially assumes that there are no joint products, this could only be an industry using one commodity to produce the same commodity as an output (cf. the simple corn model). Still less is it likely that an entire department, like Marx's department III, will qualify. Marx was thus excessively (and unnecessarily) ambitious in his analysis of the problem.

35. This question is equivalent to that of the uniqueness of R as the only economically meaningful balancing ratio, as discussed by Sraffa (1960, ch. 5).

36. Strictly speaking, system 1^a must be scaled up by multiplying each industry by $16/12$, so that the total quantity of labour used remains equal to unity. It is readily seen that this does not affect the substance of the analysis.

37. We have discussed the *methodological* arguments which led Marx, and the classical economists, to reject supply and demand theories of value above (pp. 75–6). It should be noted that the "demand" factors which we introduced in section 5.3, in the context of Bortkiewicz's analysis, have nothing at all to do with neoclassical, Walrasian demand functions. They simply express the simple reproduction equilibrium conditions that (*a*) all means of production go to replace those used up in current production; (*b*) all wage-goods are consumed by workers; and (*c*) all surplus value is spent on luxuries, which are consumed by capitalists alone. These are accounting identities, not demand functions.

38. In this sense Harcourt is wrong when he voices the neo-Ricardian claim that "it is unnecessary, in order to explain prices, to make *any* assumptions about the motives and behaviour of individual economic units, in particular, whether they are maximizers or not and, if they are, *what* it is that they maximize" (Harcourt, 1972, pp. 193–4; stress in original).

39. Neoclassical critics of Marx usually disregard the critique of "supply curves" which is implicit in the Sraffian attack on their theory of capital,

and treat this problem as equivalent to a requirement that each industry's long-run supply curve must be perfectly elastic.

40.   In principle this is a clear objection to the labour theory of value. In practice, however, expansion of plant usually involves the purchase of new and better machines, not just more machines identical to the old ones. (As we shall see in Chapter 6, Marx argues that new technology must generally be *embodied* in new machines before it can be employed.) It would be impossible to separate out those reductions in input coefficients due to technical progress — which are not inconsistent with the labour theory of value — from those due to changes in output resulting from shifts in demand. Marx's *ceteris*, that is, do not remain *paribus*.

41.   Marx was confused on this point. Sometimes he correctly excludes department III from the determination of the rate of profit (*TSV* I, 216), sometimes wrongly taking the opposite line. Yaffe (1973) argues that (*a*) Marx always took the erroneous position, and (*b*) this position is therefore correct. Both (*a*) and (*b*) are wrong, and Yaffe's argument is in any case invalid.

42.   This is not quite true, since these relations may themselves be influenced by changes in the intensity of labour, and perhaps also by changes in the length of the working day (both of which Marx correctly accused Ricardo of neglecting). For Marx there is never a complete divorce between the social and the technical.

43.   If, for example, two tractors are produced by process 1, and one tractor by process 2, total inputs of $(2)(\frac{1}{4}) + (1)(\frac{1}{2}) = 1$ tractor, and $(2)(\frac{1}{2}) + (1)(\frac{1}{4}) = 5/4$ units of labour produce a total output of 3 tractors. Thus $\lambda + 5/4 = 3\lambda$, so that $\lambda = 5/8$. If one tractor is produced by process 1, and two by process 2, then (by a similar process of reasoning) we find that $\lambda = 4/7$.

44.   This is not a problem in simple commodity production. Here the rate of profit is zero, all costs are labour costs, and cost-minimization is equivalent to minimizing the quantity of labour required to produce a commodity, and hence to minimizing its labour value. If different processes are used simultaneously, this simply means that each involves the same labour value.

45.   He adds that "a system which contained no other element of joint production besides what is implied in the presence of fixed capital would

in general have an all-positive Standard commodity, thus reproducing in this respect the simplicity of single-product industries" (Sraffa, 1960, p. 73). The q-multipliers, that is, may well be all positive.

46.   The best of all the early Marx-critiques, less famous but more honest than that of Böhm-Bawerk, itself explicitly uses and justifies the use of such a non-observable entity in order to produce a theory of value. The entity in question, however, is *utility* (Wicksteed, 1884). In this respect Wicksteed was only following one of the founders of neoclassical economics, W. S. Jevons: "Cournot does not *recede* to any theory of utility, but commences with the phenomenal laws of supply and demand" (Jevons, 1871, p. xxxi, cited by Meek, 1972, p. 502).

47.   An earlier statement puts the issue equally clearly: "Whatever the usefulness or irrelevance of the Marxian value concept as a description of 'reality' or as a guide to action, it is at least operationally meaningful" (Morishima and Seton, 1961, p. 205).

48.   Methodological critics of the labour theory of value display a certain degree of confusion here. It is not consistent to attack Marx *both* for propounding tautologies *and* for making metaphysical statements (which, being meaningless, are neither true nor false). Of course, it ill behoves an adherent to utility theory, or to the "theory" of revealed preference, to complain about the use of tautological statements in economic analysis!

49.   See the famous letter to Kugelmann (*SC* pp. 208–10), of which rather too much is made by Sowell (1967, pp. 68–9).

50.   Though, as Samuelson justly observes, it is significant that Sraffa himself does not do this, or even hint that it might be possible.

51.   Related to this, though Samuelson does not make the relation at all clear, is his argument that the transformation is essentially bogus: "In summary, 'transforming from values to prices' can be described logically as the following procedure: '(1) Write down the value relations; (2) take an eraser and rub them out; (3) finally write down the price relations – thus completing the so-called transformation process'" (Samuelson, 1970, p. 425). Samuelson's matrix algebra is itself superfluous. The point he is making is in fact clear in the much simpler Bortkiewicz analysis: for example in equation 5.1' above, x is the price/value ratio in department 1, and the arithmetic, though hardly the logic, is as Samuelson describes it.

52.   Subject to reservations on work intensity and working hours (above, p. 135).

53.   This in effect is why Sraffa defines wages as part of net output (above p. 150). Our proposal would have the attraction that wage-goods would revert to their role as means of production, rather than (as they must be for Sraffa) non-basic, "luxury" commodities (Medio, 1972, pp. 342—3). The alternative, then, is to follow Sraffa, thereby rejecting the applicability of Marx's *quantitative* theory of distribution to modern capitalism; both Meek (1973, p. 286) and Dobb (1973, pp. 269—70) find this acceptable.

54.   It is worth repeating that this problem is equally acute both for Sraffa's analysis and for *all* versions of neoclassical theory.

55.   Recent contributions to the literature on the issues discussed in this chapter are listed in the supplementary bibliography. Rowthorn (1974a), Hare (1974), and Roncaglia (1974) treat heterogeneous labour in a manner similar to that of Section 5.2 above, while Morris and Lewin (1973—4) take a quite different view. Samuelson (1974a, 1974b, 1974c) has continued his analysis of the transformation problem, and has been further criticised by Baumol (1974) and Morishima (1974). Eatwell (1974) argues that the relationship between Sraffa and Marx is a very close one, a view which is vigorously attacked by Lebowitz (1973—4) and Rowthorn (1974b).

6

The theory of capitalist accumulation

6.1 Introduction

Although Marx's theory of accumulation is largely macro-economic, he presented it in the categories of his value theory. He simply aggregated the components of each commodity value into one, two or three sectors as his purpose required[1]. The propositions of the macro-theory, however, in no way depend on these specific categories, although they obviously do depend on the relations which these categories express. This has now generally been recognized by economists familiar with Marx's work[2]. However, many have remarked on the complications which can result from such a presentation (Robinson, 1942, pp. 19–20; Harris, 1972, p. 510). Nevertheless we follow Marx here and express his theory largely in value categories, for these most clearly embody his basic assumptions about the nature of the capitalist system, as we have seen in Chapter 2.

The theory described here covers three main areas: growth, technical change, and effective demand. We have already outlined some areas of it (above pp. 116f), in discussing Marx and classical political economy. Here we develop it in much more detail, and subject it to criticism. Section 6.2 contrasts Marx's approach with that of the classical economists in terms of the role of technical change, and gives Marx's own explanation of the differences. Section 6.3 then outlines and analyses Marx's reproduction models, with attention focused on expanded reproduction. In effect this is a formal model of capitalist growth without technical change, but it provides an important framework both for a growth theory based on technical change (6.4) and for Marx's theory of effective demand and cyclical instability. Marx maintains that growth with technical change leads both to a decaying employment position and to a falling rate of profit, independently of deficient aggregate demand. Section 6.5 takes up the effective demand strand in Marx's argument to discuss his theory of the industrial cycle. Section 6.6 considers a problem thrown up by the implications of the previous sections, and of which Marx may or may not have been fully aware. We conclude with a brief analysis of Marx's theory of proletarian revolution in the light of the criticisms which are made in previous sections.

6.2 The importance of technical change in Marx's theory of accumulation

Marx's macro-economics, unlike that of Keynes, focused less on the level of macro-aggregates in the short run (a period in which capacity is fixed), than on the more ambitious task of analysing their dynamics and thus their long run timepath. In this respect Marx's model is similar to those of classical political economy. But, as we have already seen (above pp. 116f), there are important differences. One crucial aspect of these differences, that we have not so far emphasized, now becomes very important:

"[Marx's vision] of the capitalist process differs radically from that which underlies the classical theory of economic evolution. The latter is, in principle, unconcerned with changes in methods of production; economic development is viewed exclusively in terms of (gradual) quantitative changes in population, capital, wages, profit and rent. Social relations remain unaffected; the end product is simply a state of affairs in which all these rates of change equal zero. Since the Marxian view lays primary stress on changes in methods of production, it implies qualitative change in social organization and social relations as well as quantitative change in economic variables" (Sweezy, 1946, p. 94).

It is this emphasis on technical change which forms a crucially important factor distinguishing Marx's model from those of his predecessors. Marx himself was conscious of this, and explained it as resulting in part from the classics' orientation on the "manufacturing stage" of capitalist development, as opposed to that of "modern industry" on which he largely built his own macro-theory[3].

Marx characterized the manufacturing stage as the first phase in capitalist development. It is based on the handicraft technology of pre-capitalist commodity production, but goes beyond the handicraft production process in that it extends the division of labour, since capital allows an extension in the size of the workshop; the methods of production, however, are still based on the handicraft technology of the artisan workshop. Consequently Marx maintains that the period of manufacture is essentially conservative:

"History shows how the division of labour peculiar to manufacture, strictly so called, acquires the best adapted form at first by experience, as

it were behind the backs of the actors, and then, like the guild handicrafts, strives to hold fast that form once found, and here and there succeeds in keeping it for centuries" (Capital I, p. 363).

Growth in this stage could be viewed, as it was by the classical economists, in terms of quantitative expansion: a relatively smooth path of accumulation without large-scale technical change and with causes and consequences seen largely in terms of "quantitative changes in population, capital, wages, profit and rent" (Sweezy, 1946, p. 94)[4]. Thus

"Marx, in contrast to the classics systematically took into account and incorporated into his theoretical system that interrelated series of events and processes which is generally known as the industrial revolution . . . [and which for Marx] marked the transition between two essentially different periods of capitalist development, the first being characterized by the dominance of manufacture and the second by the dominance of 'modern industry' " (Sweezy, 1968, pp. 109—10).

For Marx, then, the industrial revolution was essentially a process of *mechanization*, and "modern industry" was characterized by the extensive use of machinery. This process of mechanization brought about the systematic application of the natural sciences to the production process, and thus led to continual technical change (*Capital* I, 386, 486). Consequently, and in contrast to manufacture, Marx maintains that "the technical basis of . . . [modern industry] is revolutionary" (*ibid.*, 486). "Modern industry" thus forms the technical basis for stage 3 and the subsequent stages of Marx's logical-historical typology of the phases of capitalist development (see above pp. 45—52).

Marx's macro-economics is primarily concerned to delineate the "laws of motion" of *advanced* capitalist development. In arriving at these laws he thus generally assumes the technical basis of modern industry, and the presence of large-scale technical change (which is "embodied" in new capital equipment). Marx's theory of technical change is in fact the key to important "contradictions" in the accumulation process (below pp. 199f): hence Marx's "relatively violent" characterization of the development process in advanced capitalism compared with that of classical political economy (Meek, 1968, p. 120).

These economic factors in turn reflect and create qualitative change in the social structure, the most important aspect of which, in Marx's view, is change in the composition and organization of the working class. Modern industry progressively undermines the skills which differentiate sections of the working class in the period of manufacture. It facilitates the employment of women and children and destroys the economic basis of the independent producer, forcing through technical change which creates an increasing "reserve army" of unemployed workers, reducing the economic power of the proletariat. The potential *political* power of the proletariat is simultaneously increased; its relative size is enlarged and its composition made more homogeneous. The organization and conditions of work are such as to allow proletarians to identify their interests as common interests opposed to those of the bourgeoisie, and in turn prepares them for disciplined political action. Thus the proletariat not only has an interest in revolution but is also made capable of carrying out such action by the very process of capitalist production itself. Marx's macro-economic theory essentially consists of an analysis of the dynamics of the system which mould the proletariat into such a revolutionary force (see also Chapter 1).

Before we proceed to a discussion of these "laws of motion" it is necessary to analyse Marx's models of reproduction. These models are in fact constructed on the assumption that there is *no technical change*, but they do provide a framework for understanding those parts of Marx's theory where technical change has the central role. Moreover, especially due to the increased interest in growth theory in recent years, these models have also become increasingly important in their own right.

6.3 The reproduction models

Marx constructs two reproduction models, one of "simple reproduction" and one of "extended reproduction". Simple reproduction occurs in a capitalist system which, in equilibrium, can only reproduce itself on the same scale year after year. In equilibrium, therefore, net investment is zero; there is no accumulation of capital (*Capital* I, 567). Extended reproduction concerns a capitalist system which, in equilibrium, can more than reproduce itself, and grows. The mechanism of growth is provided by the accumulation of capital, via capitalist saving out of surplus value and its investment in additional constant and variable capital (*Capital* I, 579)[5].

Marx used these models to depict crucial relations of interdependence in a capitalist economy, and in particular to derive the conditions necessary for macro-economic equilibrium to prevail. He intended to prove that, given the assumptions of the models, it was not inherently impossible for capitalism to experience continuous equilibrium and stable development. However, he also intended to prove that for such stability to prevail certain special conditions had to be met. In consequence, he argued, since there is no conscious social regulation of the economy, disequilibrium and unstable development are most probable in capitalist economies.

Simple reproduction

The model of simple reproduction was deliberately extremely unrealistic, and abstracts from many essential characteristics of capitalism, in particular from accumulation (*Capital* II, 398–9). Marx believed, however, that such a model was useful for comprehending certain aspects of the capitalist structure of economic interrelations in their clearest form. It primarily serves him in bringing leverage to bear on the more complex and realistic model of extended reproduction (though the latter is, as we shall see, also a highly abstract model). Simple reproduction is thus very largely a methodological device; as such there is an important contrast with the classical economists' conception of the stationary state (above pp. 80f), which was seen as a *real* economic state to which capitalism would eventually tend.

In outlining Marx's model of simple reproduction, we first define some terms ($i = 1,2$):

c_i: constant capital in department i
v_i: variable capital in department i
s_i: surplus value in department i
$a_i = c_i + v_i + s_i$: total value of the output of department i
$e_i = s_i/v_i$: rate of exploitation in department i[6]
$k_i = c_i/v_i$: organic composition of capital in department i

The assumptions on which the model is constructed are as follows:

1.   We are dealing with a capitalist economy with only two classes, capitalists and workers. There are no unproductive activities other than the consumption of the capitalists (*Capital* II, 401; I, 564).

2.   All commodities sell at their *values*; the model abstracts from the transformation of values into prices of production. Consequently Marx abstracts from credit and capital mobility between departments. Each capitalist uses only his own capital, and there is no borrowing or lending between departments. There is thus no tendency for the equalization of profit rates between departments (*Capital* II, 412, 505, 435; I, 564).

3.   The technology of the system is "productive", in the sense that non-negative net outputs of all commodities can be produced from the inputs; this is a sufficient condition for the system's ability, in equilibrium, to reproduce itself.

4.   The capitalists carry out zero net saving and investment, so that their whole income (surplus value) is spent on consumption goods (*Capital* I, 567).

5.   The wage rate is fixed at subsistence level, so that workers spend their entire income on wage goods. Moreover, the rate of exploitation is the same in each department (*Capital* II, 512; see also above p. 144).

6.   All industries are aggregated into two departments. Department I produces means of production (*c*), while department II produces consumption goods (*Capital* II, 372). (Marx sometimes subdivides department II into wage and luxury good sections; see, for example, *Capital* II, 406). Values provide the weights by means of which heterogeneous commodities are aggregated into the two departments (Morishima, 1973). Marx usually assumes that the two types of commodities are distinct: that is, the output of department I cannot be consumed, and that of department II cannot serve as means of production.

7.   It is implicitly assumed that "each production process is of the point-input-point-output type; inputs are made at the beginning of the production period and outputs obtained at the end of the period" (Morishima, 1973, p. 12). Thus v_i is both the annual wage bill paid by capitalists in department i and the amount of capital locked up as variable capital.

8.   Marx assumes, in effect, that all fixed capital wears out in the course of the production period (*Capital* II, 400–1). Thus c_i represents both the amortization *flow* in department i during the production period and its *stock* of constant capital at the beginning of that period.

9.   The economy is assumed to be closed, so that there is no foreign trade (*Capital* II, 474).

10.   It is assumed that there is no technical change (*Capital* II, 393). Thus there is no change in the organic composition of capital (*k*) in either department (though the organic compositions need not be the same in each department, and normally $k_1 \neq k_2$).

Marx's analysis of simple reproduction involves several numerical examples and a general algebraic formulation of the equilibrium condition. We begin with the algebraic derivation of this condition, and then provide one of Marx's numerical examples as an illustration.

The aggregate value of gross output in each department (a_i) consists of the value of the used-up means of production (c_i), the value of the labour power employed (v_i), and the surplus value generated (s_i). Thus in Marx's two sector model we have

$$a_1 = c_1 + v_1 + s_1 \qquad [6.1]$$

$$a_2 = c_2 + v_2 + s_2 \qquad [6.2]$$

Each of the elements has a dual character, since it represents an element of "aggregate demand" and simultaneously an element of "aggregate supply". Thus, for example, v_1 and v_2 represent part of each department's "supply", and also constitute the workers' "demand" for consumption goods[7].

Since both departments require means of production but only department I produces such commodities, an exchange must take place between departments. For equilibrium to prevail the sum of the means of production required in both departments must equal a_1, so that

$$c_1 + c_2 = c_1 + v_1 + s_1 = a_1 \qquad [6.3]$$

Likewise, capitalists and workers in department I cannot consume their own output, which consists of constant capital. They must therefore obtain consumer goods through exchange with department II. In equilibrium the exchange must be such that the sum of the consumption of capitalists and workers in both departments is equal to a_2[8]:

$$v_1 + v_2 + s_1 + s_2 = c_2 + v_2 + s_2 = a_2 \qquad [6.4]$$

Clearly both equations [6.3] and [6.4] reduce to

$$c_2 = v_1 + s_1 \qquad [6.5]$$

Diagrammatically the exchange relationship can be represented as

$$c_1 \quad + \quad \boxed{v_1 + s_1}$$
$$\boxed{c_2} \quad + \quad v_2 + s_2$$

Department I produces its own means of production for its replacement needs; it must obtain from department II the consumer goods needed to feed its workers and to provide for the consumption of its capitalists. Department II produces consumer goods for its own workers and capitalists; it requires means of production from department I to replace its constant capital. The boxed items figure in interdepartmental trade, and must be equal in value if equilibrium is to prevail.

Marx gives the equilibrium condition in algebraic form as equation [6.5] above (*Capital* II, 406). This can be taken further[9]. If we divide through by v_2 we obtain

$$\frac{c_2}{v_2} = \frac{v_1}{v_2} + \frac{s_1}{v_2}$$

which simplifies to

$$k_2 = \frac{v_1}{v_2}\left(1 + \frac{s_1}{v_1}\right)$$

so that, in equilibrium,

$$\frac{v_1}{v_2} = \frac{k_2}{1 + e} \qquad\qquad [6.6]$$

Thus the equilibrium condition for simple reproduction requires that the employment of variable capital in the two departments be in a specific ratio determined by the values of k_2 and e.

This algebraic formulation can be illustrated by one of Marx's numerical examples taken from *Capital* II, 401–2:

Department I : $4\,000c_1$ + $\boxed{1\,000v_1 + 1\,000s_1}$ $= 6\,000a_1$

Department II : $\boxed{2\,000c_2}$ + $500v_2 +$ $500s_2$ $= 3\,000a_2$

The boxed components are those which are exchanged between departments. Consider department I: the $4\,000c_1$ consist of means of production, which are produced by department I itself; the $1\,000v_1$ and $1\,000s_1$ consist of consumer goods, which are produced by department II. Conversely, for department II, the $500v_2$ and $500s_2$ consist of consumer goods, produced within II itself; the $2\,000c_2$ consist of means of production, produced by I. Department I must thus obtain from department II a quantity of consumer goods sufficient to pay its wage bill and to provide for the consumption of its capitalists. Department II, on the other hand, must obtain from department I a quantity of means of production sufficient to replace the constant capital used up in its production. In equilibrium, these requirements must be equal. And so they are in the example, at 2 000. It can easily be seen that equations [6.5] and [6.6] hold in this case.

Extended reproduction

Assumptions 1–3 and 5–10 of simple reproduction also hold in Marx's model of extended reproduction. The main difference between the two models is that assumption 4 of simple reproduction does not hold in extended reproduction. Capitalists are now assumed to save a portion of their income, and to invest it, thus increasing their capital and generating growth in their own departments. Marx assumes that the saving ratio is exogenously determined (*Capital* II, 507), though as we shall see he relaxes this assumption somewhat in his numerical examples so far as the savings ratio in department II is concerned[10]. Since surplus value is no longer wholly consumed, we must differentiate its various components; thus we define the following terms ($i = 1,2$):

s_{o_i} : amount of surplus value consumed in department i

s_{c_i} : amount of surplus value invested in additional constant capital in department i

s_{v_i} : amount of surplus value invested in additional variable capital in department i

$s_i = s_{o_i} + s_{c_i} + s_{v_i}$: total surplus value in department i

Assumption 2 of simple reproduction still holds, so that capitalists invest *only in their own department*. Consequently

$$I_i = \alpha_i s_i \qquad\qquad [6.7]$$

where

I_i : total investment in department i

α_i : the savings ratio of capitalists in department i (that is, the proportion of their surplus value that they save)

We still assume that there is no technical change, so that the organic composition k_1 and k_2 are constants. The allocation of investment between variable and constant capital is such that

$$I_i = \Delta c_i + \Delta v_i \qquad\qquad [6.8]$$

and

$$\frac{\Delta c_i}{\Delta v_i} = \frac{c_i}{v_i} = k_i = \text{constant,} \qquad\qquad [6.9]$$

where

Δc_i : addition to constant capital in department i ($=s_{c_i}$)

Δv_i : addition to variable capital in department i ($=s_{v_i}$)

The assumption that the investment of surplus value is restricted to the department in which it originates may seem inappropriate in the context of competition, which normally implies free mobility of capital between sectors (Robinson, 1960, pp. 62–3, 82). In fact Marx introduces the model of extended reproduction *prior* to transformation, so that it applies to the *second* stage of the logical-historical typology (above p. 49).

The wage rate is still assumed to be fixed at the subsistence level. Since we are now dealing with extended reproduction, this implies that the supply of labour power is perfectly elastic at the subsistence wage (*Capital* II, 505). Because there is no change in the organic composition of capital, employment increases at the same rate as constant capital. Since we are now dealing with a growth model, some assumption about returns to scale becomes necessary: Marx implicitly assumes constant returns to scale in both departments. Clearly, with these additional assumptions, the equilibrium condition for smooth reproduction will differ from that expressed for simple reproduction in equations [6.5] and [6.6] above. We give the algebraic derivation of their counterparts for extended reproduction below, and then analyse Marx's main numerical examples.

We can write the outputs of the two departments as

$$a_1 = c_1 + v_1 + s_{o_1} + \Delta c_1 + \Delta v_1 \qquad\qquad [6.10]$$

$$a_2 = c_2 + v_2 + s_{o_2} + \Delta c_2 + \Delta v_2 \qquad\qquad [6.11]$$

For equilibrium to prevail "supplies" must equal "demands", so that

$$a_1 = c_1 + c_2 + \Delta c_1 + \Delta c_2 \qquad\qquad [6.12]$$

$$a_2 = v_1 + v_2 + \Delta v_1 + \Delta v_2 + s_{o_1} + s_{o_2} \qquad\qquad [6.13]$$

The right-hand side of equation [6.12] shows that constant capital is required in each department both to replace that used up and to provide for growth. The right-hand side of equation [6.13] shows that consumer goods are required in both departments to support the existing and the additional workers, and to provide for the consumption of the capitalists. Equation [6.12] and [6.13] yield the same equilibrium condition:

$$c_2 + \Delta c_1 + \Delta c_2 = v_1 + s_1 \qquad\qquad [6.14]$$

This is the equilibrium counterpart for extended reproduction of equation [6.5] in simple reproduction. It is stated by Marx in *Capital* II, 521. Equation [6.14] can also be written as

$$c_2 + \Delta c_2 = v_1 + \Delta v_1 + s_{o_1} \qquad\qquad [6.15]$$

Diagrammatically the exchange relationships can be represented as follows:

$$c_1 + \Delta c_1 \quad + \quad \boxed{v_1 + s_{o_1} + \Delta v_1}$$

$$\boxed{c_2 + \Delta c_2} \quad + \quad v_2 + s_{o_2} + \Delta v_2$$

Department I produces its own means of production, for replacement and accumulation; it must obtain from department II the consumer goods needed to feed existing and additional workers, and to provide for capitalists' consumption. Department II produces consumer goods for its existing and additional workers, and for its capitalists; it requires means of production from department I to replace and extend its constant capital.

The boxed items feature in interdepartmental trade, and must be equal in value for equilibrium to prevail.

We can also derive the counterpart to equation [6.6] in simple reproduction. We define

$$g_{v_i} = \frac{\Delta v_i}{v_i} \qquad\qquad [6.16]$$

$$g_{c_i} = \frac{\Delta c_i}{c_i} \qquad\qquad [6.17]$$

where g_{v_i} is the rate of growth of variable capital in department i, and g_{c_i} the rate of growth of constant capital in department i. Dividing equation [6.14] through by v_2, we obtain[11]

$$\frac{v_1}{v_2} = \frac{k_2(1 + g_{c_2})}{(1 + e - g_{c_1}k_1)} \qquad\qquad [6.18]$$

This equation is the counterpart in extended reproduction of equation [6.6] in simple reproduction. It must be fulfilled for equilibrium growth to prevail in the system.

We can go further than this and derive a condition for *balanced* growth, in which the two departments grow in equilibrium *at the same rate*. We define

λ_{v_i} : the proportion of investment in department i (I_i) allocated to variable capital.

$1 - \lambda_{v_i}$: the proportion of I_i allocated to constant capital.

It follows from our definitions that

$\Delta v_i = \lambda_{v_i} \cdot I_i$ and

$\Delta c_i = (1 - \lambda_{v_i}) I_i$, so that

$$g_{v_i} = \lambda_{v_i}\alpha_i e \quad \text{and} \qquad\qquad [6.16a]$$

$$g_{c_i} = (1 - \lambda_{v_i}) \cdot \frac{\alpha_i e}{k_i} \qquad\qquad [6.17a]$$

If the two departments are to grow at the same rate, there must be an equal proportional increase in the value components of each department, when these departments are in equilibrium. This means that the departmental growth rates in outlays on labour power, g_{v_1} and g_{v_2}, must be the same. Using equation [6.16a], this implies that

$$\frac{\lambda_{v_1}}{\lambda_{v_2}} = \frac{\alpha_2}{\alpha_1}$$

Since we are assuming constancy in the organic compositions of capital, it must also be true that

$g_{v_i} = g_{c_i}$, so that

$$\lambda_{v_i} \alpha_i e_i = (1 - \lambda_{v_i}) \cdot \frac{\alpha_i e_i}{k_i}$$

$$\lambda_{v_i} k_i = 1 - \lambda_{v_i}$$

$\lambda_{v_i}(1 + k_i) = 1$, so that

$$\lambda_{v_i} = \frac{1}{1 + k_i} \qquad\qquad [6.19]$$

Hence

$$\frac{\lambda_{v_1}}{\lambda_{v_2}} = \frac{1 + k_2}{1 + k_1}, \text{ so that} \qquad\qquad [6.20]$$

$$\frac{\alpha_2}{\alpha_1} = \frac{1 + k_2}{1 + k_1} \qquad\qquad [6.21]$$

Equation [6.21] must be fulfilled if there is to be *balanced* equilibrium growth in Marx's model of extended reproduction.

Marx derived the equilibrium equation[6.14], but he did not go beyond it to equation [6.18], just as he did not derive equation [6.6] from equation [6.5]. Nor did he derive equation [6.21]. This extension of Marx's analysis, however, not only illuminates the properties of his model, but also provides a useful basis for the analysis of his numerical examples. We now turn to this task.

Marx presented two main numerical examples of extended reproduction. The first (*Capital* II, 514) is presented in Table 6.1. Marx assumed that α_1 is exogenously given, and makes the system expand along the equilibrium growth path shown in the table. The equilibrium equations [6.14] and [6.18] hold in every year. Note that the system exhibits a peculiar savings-investment function in department II, in that capitalists are assumed to adjust their saving and investment in such a way as to ensure equilibrium. Marx assumes that department I's savings ratio, α_1, is equal to 0.5 and is exogenously given. In this situation, given $k_1 = 4$, then in the initial year $s_{c_1} = 400$ and $s_{v_1} = 100$. Thus if there is no accumulation in department II (that is, if $\alpha_2 = 0$), the total demand for the output of department I is

$$c_1 + \Delta c_1 + c_2 = 4\,000 + 400 + 1\,500 = 5\,900$$

Table 6.1 : A numerical example of Marx's model of extended reproduction

End of year	Department	Constant capital c_i	Variable capital v_i	Surplus value s_i	Surplus value consumed s_{oi}	Surplus value invested in c ($s_{ci} = \Delta c_i$)	Surplus value invested in v ($s_{vi} = \Delta v_i$)	Total value a_i	Capitalists' savings ratio α_i
1	I	4 000	1 000	1 000	500	400	100	6 000	0.5
1	II	1 500	750	750	600	100	50	3 000	0.2
2	I	4 400	1 100	1 100	550	440	110	6 600	0.5
2	II	1 600	800	800	560	160	80	3 200	0.3
3	I	4 840	1 210	1 210	605	484	121	7 260	0.5
3	II	1 760	880	880	616	176	88	3 520	0.3
4	I	5 324	1 331	1 331	665	532	133	7 986	0.5
4	II	1 936	968	968	678	193	97	3 872	0.3
5	I	5 856	1 464	1 464	732	586	146	8 784	0.5
5	II	2 129	1 065	1 065	745	213	107	4 259	0.3
6	I	6 442	1 610	1 610	805	644	161	9 662	0.5
6	II	2 342	1 172	1 172	821	234	117	4 686	0.3

Note: All magnitudes have, where relevant, been rounded off to whole
numbers..

Since $a_1 = 6\,000$, there is a surplus of 100, so that the system cannot be in equilibrium. If instead $\alpha_2 = \alpha_1 = 0.5$, the total demand for the output of department I would be

$$c_1 + \Delta c_1 + c_2 + \Delta c_2 = 4\,000 + 400 + 1\,500 + 250 = 6\,150$$

This would lead to a deficit of 150, so that equilibrium is not possible with equal savings ratios of 0.5. In order to achieve equilibrium, Marx makes α_2 adjustable. Thus in the first year he sets $\alpha_2 = 0.2$, which does lead to an equilibrium, since

$$c_1 + \Delta c_1 + c_2 + \Delta c_2 = 4\,000 + 400 + 1\,500 + 100 = 6\,000.$$

In the second year accumulation continues at the same rate as in the previous year (that is, $\alpha_1 = 0.5$). If $\alpha_2 = 0$, so that there is no accumulation in department II, the total demand for the output of department I is

$$c_1 + \Delta c_1 + c_2 = 4\,400 + 440 + 1\,600 = 6\,440$$

Since $a_1 = 6\,600$, there is a surplus of 160, so that the system cannot be in equilibrium. If instead department II had a savings ratio of 0.2, as in the first year, the total demand for the output of department I would be

$$c_1 + \Delta c_1 + c_2 + \Delta c_2 = 4\,400 + 440 + 1\,600 + 107 = 6\,547$$

This would lead to a deficiency in the demand for the output of department I of 53. In order to achieve equilibrium Marx makes α_2 adjust to 0.3. Now we have

$$c_1 + \Delta c_1 + c_2 + \Delta c_2 = 4\,400 + 440 + 1\,600 + 160 = 6\,600.$$

The system then settles down to an equilibrium growth path, with $\alpha_2 = 0.3$ and $\alpha_1 = 0.5$.

This growth path has two properties which are especially interesting. First, the economy is *always* in equilibrium, as may be seen by an examination of the situation in years 3, 4, 5, and so on. Second, department I expands at a rate of 10 per cent in every year; department II, on the other hand, does so only from year 2 to year 3 and thereafter, while from year 1 to year 2 it expands at a rate of 6.67 per cent. Thus while there is always *equilibrium* growth, there is *unbalanced* growth in the first year, when department I grows faster than department II. This may also be seen by applying equations [6.18] and [6.21] to this case. Morishima (1973, p. 120) summarizes this second point as follows:

"It is thus seen that in Marx's economy there prevails a tendency towards balanced growth, which is much stronger than the convergence claimed by neo-classical economists such as Solow, Meade and Uzawa, because any state of unbalanced growth will disappear in Marx's economy in a single year ... such a strange conclusion is not specific to the numerical illustration used by Marx but is a logical implication of his investment function."

Marx originally began his section on the "Schematic presentation of accumulation" with the assumption that "both I and II accumulate one half of their surplus value" (*Capital* II, 511). This assumption of equality — or at least an assumption that savings ratios are *both* exogenously determined constants — is obviously the most reasonable to make within his model. As we have seen in the numerical example, however, such an assumption will normally be inconsistent with equilibrium growth. Thus in order to produce equilibrium growth Marx has to make α_2 a variable, so that department II always adjusts to the requirements of department I. There is no economic logic to this; no reason is given as to why capitalists in department II should behave as they do and thus allow the growth path to be dominated by department I. Morishima (1973, p. 125) argues that this property of the system "was invented by Marx as a *deus ex machina*"[12]. However, this artificial *theoretical* solution to the problem merely reflects what Marx saw as a problem of capitalist accumulation *in reality*. Hence no such *deus ex machina* exists in practice (see below pp. 210–23).

Conclusion

It can readily be seen that Marx's schematic models of reproduction are built on very restrictive assumptions. In particular their abstraction from technical change, so that the rate of exploitation and organic composition of capital remain constant, detracts from their relevance. They do, however, serve the purpose which Marx intended. They do show that, although equilibrium is a possibility, it is extremely unlikely in the capitalist mode of economic organization.

In showing that equilibrium reproduction was possible, and outlining some of its properties, Marx showed himself not only as an "embryonic general equilibrium theorist in advance of Leon Walras" (Bronfenbrenner, 1967, p. 628), but also an important forerunner of modern growth theory, which has concentrated precisely on the characteristics of equilibrium growth. "Modern growth theory started in the late 1930s independently of Marx, on a less refined level. . . . One may say in retrospect that . . . [Marx's model] was the beginning of modern growth theory" (Krelle, 1971, pp. 129–33)[13]. Furthermore, Marx's scheme anticipated important developments in modern planning theory, "since it directly inspired the Soviet method of balances in the 1920s, and as we now know the basic idea of the more complex input-output matrix of Leontief was derived from these balances" (Dobb, 1967, p. 537).

Marx's reproduction models, however, were designed to aid analysis of an unplanned capitalist economy, and he did not expect that such an economy would actually move along a balanced or even an equilibrium growth path. Growth in advanced capitalism, Marx observes, is *cyclical* growth (*Capital* III, 500–1), with recurrent unstable phases of expansion and relative stagnation; the causes lie in the nature of the capitalist economic process itself.

Robinson (1965, p. 163) aptly observes that the scheme of reproduction, "brilliant in its simplicity . . . provides the most secure grip on the whole savings and investment complex". The models form the basis of certain aspects of Marx's theory of crises, as we shall see (below p. 210). We can note the main point here, however, if we look at the equilibrium equations [6.6] and [6.18]. In the nature of the case capitalists cannot know the equilibrium ratio v_1/v_2. There is thus no reason why they will advance variable capital in the right proportions. As a result disruption is extremely likely, and its effects will depend on the efficiency of the "price mechanism" in bringing about adjustment. As we shall see (below p. 219), Marx is sceptical of its ability to return the system to an equilibrium smoothly.

It is not surprising, then, that there has been increasing academic interest in Marx's reproduction models. Criticism has tended to focus on the aspect of Marx's saving-investment function which we have examined above, that is, the adjustment of α_2 to ensure equilibrium; and also on Marx's further assumption that savings are invested only in the department in which they originate. Within Marx's logical-historical method, however, relaxation of the latter assumption means that there is a tendency for the rate of profit to be equalized, so that the model must now be based on prices of production, and not values. Marx never returned to the reproduction models after *Capital* II, and consequently never produced such a model based on prices of production and an equal rate of profit.

Formulations of Marx's models assuming capital mobility and exogenously determined savings ratios in *both* departments are, however, easily produced, as a number of authors have shown (Naqvi, 1960; Harris, 1972; Krelle, 1971; and Morishima, 1973). These more sophisticated models by no means invalidate Marx's conclusion that, although equilibrium and balanced growth is possible, it is "an accident owing to the spontaneous nature of this production" (*Capital* II, 499).

Marx's macro-economic theory takes up the two main conclusions drawn from the reproduction models – that equilibrium growth is *possible*, but *unlikely* – in order to analyse the "contradictions of capitalism". Marx's theory of technical change is based on the assumption that the economy is on an equilibrium growth path, and the theory is thus worked out independently of deficient demand considerations. Marx's theory of effective demand then considers the cyclical fluctuations exhibited by any actual capitalist growth path. Sections 6.4 and 6.5 deal in turn with these two questions.

6.4 Marx's theory of technical change

In developing the main aspects of his theory of technical change in capitalism, Marx abstracts from problems concerned with the realization of surplus value. His analysis thus assumes that the economy moves along an equilibrium growth path. As such it represents Marx's attempt to deal with the economic contradictions of capitalism independently of the realization problems which in practice, as he knew very well, capitalism encounters (see Shoul, 1957).

Marx now departs from the assumption, made in the analysis of reproduction, that the organic composition of capital is constant. The organic composition is assumed to rise in the course of capitalist development, reflecting the tendency inherent in capitalism for technical change to be biased towards labour-saving (capital-using) innovations. Since the organic composition rises, the equilibrium growth path is *not* balanced: department I produces an increasing proportion of total output. This also means that the rate of exploitation is not constant. Given the subsistence wage, the relative share of the proletariat in net output declines.

As in the reproduction models, Marx abstracts from the division of surplus value into interest, rent, mercantile profit and industrial profit, and assumes that all surplus value takes the form of industrial profit. Moreover, for most of the analysis Marx aggregates capitalist industry into a single sector, and ignores the distinction between the two departments made in the reproduction models. Since, however, an important part of Marx's argument concerns the impact of capitalism on the *pre-capitalist* sector, the overall model is a two-sector one. Thus Marx does not assume that the economy is entirely capitalist from the start, but that capitalism progressively extends itself into the pre-capitalist sector.

Marx's analysis of technical change is considerably less formal than his theory of reproduction. In dealing with such a complex and difficult subject this is an important limitation of his analysis. The assumptions which we have outlined are not always rigidly adhered to. Thus, although they do generally apply, Marx does refer repeatedly to cyclical fluctuations and at odd points to money capital and credit. Overall the model is one of advanced, freely competitive capitalism, but this does not preclude the existence of a large pre-capitalist sector.

Marx's definition of technical change
Marx's analysis is built on his view that technical change in capitalism is predominantly labour-saving (capital-using). Capital-saving (labour-using) innovation is recognized and analysed, but Marx expects the *overall* or net effect to be in the former direction over the long period. He identifies this with an increase in the productivity of labour.

He does not, however, define productivity as the ratio of *net* output in a given period (measured in terms of prices of production) to the total labour force employed. Instead he states that "the degree of productivity of labour in a given society, is expressed in the relative extent of the means of production that one labourer, during a given time, with the same tension, turns into products" (*Capital* I, 622). This ratio is in turn defined as the "technical composition of capital", which he states elsewhere as "the relation between the mass of the means of production employed, on the one hand, and the mass of labour necessary for their employment on the other" (*ibid*, I, 612). He proceeds to argue that these changes in the technical composition of capital are reflected in the "value composition of capital", which is "the proportion in which it is divided into constant capital or value of the means of production, and variable capital or the value of labour power". Marx argues that "between the two there is a strict correlation. To express this, I call the value composition, in so far as it is determined by its technical composition and mirrors the changes in the latter, the *organic composition* of capital" (*ibid*, I, 612).

We can attempt to clarify this rather confusing argument through the use of a simple model of an economy producing two commodities, a means of production (tractors) and a consumer good (corn)[14]. These are equivalent to Marx's departments I and II of the reproduction models. We assume that *either* all the assumptions of simple reproduction *or* all the assumptions of extended reproduction hold. We can write the value of the total output of each sector as follows:

$$b_1 X_1 = l_1 X_1 w b_2 (1 + e) + d_1 X_1 b_1 \qquad [6.22]$$

$$b_2 X_2 = l_2 X_2 w b_2 (1 + e) + d_2 X_2 b_1 \qquad [6.23]$$

where

$(i = 1,2)$

d_i : quantity of the means of production required to produce one unit of commodity i

l_i : quantity of labour needed to produce one unit of commodity i

b_i : *value* of one unit of commodity i

w : quantity of the consumer good (corn) needed to pay one unit of labour at the subsistence wage rate (that is, the *real* wage)

X_i : output of commodity i.

The "technical composition of capital" in industry i may then be defined as $(i = 1,2)$

$$\frac{d_i X_i}{l_i X_i} = \frac{d_i}{l_i} \qquad [6.24]$$

The "value composition of capital" is defined as

$$\frac{c_i}{v_i} = \frac{d_i X_i b_1}{l_i X_i w b_2} = \frac{d_i b_1}{l_i w b_2} \qquad [6.25]$$

The *average* "technical composition of capital" is

$$\frac{d_1 X_1 + d_2 X_2}{l_1 X_1 + l_2 X_2} \qquad\qquad [6.26]$$

The corresponding *average* "value composition" is

$$\frac{\sum\limits_{i=1}^{2} c_i}{\sum\limits_{i=1}^{2} v_i} = \frac{b_1(d_1 X_1 + d_2 X_2)}{b_2(l_1 X_1 + l_2 X_2)w} \qquad\qquad [6.27]$$

On Marx's definition, labour-saving technical change increases the "technical composition of capital". In terms of our *two-sector* model this is straightforward enough: the numerator of equation [6.26] rises relatively to the denominator. In terms of a multi-commodity model with *diverse* constant capital inputs, however, the technical composition has no clear meaning, for the numerator is made up of diverse commodities measured in equally diverse physical units[15].

But even in the simple two commodity model there are problems in Marx's argument, for there is unlikely to be a "strict correlation" between changes in the technical composition and the value composition, if this is taken to mean that the value composition changes in the same proportion as the technical composition. This is because changes in the technical composition—resulting from changes in the input coefficients d_i and l_i—will almost certainly change relative labour values, that is, the ratio b_1/b_2 in equation [6.27]. Such changes will *not* occur only if there are special types of technical progress (Morishima, 1973; Heertje, 1972), and there is no *a priori* reason to suppose that this will be so.

But Marx did not seem to interpret the relationship between the technical and value compositions in this strict sense. In effect he assumes only that the value composition will at least move *in the same direction* as that in which labour-saving technical change is pushing the technical composition, which he takes to be upwards, even though these changes need not be of the same magnitude (*Capital* I, 623). Marx's definition of the organic composition as a "mirror" of changes in the technical composition must presumably be understood in this sense, though his argument and its mode of expression are far from clear.

Nevertheless his procedure is still not free from objection. Labour-saving technical change which increases the technical composition of capital — equation [6.26] — will *not* necessarily lead to an increase in the value composition. It is quite possible for the value composition of capital to move in the *opposite* direction as a result of a change in the technical composition. What actually does happen will depend on the *specific form* of technical progress[16]. Marx nowhere seems to have realized this. His belief that the technical composition of capital increases with the development of capitalism is thus neither a necessary nor a sufficient condition for an increase in the value composition.

Even apart from these problems, Marx does not always use the concept of the organic composition in an unambiguous way. It is best understood as a *stock* concept rather than a flow concept. The simplest way in which this can be done is to assume, firstly that all constant capital is fully used up during one production period, so that the amortization flow equals the stock at the beginning of the period; and secondly that the wage bill for the period of production equals the stock of variable capital. Stocks and flows per period are then identical. With a constant wage rate the organic composition of capital is then proportional to constant capital per worker, which is also a ratio of two stocks.

Alternatively, we can divide the amortization flow and the wage bill by the appropriate rates of turnover when these differ from unity, again obtaining the ratio of the stock of constant capital to variable capital. In this case the ratio is also proportional to constant capital per worker, and if we ignore the stock of variable capital as negligibly small we can reduce this simply to the stock of capital per worker. (At all times capital is measured in terms of labour values.) Marx was fully aware of these points (see *Capital* II, Part II). He did, however, move between stocks and flows without warning, and this has often been a legitimate source of complaint (Robinson, 1942, p. 7; Blaug, 1968, p.228).

The industrial reserve army

If technical change is labour-saving, the employment of labour power will grow less rapidly than constant capital. The demand for labour power is a function of the accumulation of capital; since accumulation increases the organic composition, the growth in the demand for labour power must be slower than the growth of constant capital. Marx argued that this will increase the rate of unemployment as constant capital progressively replaces the employment of labour and reduces the number of workers employed by a capital of a given magnitude (*Capital* I, ch. xxv). This form of unemployment is *not* due to deficiencies in aggregate demand, and must therefore be distinguished from Keynesian unemployment. It is a form of unemployment which exists *when all existing capital is fully manned* (see Robinson and Eatwell, 1973, p. 117)[17].

As it stands this argument is incomplete, for nothing has been said about the rate of growth of population. Marx assumes that the decline in variable capital (and hence in employment) is "relative" to the growth of constant capital, and normally assumes that the absolute level of employment increases over time (*Capital* I, 629). Thus an increasing rate of unemployment will *not* occur as long as the rate of growth in the demand for labour power is greater than or equal to population growth. Marx in fact made no particular assumption about the rate of population growth, except to imply that it is normally positive, as is the rate of growth of demand for labour power.

He does supplement his argument, however, by pointing out that the process of accumulation is associated with the centralization of capital (*Capital* I, 626ff). This, he argues, "extends and speeds those revolutions in the technical composition of capital which raise its constant portion at the expense of its variable portion" (*ibid*, I, 628). This leads to "a more accelerated diminution of its variable, as compared with its constant constituent" (*ibid*, I, 630). But, as it stands, this argument certainly does nothing more to establish the case for increasing unemployment over time. The decline in the rate of growth in the demand for labour power is still only "relative" to that of constant capital. The growth of variable capital must therefore be slower than that of constant capital. But this is still perfectly compatible with a constant or even an increasing rate of growth of employment.

This can easily be seen. We know from the previous section (above p. 190) that

$$g_v = \lambda_v \alpha e \qquad [6.16a]$$

where g_v is the rate of growth of variable capital, λ_v the proportion of investment allocated to variable capital, α the capitalists' savings ratio, and e the rate of exploitation. Marx's argument is that λ_v declines at an increasing rate with the centralization of capital. But we are still not assured of a decline in g_v unless (αe) changes at an appropriate rate. If α is assumed constant, then g_v depends critically on the rate of growth of e. If the (positive) rate of growth of e is equal to the (negative) rate of growth of λ_v, for example, we have a constant g_v. In order for g_v to decline, the absolute rate of growth of e must be less than the absolute rate of growth of λ_v.

Marx argues later, as we shall see, that the rate of growth of e may progressively decline, so that, if the rate of decrease of λ_v accelerates, there must come a point after which g_v falls. This point may, however, be a long way off; and in any case this particular argument is part of Marx's theory of the falling rate of profit which, as we shall see (below pp. 203f), is invalid. Even if it were the case, however, an increase in α—which is not unlikely if centralization occurs[18]—could offset this effect. And even if

g_v did decline, population growth would still have to exceed g_v in order to produce increasing unemployment.

We may conclude that simply postulating an increasing organic composition of capital by itself tells us nothing about unemployment, even though Marx himself often assumes that it does (see for example *Capital* I, 630). Thus his argument points only to one *possible* cause of unemployment, and one is tempted to conclude that his theory of increasing relative unemployment was unsupported. This, however, would be incorrect. Marx gives two other reasons why high unemployment will be maintained and increase. Both are associated with technical change and a rising organic composition.

First, it is not the rate of population growth that is the crucial "supply" variable, but rather the rate of growth of the supply of labour power to the *capitalist* sector of the economy. The efficiency of the capitalist sector leads to its expansion at the expense of the pre-capitalist sector. Since labour productivity is higher in the capitalist sector, more workers are released through the decline in the pre-capitalist sector than can be absorbed in the expansion of the capitalist sector (see, for example, *Capital* I, 640ff)[19]. This is enhanced by the fact that mechanization increases the possibilities of employing female and child labour (*ibid*, I, 394ff). Moreover centralization itself reduces the number of capitalists while increasing the size of the proletariat.

Secondly, Marx anticipates in several places the modern idea that the rate and form of technical change is conditioned by the relative scarcities of appropriate inputs. Thus if there is at any period excess demand for labour, so that wages increase and reduce the rate of profit, the application of labour-saving innovations will be accelerated, thus reducing the demand for labour power:

"Between 1849 and 1859, a rise in wages practically insignificant, though accompanied by falling prices of corn, took place in the English agricultural districts. ... What did the farmers do now? Did they wait, until, in consequence, ... the agricultural labourers had so increased and multiplied that their wages must fall again, as prescribed by the dogmatic economic brain? They introduced more machinery, and in a moment the labourers were redundant again in a proportion satisfactory even to the farmers. There was now "more capital" laid out in agriculture than before and in a more productive form. With this the demand for labour fell, not only relatively but absolutely" (*Capital* I, 638; see also *Capital* I, 436; II, 505)[20].

This mechanism will furnish a reserve army in Marx's model, as he postulates that wages begin to increase long before the reserve army is fully absorbed. It will increase the relative size of the reserve army, however, only if this mechanism continually leads to an *overcompensation*, as Marx seems to imply[21]. He concludes as follows:

"The greater the social wealth, the functioning capital, the extent and energy of its growth, and, therefore, also the absolute mass of the proletariat, and the productiveness of its labour the greater is the industrial reserve army. The same causes which develop the expansive power of capital, develop also the labour power at its disposal. The relative mass of the industrial reserve army increases, therefore, with the potential energy of wealth. But the greater this reserve army, the greater is the mass of a consolidated surplus population, whose misery is in inverse ratio to its torment of labour. The more extensive the lazarus-layers of the working class, and the industrial reserve army, the greater is official pauperism. This is the absolute general law of capitalist accumulation" (*Capital* I, 644).

Marx's term, the "absolute general law", should not be taken to mean an unqualified law always operative without modification. On the contrary, he means here that the law is based on highly abstract analysis, and consequently that "it is modified in its working by many circumstances the analysis of which does not concern us here" (*Capital* I, 644; see also Sweezy, 1946, p. 19, and Schumpeter, 1954, p. 685). Thus Sweezy argues that the analysis of the reserve army is "provisional", in the sense that the analysis is necessarily modified in *Capital* II and III. While this is true of much of Capital I (above pp. 45–52), is does not apply to any significant extent to the theory of the reserve army. We may therefore take Marx's theory of the reserve army as a concrete long run prediction, as he himself did (*Capital* III, 236).

The reserve army allows the complete domination of capital over labour (*Capital* I, 645). It is the key economic force tending to keep the real wage down to subsistence level, ensuring that the methods of increasing the productivity of labour increase the rate of exploitation and thus the relative share of the capitalist class in net output (*ibid*, I, 604, 645, 652). Hand in hand with this process there occurs the centralization of capital (*ibid*, I, 626ff), so that the increasing relative share of net output appropriated by the capitalist class increases the share of the *surviving* capitalists to an even greater extent. There is thus an increasing polarization of the class structure.

How are we to evaluate Marx's arguments about the reserve army? We have already seen that an increasing organic composition in itself only establishes at most one *possibility* of increasing unemployment, since the actual effect depends on the rate of population growth. This possibility, however, is clearly likely to be particularly important in the context of rapid population growth, as in the industrial revolution and its aftermath in Britain. This, of course, was precisely Marx's major historical reference point in his analysis of capitalism. Thus, despite the lack of rigour in his presentation of his argument, there is an important strand of historical relevance in it, and it may be usefully applied to capitalist development. It would, however, seem to have little relevance to contemporary capitalism in the West.

This point is given added weight by Marx's other argument, which stresses the unemployment resulting from the extension of capitalist industry into the pre-capitalist sector. This was quite clearly an important analytical insight. Again, however, the argument loses its force with the progressive increase in the size of the capitalist sector relatively to that of the pre-capitalist sector. The generation of surplus labour power must become a declining force with the increasing dominance of capitalist over pre-capitalist production, and eventually lose its significance altogether. We may therefore conclude, with Meek (1968, p. 122), that Marx "generalized too extensively on the basis of a historical process of this sort, elevating to the status of basic features of capitalism certain things which were in fact basic only to the particular stage of the development of capitalism in which he happened to be living"[22].

We are left with Marx's argument that it is the intensification of labour-saving innovations, in the face of increasing wages deriving from a labour shortage, that maintains and, if there is overcompensation, actually increases the reserve army. This argument is clearly not historically relative in the way that the previous two are. However, we can use elements of Marx's own theory of technical change to show a weakness in this argument.

As we have seen (above p. 201), Marx shows how capitalists use technical change to restore profitability in the face of labour shortages and rising wages. It is clear, however, that on this argument the interests of capital will lie in adopting labour-using (capital-saving) innovations when there is a relative shortage of *capital*. And indeed Marx explicitly recognizes that there are many economic forces operating to make capital-saving innovations relatively more profitable than labour-saving innovations. One such force is the reserve army of the unemployed itself, which operates to keep wage rates from rising relative to the rate of profit (*Capital* I, 390; III, 114, 236–7, ch. IV, V and XIV). Thus Marx provides no proof that technical progress will have a labour-saving bias sufficiently strong to produce an increasing reserve army[23].

The falling rate of profit

Marx's theory of technical change leads him to postulate a decaying employment position over time, which depresses the relative share of labour and increases that of the capitalist class. *The same mechanism*, Marx argues, also produces a tendency for the *rate of profit* to fall. Thus Marx's account of the falling rate of profit, like that concerning the reserve army of the unemployed, does *not* rest on any deficiency in aggregate demand (see above pp. 195—6).

Marx's argument is as follows[24]. The rate of profit is given by the formula[25]:

$$r = \frac{s}{c+v} = \frac{s/v}{c/v+1} = \frac{e}{k+1}$$

The rate of profit is thus directly related to the rate of exploitation, and inversely related to the organic composition of capital. We have seen that Marx argues that the organic composition increases (and at an increasing rate) with capitalist development. Given only this piece of information, however, we can infer *nothing* about the rate of profit. Although the organic composition increases this will, given a fixed subsistence wage, itself produce an increasing rate of exploitation, since net output per man is growing. Thus the net effect will depend on the respective magnitudes of change in the organic composition and the rate of exploitation.

Marx argues, however, that although the rate of exploitation increases with the organic composition, it will after some point increase *less rapidly*, so that there must come a point after which the rate of profit will begin to fall:

"The compensation of a decrease in the number of labourers employed, or the amount of variable capital advanced, by a rise in the rate of surplus value, or by the lengthening of the working day, has impassable limits. Whatever the value of the labour power may be ... the total value that a labourer can produce, day in, day out, is always less than the value in which 24 hours of labour are embodied. The absolute limit of the average working day — this being by nature always less than 24 hours — sets an absolute limit to the compensation of a reduction of variable capital by a higher rate of surplus value" (Capital I, 305).

He argues further that as capitalism develops and the rate of exploitation rises, it becomes increasingly more difficult to shorten the necessary labour time by an increase in productivity and thus raise the rate of surplus value yet further:

"The larger the surplus value of capital ... or, the smaller the fractional part of the working day ... which expresses necessary labour, the smaller is the increase in surplus value which capital obtains from the increase of productive force. Its surplus value rises, but in an ever smaller relation to

the development of the productive force. . . . The smaller already the fractional part falling to necessary labour, *the greater the* surplus labour, *the less can any increase in productive force perceptibly diminish necessary labour" (Grundrisse,* p. 340).

Thus, in Marx's view, not only are there "certain insurmountable limits" to the rate of increase of the rate of exploitation, while there are no such limits to the rate of increase of the organic composition; but an increasing organic composition at an increasing rate due to the centralization of capital is coupled with a tendency for the rate of exploitation to decelerate over time. Thus, Marx argues, if the organic composition continues to take the path he expected, there must come a point after which the rate of profit declines. This mechanism, as with the case of the reserve army, operates independently of any considerations of effective demand. It concerns the *production* of surplus value, not its *realization*.

At this point it might be asked why the capitalist class carries on the accumulation process beyond the point where the rate of profit begins to fall. Why should they progressively increase the organic composition in the face of diminishing returns to this investment? Marx himself poses this question, and answers it as follows:

"No capitalist ever voluntarily introduces a new method of production, no matter how much more productive it may be and how much it may increase the rate of surplus value, so long as it reduces the rate of profit. Yet every such new method of production cheapens the commodities. Hence, the capitalist sells them originally above their prices of production, or perhaps, above their value. He pockets the difference between their costs of production and the market prices of the same commodities produced at higher costs of production. He can do this, because the average labour time required socially for the production of these latter commodities is higher than the labour time required for the new methods of production. His method of production stands above the social average. But competition makes it general and subject to the general law. There follows a fall in the rate of profit . . . which is, therefore, wholly independent of the will of the capitalist" (Capital III, 264—5).

Marx does deal with five main "counteracting influences" to the law of the falling rate of profit, which help to explain why the rate of profit may not decline as rapidly as his original argument suggests (*Capital* III, 232)[26]. These are:

1.   Increasing the intensity of exploitation (*Capital* III, 232). Here Marx is concerned with those influences which increase the rate of surplus value *independently* of any increase in the organic composition of capital. This

involves in particular the lengthening of the working day. (He has, of course, already taken into account within his exposition of the law itself the increase in the rate of exploitation that results from an increased organic composition.)

2. Depression of wages below the value of labour power (*ibid*, III, 235). This increases the rate of exploitation, though it cannot be a permanent force unless real wages continually decline.

3. Cheapening of the elements of constant capital (*ibid*, III, 236). This refers to capital-saving innovations, which *reduce* the organic composition of capital.

4. Relative overpopulation (*ibid*, III, 236). "The cheapness and abundance of disposable or unemployed wage-labourers", maintained by the growth of the industrial reserve army, encourages the expansion of industries with a low organic composition of capital, especially in the luxury trades, and hence slows down the rate of growth of the *average* organic composition.

5. Foreign trade (*ibid*, III, 237). This can cheapen the elements of both constant and variable capital, thus reducing the organic composition and increasing the rate of surplus value.

Marx argues that these forces do not "abolish the general law" (*Capital* III, 236), but only act as checks which "hamper, retard and partly paralyse" the decline, reducing its character to that of a "tendency" (*ibid*, III, 239). However, "Marx's analysis is neither systematic not exhaustive" (Sweezy, 1946, p. 100), so that in fact he provided no rigorous argument to show that "one set of influences would necessarily surmount the other" (Dobb, 1940, p. 109). We can be more conclusive than this, and now proceed to demonstrate — partly on the basis of Marx's own argument — that the theory of the declining rate of profit is invalid.

There are three broad criticisms that can be levelled against Marx: one is minor, while the other two are more substantial. The minor problem, firstly, concerns his formula for the rate of profit, given above (p. 204). Now as we have seen (above pp. 143f), when we carry out a Bortkiewicz transformation procedure the resulting rate of profit in the price system will not in general be given by Marx's formula. This is because, *inter alia*, Marx's formula includes luxury industries, while these in fact play *no* part in determining the rate of profit. Thus Marx's formula gives the correct rate of profit only under special circumstances[27].

If, however, Marx's argument about the falling rate of profit were valid, its validity would not be affected by this error in his formula. The relations between the rate of profit, the rate of exploitation, and the organic composition still hold even when the formula for the rate of profit does not. In particular, the rate of profit is still a positive function of the rate of surplus value and a negative function of the organic composition of capital (see Medio, 1972, pp. 339—40; Okishio, 1963; Morishima, 1973).

Secondly, and much more important, is the criticism of Marx's theory which is applied by his own exposition of the law, as Meek (1967, pp. 134—5) observes:

"Marx can . . . be justly criticized for a certain lack of rigour in his argument. In some contexts he speaks of the falling tendency of the rate of profit in terms which suggest that he believed that it would tend to fall more or less continuously as organic composition increased[28]. In actual fact, however, all that his own argument as it stands really allows us to say is that as organic composition increases and the number of men employed with a given capital diminishes there will eventually come a point beyond which no conceivable rise in the rate of surplus value — not even a rise to infinity — could possibly prevent the mass of surplus value produced by the given capital (and thus the rate of profit) from falling below its original level. It is true, of course, that in the real world, the rate of profit will probably begin to fall before this point is reached since the rate of surplus value cannot in fact rise to infinity . . . it is also clear that in the intervening period . . . the rate of profit may well rise above its original level. Marx's argument as it stands in Capital *requires a certain amount of modification and elaboration before anything like a law of the falling tendency of the rate of profit can properly be based on it."*

Cogoy (1973) provides an algebraic formulation which claims to vindicate Marx's analysis. It has been shown, however, that Cogoy's "proof" is internally inconsistent, since it requires accumulation to proceed so rapidly that investment becomes larger than the surplus value which is available to finance it. This flaw in Cogoy's argument is exposed by Himmelweit (1974). In consequence, Meek's conclusion has yet to be successfully refuted.

The third criticism takes this point much further by showing that, if capitalists behave rationally (as, according to Marx, they do); if there is only one non-reproducible input, labour (thus excluding any Ricardian factors operating to reduce the rate of profit, as they are excluded in Marx's own argument); if the wage is fixed (as it is by the reserve army); and if the economy is closed (to which Marx would not object, since for him foreign trade functions only as a "counteracting influence"); then the system will never proceed beyond the point where the rate of profit begins to fall, or, more strictly, the system will revert to the technology in operation before the rate of profit began to fall.

This argument can be demonstrated by the use of a version of the model used in section 6.4, but this time expressed in *price* rather than value terms (see Garegnani, 1970). We rewrite equations [6.22] and [6.23] in this way, and derive:

$$p_1 X_1 = l_1 w p_2 X_1 + d_1 p_1 (1 + r) X_1 \qquad [6.28]$$

$$p_2 X_2 = l_2 w p_2 X_2 + d_2 p_1 (1 + r) X_2 \qquad [6.29]$$

These two equations represent the equilibrium conditions that, in each department, the price of the output must equal total labour costs plus total "capital costs", including the prevailing rate of profit (r), which is equal in both departments. The price of the output of each department is represented by p_1 and p_2 respectively.

By a tedious but straightforward process of substitution demonstrated in Appendix 1 (section 6.8, pp. 227–8) – we obtain an expression for the wage (w) in terms only of the rate of profit (r) and the technical coefficients of production (d_i, l_i):

$$w = \frac{1 - d_1(1 + r)}{l_2 + (l_1 d_2 - l_2 d_1)(1 + r)} \qquad [6.30]$$

It is also shown in Appendix 1 (section 6.8, pp. 227–8) that the "wage curve" of equation [6.30] is inevitably downward-sloping, so that w and r are inversely related[29].

There may well be different pairs of techniques available, each with their own technical input coefficients and also, therefore, their own wage curve. The envelope of these curves forms the *wage frontier*, which shows the maximum rate of profit associated with each level of the wage. One such frontier is illustrated by the unbroken "curve" in Fig. 6.1. Competition will force capitalists to operate on, rather than inside, the frontier. In Fig. 6.1, with a fixed subsistence wage at w^*, capitalists will be forced by competition to employ that pair of techniques which yields the maximum rate of profit (r^*); that is, at point A on the frontier.

Using Fig. 6.1, we are now in a position to see the error in Marx's argument. Technical change, he suggests, will lead to a decline in r for a constant w. But then the new technology must have a wage curve which lies *inside* the frontier at the given subsistence wage w^* (for example, at point B in Fig. 6.1). But the switch to this new technology could never be more than temporary. If for some reason the new technology were adopted, and capitalists moved from A to B, they would have an obvious incentive to switch *back* to A and return to the frontier: this would be more profitable for them. Faulty expectations or misinformation could lead to such temporary unprofitable moves, but unless technical change is

Fig. 6.1: The wage frontier

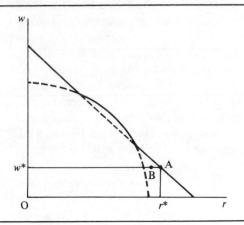

inherently *irreversible* it is difficult to see why a reversion to the old technology would not occur[30]. If the new technology is to be viable in the long run its wage curve must lie *outside* the old frontier in the relevant range; and this means, given that the wage remains at the subsistence level w^*, that it must yield a *higher* rate of profit[31].

Thus the only way in which the rate of profit could fall, at least in the long run and assuming no irreversibility, is by abandoning at least one of the assumptions on which Marx's law is based: in particular, by allowing real wages to increase over time, or by bringing in Ricardian diminishing returns. But Marx assumed constant real wages at subsistence level, as his theory of the reserve army demands. And as we have seen (above pp. 116—19), he explicitly rejected Ricardo's model of the falling rate of profit[32].

This certainly does not mean that the rate of profit may not show a declining long run tendency. It does mean, however, that *Marx's* theory of the falling rate of profit is invalid. If we abstract from Ricardian arguments, an increase in real wages is a necessary condition for a decline in the rate of profit. Thus, even though it appears that the rate of profit actually has been in secular decline (see Feinstein, 1968), this does not support, nor can it be explained by, Marx's theory.

Conclusion

This discussion has obvious and serious implications for Marx's theory of economic development. The criticism levelled against his theory of the reserve army is especially damaging. The reserve army is the linchpin of Marx's theory of distribution, and without it there is no mechanism to keep wages at subsistence level. Thus Marx cannot sustain a thesis of absolute impoverishment[33]. More important, an argument for *relative* impoverishment is contingent on many economic and political factors which Marx does not analyse in depth. Technical change can still be employed against the interests of the working class, as he so clearly saw, but whether it is or not depends on particular historical circumstances concerning the rate of population growth relative to the pace of accumulation, and the extent of capitalist penetration into pre-capitalist sectors. And it is at *all* times not in the economic interests of the capitalist class to react against an increase in wages in the manner postulated by Marx without considering the costs of alternative techniques.

Our criticism of the theory of the falling rate of profit is, on the surface, even more damaging to Marx, for, *on his argument* there is *no* possibility of a long-run decline in the rate of profit. From an overall perspective, however, the damage to his system is less serious. The primary significance which he attached to the falling rate of profit was at a very high level of theoretical abstraction. He seems to view it as a vindication of his general theory of historical materialism by showing that capitalism faces a barrier to accumulation which in turn implies that it is not an absolute mode of production, but is historical and relative. He does not use his theory of the falling rate of profit to argue for any mechanical "breakdown" theory of capitalism, for Marx has no such theory.

The concrete effect which the falling rate of profit seems, for Marx, to have on the operation of capitalism is through the trade cycle, which depends on deficiencies in aggregate demand (see below pp. 214–15). Since Marx brings in other elements, which in this context have the same effect as the falling rate of profit, the criticism of the latter must be seen as relatively minor.

But criticism of the theory of the reserve army and the falling rate of profit raises another question. Can the economic contradictions of advanced capitalism be demonstrated independently of the existence of deficient aggregate demand, as Marx's argument suggests that they can? We have shown that *on Marx's argument itself they cannot.* Thus we now turn to his theory of cyclical crises, where recurrent deficiencies in aggregate demand now move to the centre of the analysis.

6.5 Marx's analysis of cyclical fluctuations

Marx was extremely conscious of the periodic fluctuations in economic activity which take place as a capitalist economy grows. There are many *descriptive* outlines of this cycle in his work, together with detailed descriptions of each phase (see, for example, *Capital* I, 453). Marx's *theoretical* analysis of the trade cycle, however, remains an "unwritten chapter" (Schumpeter, 1954, p. 747), in that although there are numerous hints the analysis is never integrated into a coherent whole[34].

This is partly explained by Marx's method. As we have seen, he believed that economic analysis should consist of a hierarchical series of logical-historical stages which successively lower the level of abstraction, moving from the most abstract and essential to the most concrete aspects of economic phenomena (above pp. 45f). Cycles, especially in the crisis phase, are considered to be one of the most concrete aspects of capitalist production. Thus in the plan of his work written in 1857 (*Grundrisse*, p. 108) crises appear with the "world market" as the final task of analysis.

This reflects Marx's view that with the development of capitalism crises are increasingly world market phenomena[35]. As such, crises are very complex. In fact Marx goes so far as to state that the "world market crisis" is "the most complicated phenomenon of capitalist production" (*TSV* II, 501). He would, therefore, have considered it methodologically inappropriate to give a complete analysis of the cycle within the confines of the three published volumes of *Capital*. He never succeeded in undertaking the final stages of his work foreshadowed in the *Grundrisse*.

But this is probably not a complete explanation. As we shall see, although Marx made great strides forward in his cycle theory, there are areas in which he did not put forward satisfactory explanations. One is struck, in fact, by the similarity with his analysis of the transformation of values into prices of production. In both cases the complexity is recognized, the problem stated, and strong hints of a solution outlined, but in neither is such a solution adequately worked out.

Such a solution must attempt to explain the whole series of phenomena which are reflected in cyclical oscillations. In particular the theory of the cycle must seek to answer the following questions. Why does the period of rapid expansion in the boom come to an end? Why does the economy then not simply level out, rather than take an actual downturn in activity? What stops the process of contraction and determines the level of the floor? Why does the economy at some later point begin a recovery? What accounts for the specific length of the cycle, that is, its periodicity? What is the long-run tendency in the amplitude of the cycle, and are there any methods by which it may be controlled? Our outline of Marx's theory is organized on the basis of the answers which he gave (and failed to give) to these questions.

Crises

His recognition of the complex nature of crises led Marx to take special care in discussing the causes of crises. He therefore dealt at length with the important distinction between those factors which allow the *possibility* of crises, those factors which *cause* crises, and those factors which are merely *symptoms* of crises (Schumpeter, 1954, p. 748). We have already mentioned this distinction in dealing with Marx's attack on Say's Law (above pp. 119–22). We saw there that, for Marx, the possibility of crises appears only with commodity production and the use of money. It is only in such a system of social relations that the separation of sale from purchase can take place. The actual occurence of crises, however, is not inevitable simply because of the existence of the conditions for their possibility. Marx argues that crises occur only with *capitalist* commodity production, and then at a relatively late stage (above p. 120). Having laid this groundwork, we deal here with the specific *causes* which, Marx believes, actually generate crises.

The first point to be clarified concerns the general nature of crises. Marx makes it quite clear that cyclical movements involving crises are endogenous; cumulative movements in one direction set up forces that will cause a reversal of that movement (*TSV* II, 497–8; *Capital* III, 255, 489). He recognizes, however, that such cycles are "complicated by irregular oscillations" (*Capital* I, 637); although he could not accept a general "random disturbance" theory of crises, he did see that such factors might have an important part to play in explaining the actual historical course of the cycle. Furthermore, he nowhere appears to conceive of crises independently of a deficiency in aggregate demand; changes in supply conditions are not considered to be especially important:

"If purchase and sale do not get bogged down and, therefore, do not require forcible adjustment . . . no crisis exists. No crisis can exist unless sale and purchase are separated from one another and come into conflict" (*TSV* II, 512; see also *ibid*, II, 507–8, 514).

"Crisis results from the impossibility to sell. The difficulty of transforming the commodity *. . . into . . . money . . . lies in the fact that . . . the person who has effected a sale . . . is not compelled to buy again at once"* (*TSV* II, 509).

Thus crises are characterized as periods of "overproduction", in the sense that too much is produced in relation to effective demand (*TSV* II, 505–7). Thus every crisis is a "realization crisis", in that there is a failure to realize the full value and, therefore, the full surplus value of commodities in the form of money (*TSV* II, 503; *Capital* II, 322). In consequence, crises represent the phase of disturbance or interruption in the process of reproduction (*TSV* II, 503). Crises are characterized, *inter alia*, by a decline in output (*Capital* II, 328, 494, 524)[36].

In Marx's view, however, this does not explain the *cause* of crises, for it does not tell us why the imbalance between purchase and sale initially occurs and then spreads[37]. It only *defines* a crisis as that which results from such an occurrence[38]. In taking his analysis of causation toward the actual precipitating factor, Marx points to the pivotal importance of the rate of profit. He regards the rate of profit as the key motivational variable of the capitalists, and states that

"If, therefore, through any circumstance or combination of circumstances, the market prices of commodities (of all or most of them, it makes no difference) fall far below their cost prices, then reproduction of capital is curtailed as far as possible. Accumulation . . . stagnates even more" (*TSV* II, 494; see also *ibid*, II, 513, and *Capital* III, ch. xv)[39].

This is explained by the *expectations* of capitalists. If they do not achieve their expected rate of profit, they hold back from continuing production at the prevailing level, the more so the greater any expectation they have of an increased rate of profit in the future (*Capital* II, 424—5, 449)[40]. In reducing production, capitalists thus create or extend an imbalance between purchase and sale. They seek to hold capital in its money form, rather than employ labour power and means of production; that is, they "hoard" money.

Marx's emphasis on the critical role of changes in the rate of profit brings his analysis one step closer to the concrete causal factors involved in crises. Commodity production and the use of money contain the possibility of crises. Capitalism *actualizes* these possibilities in so far as the requisite changes in the rate of profit occur. Marx expresses this point in a more general way by pointing out that capitalist production is not production for use. Capital does not circulate in the form C — M — C, but in the form M — C — C' — M'. It is precisely because pre-capitalist commodity production is still production for use, C — M — C, though not production for direct personal needs (*TSV* II, 509), that crises are not actualized in this stage[41].

Given the importance of changes in the rate of profit as the initial trigger of crises, we must now pose the question of why such changes should actually take place. Marx's analysis refers to many circumstances which could bring this about (see, for example, *Capital* II, 499; *TSV* II, 492, 503, 533). We can, however, subdivide these into two main categories: first, those which form *general* factors in the sense that they seek to explain crises within the main trend or regular oscillations of the cycle; and second, those factors which seek to explain the irregularities through randomly distributed erratic shocks. Marx does not explicitly make this distinction when discussing causation. He makes the distinction elsewhere, however (*Capital* I, 637), and was aware of its importance in theoretical analysis (Leontief, 1938, p. 91); and the many causes he enumerates, and the emphasis given to each, suggests that he had this distinction in mind.

Within those factors explaining crises as a regular occurrence, Marx develops two types of theory. The first stems from those factors in the *production* of surplus value which reduce the rate of profit but can also lead to an imbalance between sale and purchase, and thus to a crisis. The second concentrates on those factors which lead to a reduction in the rate of profit as a *direct result* of an imbalance between the production of surplus value and the circulation process which will allow its full realization[42].

Marx refers to the long-run mechanism of the declining rate of profit as causing crises at many points in his work (*Grundrisse*, p. 749; *Capital* III, 242, 250–9; *TSV* II, 510). Since, however, the law of the declining rate of profit is for Marx a long-run phenomenon (*Capital* III, 239), it has led some commentators to devalue its significance in Marx's theory of crises (see, for example, Sowell, 1967, p. 64; Sherman, 1967, p. 492). But this contradicts Marx's explicit references, and fails to note that although the law is of a long-run nature its manifestation is not smooth or regular. Marx sees accumulation, which he believes to produce the declining rate of profit, as coming in bursts (*Capital* I, 613, 632–3), and implies that the rate of profit will display a similarly irregular decline (*Capital* III, 249, 263). This in itself, however, will not create crises: as we have seen, the argument for the declining rate of profit is developed on the assumption that there is no deficiency in aggregate demand. For Marx the decline in the rate of profit results from a decrease in the production of surplus value relatively to the value of the capital stock, and not from a failure to realize the surplus value which has been produced.

Marx overcomes this objection in the following manner. In linking the declining rate of profit theory to crises, which *always* involve deficient aggregate demand, he strongly implies that capitalists react *as if* they experience realization difficulties, and by so doing actually *create* those difficulties[43]. On this argument, then, a decline in the rate of profit due to factors inherent in production is mistaken by capitalists for a realization problem. This leads to a cutback in production, and creates a break between purchase and sale[44]. It is true that Marx does not explicitly formulate the argument in these terms, but the context of his argument supports this interpretation (*Capital* III, ch. xv), and it is certainly consistent with his repeated stress that capitalists are unaware of the laws of their own system (*Capital* III, Part VII).

If one accepts the logic of Marx's theory of the falling rate of profit, this does provide a basis for explaining crises. But it provides only a *basis*, because the argument thus far does not include a precise theory of the turning point. It must therefore be extended to show at exactly what point disruption occurs; and Marx did not do this.

Now we have seen above (pp. 206–9) that Marx's argument for the declining rate of profit is invalid. Does this imply that the utilization of this theory to explain crises is illegitimate? Strictly, of course, it does. But we must note the more general and valid point that our interpretation of Marx's argument suggests. If the rate of profit should fall because of problems arising in production, as opposed to realization, then a deficiency in aggregate demand may quickly loom to the surface because of the way in which capitalists react to it, and a realization crisis will ensue.

In the light of the inadequacy of Marx's theory of the falling rate of profit, Sweezy (1946, ch. 9) emphasizes that Marx also had a theory of crises in which the causal agent inducing the rate of profit to fall is *an increase in real wages*. This may occur when accumulation is rapid enough sharply to reduce the size of the reserve army, and thus to allow wages to rise above the subsistence level. There are frequent references in *Capital* I to such a possibility, and although Marx regards such an increase in real wages as only a *temporary* phenomenon, this might well be enough to spark off a crisis in the manner described above.

There are two major problems associated with Sweezy's interpretation. In the first place, Marx himself discusses this possibility most clearly in the context of the "absolute overproduction of capital" (*Capital* III, 251–2). This is a situation in which the absolute volume of surplus value produced is declining, so that an increase in real wages could have a devastating effect on the rate of profit. But the "absolute overproduction of capital" results from the operation of Marx's original (and faulty) theory of the declining rate of profit, so that the whole argument is deeply suspect. The second problem is empirical: the evidence appears to show that the wage share in net output — which serves as a very approximate measure of the rate of exploitation — *diminishes*, rather than increases, in a boom[45]. Thus the relevance of Sweezy's argument is questionable.

We now turn to the second factor which Marx introduces to explain the general course of the cycle; that is, the deficient aggregate consumption of workers and capitalists[46]:

"Contradiction in the capitalist mode of production: the labourers as buyers of commodities are important for the market. But as sellers of their own commodity — labour power — capitalist society tends to keep them down to the minimum price.

Further contradiction: the periods in which capitalist production exerts all its forces regularly turn out to be periods of overproduction, because production potentials can never be utilised to such an extent that more value may not only be produced but also realized; but the sale of commodities, the realization of commodity capital and thus of surplus value, is limited, not by the consumer requirements of society in general, but by the consumer requirements of a society in which the vast majority are always poor and must always remain poor" (*Capital* II, 320).

Marx did not, however, accept the arguments of "underconsumptionist" theorists like Malthus, Rodbertus, Sismondi and Chalmers. He saw crises as periodic, occurring at "definite periods" (*TSV* II, 36), whereas the arguments of these others represented theories of secular stagnation (Schumpeter, 1954, pp. 740 and 750; Blaug, 1968, ch. 5). Furthermore, Marx rejected the hypothesis on which their arguments were based. In particular they argued that, since workers did not receive sufficient in wages to purchase their own products, there would necessarily be deficient demand unless there was some special offsetting factor (for Malthus, for example, consumption by the "unproductive class" of landlords). Marx's criticism of this approach was based on his own analysis of reproduction, which clearly showed its error (see, for example, *TSV* III, ch. xix).

Marx's own theory of the forces making for deficient aggregate consumption in capitalist economies is itself far from clear. Robinson (1942, p. 49) has probably come closest to Marx's own ideas in writing that the passages quoted above

"combined with the equations of reproduction, suggests that Marx intended to work out a theory on some such lines as this: consumption by the workers is limited by their poverty, while consumption by the capitalists is limited by the greed for capital which causes them to accumulate wealth rather than enjoy luxury. The demand for consumption goods . . . is thus restricted. But if the output of the consumption good industries is limited by the market, the demand for capital goods, . . . is in turn restricted, for the constant capital of the consumption-good industries will not expand fast enough to absorb the potential output of the capital-good industries. Thus the distribution of income between wages and surplus is such as to set up a chronic tendency for a lack of balance between the two groups of industries."

The reproduction models certainly show that the relation of the capital good industries to the consumption good industries was considered by Marx as crucial to the instability of capitalism. Any disproportionate relation between these two sectors would make itself felt in a change in the rate of profit which, if downward, could quickly spark off a crisis[47].

Again, however, Marx does not seem to deal with the turning-point mechanism. In other words, he gives no reason why a burst of accumulation, when once under way, must necessarily slow down or come to an end so as to create the crisis. In the chapter on the reproduction models he strongly suggests that it is the instability in the demand for means of production which is the root cause of such a crisis. Heavy demand for capital goods leads to a boom, but when this declines the maldistribution of income is such that consumption will not expand sufficiently rapidly to absorb the resources previously employed in the industries producing capital goods.

Here Marx was indeed pointing to the significant variable, as both modern theory and empirical evidence show that it is the volatility of investment expenditures that are the key to cyclical fluctuations (see, for example, Matthews, 1959, for a good survey). But Marx still gives no reason to explain why the relationship between departments I and II necessarily slows down or brings to an end the accumulation process once it has started. The obvious solution is to bring in the rate of change of consumption and its effects on changes in the capital stock via the rate of profit, so that at a certain point crises are triggered off (see, for example, Samuelson, 1939). Marx may have been working towards such a theory, as the following passage suggests:

"It is sheer tautology to say that crises are caused by the scarcity of effective consumption, or of effective consumers. The capitalist system does not know any other modes of consumption than effective ones. . . . That commodities are unsaleable means only that no effective purchasers have been found for them . . . But if one were to attempt to give this tautology the semblance of a profounder justification by saying that the working class receives too small a portion of its own product and the evil would be remedied as soon as it receives a larger share of it and its wages increase in consequence, one could only remark that crises are always prepared by precisely a period in which wages rise generally and the working class actually gets a larger share of that part of the annual product which is intended for consumption. From the point of view of these advocates of sound and 'simple' (!) commonsense, such a period should rather remove the crises. It appears, then, that capitalist production comprises conditions independent of good or bad will, conditions which permit the working class to enjoy that relative prosperity only momentarily, and at that always only as the harbinger of a coming crisis" (*Capital* II, 414–15).

Clearly, however, one cannot be definite on this question.

Together with these two arguments for crises (the falling rate of profit and "under-consumption"), which we interpret as theories attempting to account for the regularity of crises, there are numerous references in Marx to random shocks that send the system into crisis before the main and more powerful mechanisms fully work themselves out. Thus he points out that each market experiences fluctuations due to its own specific nature (*Capital* I, 478). More concretely he refers to crises that can result from large changes in the composition of demand (*TSV* III, 122), and crises resulting from a shortage of particular commodities and the attendant price fluctuations (*TSV* II, 516; Sherman, 1967, 1971).

Marx realizes that such disruptions need not always lead to crises, and that reductions in particular profit levels may only lead to partial crises without widespread ramifications (*TSV* II, 521). He does state, however, that if such problems affect the "principal items of commerce" this is likely to generate a general crisis (*TSV* II, 505, 523, 529). Although this is rather vague, it expresses Marx's general view that in the anarchic conditions of capitalist production crises were a continual threat.

In examining the transition from a partial crisis to a general crisis, either as a result of random shocks or because the more general mechanisms initially make themselves felt in particular sectors, Marx reveals himself at his best. Here we have an explicit and quite well developed theory of the downturn from an initial point of crisis. Money plays a key role: it is the mechanism which intensifies the disequilibrium. A decline in the rate of profit generates a demand to hold capital in its money form, that is, to "hoard", and a consequent failure to recirculate it. This in turn creates other price-profit changes, and thus further disruption in other industries (*Capital* II, 106; *TSV* II, 522–3). The demand for money increases as the decline in profitability renders the capitalist incapable of meeting fixed obligations (*TSV* II, 516). The credit system is then undermined, and its contraction leads to a further fall in aggregate demand (*Capital* III, 254). Even commodities which were not initially overproduced may now face a sharp fall in demand (*TSV* II, 253). All this further intensifies the demand for money (*Capital* III, 490), and reduces still more the demand for non-monetary commodities. This expresses Marx's view that money is not merely a means of exchange. It also has the role of uncertainty bearer, providing the least uncertain store of value between the present and the future (see, for example, *TSV* II, 504; Somerville, 1933). There is here a marked similarity with the views of Keynes.

These changes in turn have international ramifications through foreign trade relations (*Capital* II, 472–3, 321; III, 491, 547, 575; *TSV* II, 500, 534). In believing that production for the world market becomes increasingly important with the development of capitalism, Marx implies that the international transmission of the trade cycle becomes stronger over time.

Thus crises form an important method of disequilibrium adjustment. At the most general level of Marx's theory, they can be said to spring from the unplanned, anarchic character of capitalist production. *Ex ante* coordination, and the discovery of equilibrium proportions prior to production and circulation, is impossible in capitalism. There is in reality no perfect information, as neoclassical theory assumes (*Capital* I, 36, 130; III, 539). Price-profit changes bring about an *ex post* coordination, but this mechanism produces crises rather than a smooth transfer of resources (*ibid*, II, 319). Thus crises reflect the absence of conscious social control over economic relations (*ibid*, II, 176, 473), and manifest in the clearest fashion the alienated social relations of capitalist commodity producers (*ibid*, III, 257).

The slump, the lower turning point and periodicity

In his analysis of the cycle Marx gave no theory which would allow the determination of the point at which the level of economic activity ceases to fall. He did, however, deal with the lower turning point, at which the economy begins the upturn to the boom. There seem to be three main factors causing this revival. As we would expect in view of the previous section, all work by directly or indirectly bringing about an increase in profitability.

Of most importance in the light of modern theories of the cycle is the physical destruction of capital through depreciation. Marx maintains that the investments which were bunched together at the peak of the cycle, or at least large portions of these investments, come up for renewal almost simultaneously, because of similarities in the period of amortization. Replacement demands are thus bunched, and give rise to disproportionality by generating "purchases without sales". This has reflationary effects, and raises profitability. Marx believed that the durability of much of the fixed capital in the most important industries was about ten years, and used this to explain the definite periodicity of the cycle (*Capital* II, 188–9, 318–20, 454; *TSV* II, 495). Thus as in his analysis of the upper turning point — though much more clearly here — Marx was on the right track in that "variations in investment are the key to the trade cycle" (Robinson, 1942, p. 46).

These echo effects are unlikely to provide a general explanation of the causes of recovery and periodicity, since such a mechanism is dependent on a uniform lifespan of a significant proportion of fixed capital. This is unlikely to be the case unless the industrial sector of the economy is highly specialized. But since the British economy between 1820 and 1870 did experience an extremely regular ten-year cycle, and was very highly specialized, the dynamics of capital investment may well have generated significant echo effects along the lines suggested by Marx.

Marx also maintains that profitability is restored by the destruction of capital *values* which results from the decline in prices in crises. The bankruptcy of weaker capitalists and their forced sale of assets on a depressed market allows the more strongly placed sections of the class to buy in anticipation of large capital gains when an upturn occurs. This transfer of wealth will thus tend to raise the rate of profit and aid recovery (*Capital* III, 233–5; *TSV* II, 495–6).

Marx argues, thirdly, that the stagnation of production which occurs in the slump will increase the reserve army of the unemployed and lead to reductions in real wages from the high point reached in the boom, when unemployment was at its lowest (*Capital* III, 254–5). In Marx's theory wages and profits are inversely related, so that this would tend to increase profitability and encourage the re-expansion of production.

This last argument seems rather unsound in the light of Keynesian theory, according to which a reduction in real wages is likely to reduce effective demand by diminishing workers' consumption; this in turn is likely to reduce the rate of profit, and not to increase it. Despite strong doubts on the validity of this third argument, however, Marx's other two arguments, and in particular the first, show that he pinpointed important forces working for revival in the slump, and accounting for a definite periodicity of the cycle when random disturbances are unimportant.

The secular tendency of the cycle
It is clear from what we have already said that Marx did not foresee a secular stagnation of economic activity under capitalism. He says quite clearly that "permanent crises do not exist" (*TSV* II, 497). Engels, in editing *Capital* after Marx's death, did not seem to share this view (*Capital* I, 6; III, 489), but there is no evidence that Marx changed his mind on this matter.

There are, however, certain hints in Marx's work that crises and depressions will get more severe as capitalism develops (*Grundrisse*, pp. 749–50). As we have seen, the general basis on which crises arise is for Marx the inadequacy of any *ex ante* coordination between interdependent sectors of the economy. Marx's frequent references to the increasing "socialization" of production which takes place with the development of capitalism can thus be taken to imply that maladjustments would increase in their intensity, resulting in a cycle of increasing amplitude[48]. More concretely, Marx pointed out that the development of credit can intensify the disruptive potentialities of the system, as his theory of the downturn would in fact suggest. Moreover, he states that crises become more severe as the working period lengthens and speculation increases (*Capital* II, ch. xii; 441, 504; III, pts. III and V). These points are not, however, developed into any systematic theory, and it is probably wrong to give them too much weight.

As for the control of cyclical fluctuations, Marx maintains that they can be alleviated but *not* eradicated. Many modern economists would agree with him on this. They would certainly disagree with him, however, about the *degree* to which cyclical instability can be contained. Marx discusses this question in the context of the bank legislation of the 1840s, which he rightly saw as intensifiying the effects of crises. But for Marx monetary disturbances are not the *cause* of crises but rather their *symptoms*, and he is adamant that more systematic economic control than is implied by tinkering with the banking system would be incompatible with the structure of capitalist production itself (*Capital* I, 633; III, 120, 490, 515, 547, 554–5, 560–2; see also Fan-Hung, 1939).

This raises a fundamental problem inherent in Marx's theory of capitalism, with which he never explicitly or systematically comes to terms. What prevents the capitalist class from agreeing to use the state's many instruments of economic control to bring about a significant reduction in the amplitude of the cycle? Marx argues that this is not possible, but provides little justification for this view. His own models of reproduction indeed strongly suggest that it is *technically* possible. Moreover he provides no convincing argument to demonstrate that it is *sociologically* impossible for the capitalist class to initiate or concur in such policies. Indeed his emphasis on the rationality of capitalists, his theory of the centralization of capital, and his theory of class consciousness should have suggested to him that such policies were likely to emerge with the development of capitalism.

Conclusion

We should emphasize that this account, and particularly the section relating to crises, is very much an interpretation rather than a simple exposition of Marx's many references on this subject. These references allow no more than an interpretation, and it is obviously not possible to take the view that there is enough evidence to rule out other interpretations.

Marx's theory was well in advance of its time. He saw very clearly that cyclical phenomena were endogenous to the capitalist system, in contrast to the emphasis placed by classical political economy on exogenous disruption caused by wars and government regulation. Those who *had* criticized Say's Law revealed no more than the *possibility* of crises, rather than their *causes*. Post-classical economics tended to concentrate their explanation on monetary and credit phenomena, which Marx rightly saw were only *symptoms* of crises.

Such a typology itself is important, as Schumpeter (1954, p. 748) has explained:

"It stands to reason that neglect of these distinctions must be a fertile source of errors in analysis and of futile controversy 'and that this methodological contribution is itself sufficient to give to Marx high rank among the workers in this field."

Prior to Keynes, in fact, Marx was the most rigorous and effective in criticizing Say's Law and developing that criticism into an overall theoretical structure. Furthermore, in putting his criticism into historical perspective, Marx is indeed much superior to Keynes, whose own analysis bore close resemblance to the ahistorical conceptions of the neoclassical theory out of which it grew (above p. 27).

As we have seen, there are elements of real perception in Marx's analysis of the cycle itself. His emphasis on the key role of the rate of profit; on aggregate demand and the special volatility of investment; its relation to periodicity; the maldistribution of consuming power; the mechanism of the downturn and the role of money; all of these elements show that Marx was on the frontier of cycle theory well after his own time.

Nevertheless it should also be clear, on our interpretation of Marx's analysis, that his theory is far from complete and has major limitations. In particular the two main mechanisms – the declining rate of profit and "underconsumption" – are not really related to each other. The former rests on analysis the validity of which is highly suspect; in both the answer to the most important question of all, the mechanism of the upper turning point, is not clearly given.

Modern theory shows that the development of economics has not in fact made major progress over Marx in the sense that it has not developed anything approaching a satisfactory theory which would explain the complexity of the cycle's historical course. What the development of economics has provided, however, is a large number of particular theories, the content of which is much richer, though little more systematic, than Marx's own analysis. That economic theory has not progressed further than this is partly due to its neglect of this important problem in favour of the trivia of the subject; but it is also due to the inherent complexity of the problem, which Marx himself recognized. Each cycle is in a sense a "historical individual", and although the key to each is likely to be changes in profitability and investment, which are emphasized both by

Marx and by modern theory, this in turn is only another way of stating the complexity of the problem. The investment function is the most difficult of macro-economic functions to specify precisely, as is the related problem of accounting for changes in expectations.

6.6 Another aspect of Marx's theory of deficient aggregate consumption

In the light of the last three sections it is interesting to inquire further into Marx's analysis of the growth path in advanced capitalism. In particular, we ask here whether such a growth path is possible over a long historical period.

Table 6.2 shows a numerical example in which Marx's assumptions of a constant subsistence wage and an increasing organic composition which raises labour productivity are embodied. It can be seen that the profit share in net output increases over time. If the capitalists' saving propensity is constant or increasing[49], a rising proportion of net output is devoted to the production of constant capital, and the share of consumption declines. The ratio of investment in constant capital to net output approaches the capitalists' savings ratio, and the profit share approaches unity as the wage share tends towards zero.

Table 6.2 implies that the increasing investible surplus in the hands of the capitalist class is increasingly invested in constant capital to produce more constant capital to produce yet more constant capital, so that the ratio between constant capital and consumption increases. There are strong hints in Marx to suggest that it may not be possible for capitalism *continually* to grow in this fashion.

As we have seen, Marx's theory of crises is not simply a theory of deficient aggregate demand. It is a theory of deficient demand that emphasizes that the dominant factor is the limited consuming power inherent in the capitalist system due to the subsistence wage and the high propensity of capitalists to accumulate. Thus, unlike much of modern theory, Marx's references to deficient demand often relate accumulation to consumption rather than to income (*Capital* III, 244, 250, 256–8, 484; *TSV* II, 492, 522, 525, 528, 535; *TSV* III, 56, 122). Furthermore, what is implicit in such references is made explicit at one point:

"Continuous circulation takes place between constant capital and constant capital (even regardless of accelerated accumulation). It is at first independent of individual consumption because it never enters the latter. But this consumption definitely limits it nevertheless, since constant capital is never produced for its own sake but solely because more of it is needed in spheres of production whose products go into individual consumption" (Capital III, 304–5)[50].

In such a situation there may well be a problem in maintaining the growth path which, Marx believed, advanced capitalism followed. If the "appropriate" or "desired" constant capital/consumption ratio[51] is attained, the form of the growth path must change.

This did not show up in Marx's analysis of extended reproduction, of course, because the growth path there is based on the assumption that there is no technical change, and hence no increase in productivity. In this case the rate of exploitation stays constant, and in Marx's examples, after one year, growth is balanced and all variables grow at the same rate. Marx never developed his reproduction models in terms of technical change, although he considered this case most relevant to advanced capitalism. Consequently we do not know whether he realized the implications outlined above.

Had Marx realized these implications, he would probably have stated them explicitly, for it is precisely in such a situation that his analysis of the "absolute overproduction of capital" would become relevant (above

Table 6.2. Growth with technical progress and a constant real wage*

End of year	Net output per worker (Y)	Wage per worker (W)	Profit per worker $(P = Y - W)$	Constant capital per worker (K)	Investment per worker $(I = sP)$	Consumption per worker $(C = W + (1 - s)P)$
1	20.000	10.000	10.000	100.000	5.000	15.000
2	21.000	10.000	11.000	105.000	5.500	15.500
3	22.100	10.000	12.100	110.500	6.050	16.050
10	33.579	10.000	23.579	167.897	11.790	21.790
20	71.159	10.000	61.159	335.795	30.580	40.580
60	2 778.015	10.000	2 768.015	13 890.075	1 384.007	1 394.007
70	7 189.518	10.000	7 179.518	35 947.589	3 589.759	3 599.759

End of year	Ratio of investment : income (I/Y)	Wage share in net output (W/Y)	Ratio of constant capital : consumption (K/C)	Ratio of constant capital : net output (K/Y)
1	0.250	0.500	6.666	5.000
2	0.262	0.476	6.774	5.000
3	0.274	0.452	6.885	5.000
10	0.351	0.298	7.705	5.000
20	0.430	0.141	8.768	5.000
60	0.498	0.004	9.964	5.000
70	0.499	0.001	9.986	5.000

* For simplicity we assume a one-sector corn model; all magnitudes are thus measured in terms of corn. We further assume that K/Y is constant; that capital lives for ever; and that the gestation period of investment is one year. The capitalists' savings propensity, s, equals 0.5. All investment decisions are made at the beginning of the year.

p. 215). In the face of such a drastic fall in the rate of profit, capitalism would breed cutthroat competition, with all its resulting chaotic effects: an increased rate of bankruptcy, unemployment and idleness of capital (*Capital* III, 250—9).

Even if this did not occur, and the growth path switched to that of Marx's model of extended reproduction, there might still be problems. If the growth rate exceeded the rate of growth of labour power[52], there would be a decline in the rate of profit as wages increased. This would provide a potential source of crises.

Marx does not, however, use such an analysis in this context. He does say, though, that capitalism has an "innate necessity ... for an ever-expanding market" (*Capital* III, 237), and relates this to his "underconsumption" theory (*ibid*, III, 244—5). This may explain the emphasis he gave to the inherent urge of the capitalist system to engage in foreign expansion. We return to this question in the next chapter.

The fact that these problems have not materialized is probably explained by the long-run increase in the real wage. This has kept the consumption requirements of the system roughly in line with the expanding stock of constant capital. Thus the organic composition could have risen without meeting the constraint which we have discussed (though there have, of course, been periodic realization crises). We therefore conclude this section with the paradox that although the struggles of the trade unions may not greatly have reduced the relative share of profits in net output, they do "save the capitalists from the ill effects of increasing it" (Robinson, 1942, p. xiv).

6.7 Conclusion

This review of Marx's macro-economics shows it to be a mixed bag. Its stress on the pivotal role of technical change makes it relevant today as none of the theories of Marx's predecessors, contemporaries or immediate successors can be. His models of reproduction were a superb achievement, and his theory of the trade cycle was full of insights. At the same time it is precisely the *theory* of technical change that is its main weakness. The theory of the reserve army is at best historically specific to one particular stage of capitalist development, while the theory of the falling rate of profit is based on an inadequate analysis. Here we consider how serious all this is for Marx's theory of proletarian revolution, which we outlined in Chapter 1.

It is clear that Marx considered that the transcendence of capitalism would result from the system's own contradictions, and that the root cause of these contradictions lay in the economic structure. Marx expresses these contradictions in different ways in different contexts from alternative perspectives, but the essential idea is invariant. It stresses that, due to their own structure, societies create within themselves conflicting forces which ultimately lead to a qualitative structural change; and that the key to these forces lies in the economy. This general conception is immensely fertile as a guide to research, and is now generally recognized as such (Bottomore and Rubel, 1963, pp. 44—63).

Marx's own application to the economic structure of capitalism clothes it with specific empirical content, as we have seen in previous sections. In terms of this we can try to pinpoint what Marx considered to be the most important underlying economic forces making for proletarian revolution.

The answer cannot be given with complete certainty, but it does appear that Marx considered the twin processes of the centralization of capital and the growth of the reserve army as the most important structural factors that would bring class conflict to a revolutionary pitch. Certainly the most explicitly revolutionary passages in *Capital* appear in Volume I, in the context of class polarization due to these economic forces (see especially *Capital* I, chs. xxv and xxxii). It is true that periodic crises are repeatedly referred to when Marx is discussing the reserve army, but it is probable that he considered that they only intensified the revolutionary consequences of the main forces of polarization[53]. The falling rate of profit appears to play no direct role in itself, and was in Marx's view only a partial explanation of crises.

In concentrating on the reserve army, then, Marx emphasizes a factor which we have seen to be historically specific at most only to a certain stage in capitalist development; its applicability to modern capitalism is extremely limited. This does not of course mean that modern capitalism is the best of all possible worlds; that it is subject to no tensions which can form the basis of a radical political movement; or that the working class must necessarily remain conservative. But it does mean that Marx's own view of the causes of revolution is of limited relevance today. Modern revolutionaries would therefore be wise to think for themselves and act in terms of their own analysis if either their theory or their practice is to have the relevance it requires[54].

6.8 APPENDIX 1

We start with equations [6.28] and [6.29] on p. 208:

$$p_1 X_1 = l_1 w p_2 X_1 + d_1 p_1 (1 + r) X_1 \qquad [6.28]$$

$$p_2 X_2 = l_2 w p_2 X_2 + d_2 p_1 (1 + r) X_2 \qquad [6.29]$$

Divide both sides of equation [6.28] by X_1, and both sides of equation [6.29] by X_2, to obtain:

$$p_1 = l_1 w p_2 + d_1 p_1 (1 + r) \qquad [A26]$$

$$p_2 = l_2 w p_2 + d_2 p_1 (1 + r) \qquad [A27]$$

Now divide both equations by p_2, and write $p_1/p_2 = p_1{}^*$, the relative price of commodity 1 in terms of commodity 2. Thus:

$$p_1{}^* = l_1 w + d_1 p_1{}^* (1 + r) \qquad [A28]$$

$$1 = l_2 w + d_2 p_1{}^* (1 + r) \qquad [A29]$$

228

Equation [A28] may be written as

$$p_1^* = \frac{l_1 w}{1 - d_1(1 + r)}$$ [A30]

Similarly, equation [A29] may be written as

$$p_1^* = \frac{1 - l_2 w}{d_2(1 + r)}$$ [A31]

Now equate [A30] and [A31], and cross-multiply, to obtain

$$w\{l_2 + (l_1 d_2 - l_2 d_1)(1 + r)\} = 1 - d_1(1 + r)$$ [A32]

from which we derive the wage curve:

$$w = \frac{1 - d_1(1 + r)}{l_2 + (l_1 d_2 - l_2 d_1)(1 + r)}$$ [6.30]

For convenience we write the constant term

$$(l_1 d_2 - l_2 d_1) = A$$ [A33]

so that equation [6.30] may be written as:

$$w = \frac{(1 - d_1) - d_1 r}{(l_2 + A) + Ar} \text{ so that}$$ [A34]

$$\frac{dw}{dr} = \frac{1}{\{(l_2 + A) + Ar\}^2} \{-d_1[(l_2 + A) + Ar] - A[(1 - d_1) - d_1 r]\}$$ [A35]

which yields

$$\frac{dw}{dr} = \frac{-l_1 d_2}{\{l_2 + A(1 + r)\}^2}$$ [A36]

Thus the wage curve is downward sloping.

Notes

1.   For a clear analysis of Marx's procedure in terms of modern aggregation theory see Morishima (1973, especially ch. 8).

2.   For a contrary view see Lowe (1954) and Thweatt (1962).

3.   This is brought out superbly by Sweezy (1968).

4.   Hence Marx argued that "political economy, which as an independent science sprang into being during the period of manufacture, views the social division of labour only from the standpoint of manufacture" (*Capital* I, 364).

5.   The models are presented in their most developed form in *Capital* II, chs. xx—xxi. Preliminary forms are also to be found in Marx's letter to Engels of 6 July 1863 (*SC*, pp. 142—5). In developing these models Marx was heavily influenced by the Physiocrat, Francois Quesnay, whose *Tableau Economique* was published in 1758. Marx said of the *Tableau* that it was "incontestably the most brilliant ... [conception] for which political economy had up to then been responsible" (*TSV* I, 344).

6.   When there is free labour mobility, the rate of exploitation will tend to equality in all sectors of the economy. In the rest of this chapter we assume that this is so, so that $e_1 = e_2 = e$, the *economy-wide* rate of exploitation.

7.   Care must be taken in interpreting the meanings of "supply" and "demand" in this context; see above, p. 176 note 37.

8.   See also above, p. 145, where the equilibrium conditions for a *three*-sector model of simple reproduction are shown.

9.   This paragraph, and much of the discussion of extended reproduction which follows, draws heavily on Harris (1972).

10.   The assumption that the savings ratio is exogenously determined may be accepted as a legitimate simplification in this highly abstract model. A complete growth model, however, would require the specification of the endogenous determinants of this ratio. Marx's failure to do so at any point in *Capital* is a serious omission. Modern economists in fact do no better: they simply conceal the omission in the tautologies of utility theory.

230

11.   Equation [6.18] is easily derived if it is remembered that the following identities hold:

$$\frac{\Delta c_1}{v_2} \equiv \frac{\Delta c_1}{c_1} \cdot \frac{c_1}{v_1} \cdot \frac{v_1}{v_2}$$

$$\frac{\Delta c_2}{v_2} \equiv \frac{\Delta c_2}{c_2} \cdot \frac{c_2}{v_2}$$

$$\frac{s_1}{v_2} \equiv \frac{s_1}{v_1} \cdot \frac{v_1}{v_2}$$

12.   Marx's second main numerical example (*Capital* II, 518) is based on the same form of saving-investment function as that used in the first example outlined above.

13.   See also Blaug (1968, p. 255); Samuelson (1967, p. 618); Erlich (1967, p. 607); and Morishima (1973, p. 125).

14.   This model is similar to that of Garegnani (1970), but is expressed in terms of values rather than prices of production; the notation is also rather different.

15.   The numerator of equation [6.26], for example, would read $d_1^1 X_1 + d_1^2 X_1 + d_2^1 X_2 + d_2^2 X_2$, where the superscripts (1,2) refer to two different types of means of production (for example, tractors and machines). In consequence, if they do not rise in the same proportion, or if new d^i's enter and old ones drop out, we cannot say by how much the "technical composition" has changed.

16.   Heertje (1972) provides examples in which the technical organic composition rises simultaneously with a *decline* in the value composition.

17.   This distinction is clear when capital capacity is clearly defined. In a situation where the manning of existing capacity can easily be increased the distinction becomes blurred, as unemployment could then be reduced by increasing effective demand. Since Marx assumed that substitution possibilities are extremely limited, however, except through changing the technical structure of capital equipment, these difficulties are not very serious.

18.   As Marx himself recognizes (see *Capital* III, 245, 251).

19.   This mechanism would be extremely powerful in a closed economy. If foreign trade is introduced, however, expansion may take place at the expense of *overseas* pre-capitalist producers, and export growth may result in a contraction of the reserve army. Marx does not seem to have given this question any explicit consideration, and we continue to assume that it is insufficiently powerful to offset the expansion of unemployment (but see below pp. 239–41).

20.   The "dogmatic economic brain" is a reference to the Malthusian population theory.

21.   It will also increase the relative size of the reserve army if the relationship between unemployment and the rate of increase in the real wage shifts upwards over time. However, Marx makes no explicit reference to this possibility.

22.   Marx may well have recognized the historical relativity of his argument, but have neglected it due to a belief that the reserve army would lead to a revolution before it was even close to exhaustion; and/or that, in the event of the drying up of *domestic* labour reserves, there was a virtually infinite supply available on a world scale. On this, however, he is nowhere explicit.

23.   Marx's overall theory of technical change is similar to neoclassical ideas of input substitution in the face of changes in relative input prices. Blaug (1960, 1968), draws out these implications of Marx's argument and uses them to derive a neoclassical theory of "neutral" technical progress. His argument against Marx is certainly more relevant than the standard neoclassical view, as it implies that input substitution takes place through technical change, rather than by substitution within a *fixed* technology. But Blaug's argument is a simple application to the process of technical change of the neoclassical static argument that an increase in the wage rate relative to the rate of profit will cheapen "capital-intensive" techniques relatively to "labour-intensive" techniques, while a persistent and significant bias towards the use of "capital-intensive" techniques will create forces which cheapen the more "labour-intensive" techniques. This cannot be valid as a *general* theory of technical change, however, for we know conclusively that in a stationary state an increase in the wage rate may cheapen the *less* "capital-intensive" technique, and *vice-versa* (Sraffa 1960; Garegnani 1970). This clearly undermines the static neoclassical theory of substitution; since Blaug's argument rests on this basis, it undermines *his* argument too.

24.   Marx nowhere gives a fully integrated exposition of his theory of the falling rate of profit. The best secondary interpretation is that of Meek (1967, pp. 129—42).

25.   The organic composition is measured on a stock basis, and is thus proportional to constant capital per man. The rate of exploitation, then, refers to the annual rate of exploitation, and is proportional to surplus value per man employed per period of production.

26.   Since the mechanism which produces the declining rate of profit is also that which progressively increases the relative size of the reserve army, these counteracting influences may also act as "modifications" to the latter. We have already used elements of Marx's argument about "capital-saving" innovations to criticize his theory of the reserve army (above p. 203). Marx himself, however, discusses these counteracting influences only in the context of his theory of the declining rate of profit.

27.   A sufficient condition for Marx's formula to hold is that there are no "non-basic" or luxury commodities produced. Sraffa's "Standard commodity" is composed entirely of "basics" (see above pp. 149—56).

28.   See, for example, *Capital* III, 213.

29.   On this and other properties of the wage curve, see Garegnani (1970).

30.   Thus irreversibility is a necessary condition for Blaug's (neoclassical) demonstration that a falling rate of profit may occur with a constant real wage (see Blaug, 1968, pp. 259—60).

31.   This argument seems to have originated with Samuelson (1957, 1960, 1972, 1973); for a more formal statement, see Okishio (1961, 1963).

32.   Rosdolsky (1956), Erlich (1967) and Güsten (1965) have suggested that Marx did supplement his argument with Ricardian elements. There seems to be some evidence for this. But Marx's *main* argument is certainly that which we have outlined above, and in any case such evidence conflicts with his very explicit critical position on Ricardo. It does appear, however, that Marx was not entirely consistent on this issue.

33.   There are places in *Capital* which support such an imputation; see, for example, I, 556, 599; III, 599.

34.   The nearest Marx comes to doing this is in *TSV* II, ch. xvii; see also *Capital* II, chs. xx—xxi, and III, chs. xv and xxx.

35.   This is based on Marx's view that crises are historically specific to capitalism, and that national capitalisms become increasingly dependent on the world market (*Capital* I, 453; II, 113; III, 333, 336). See also Chapter 7.

36.   These points have been repeatedly questioned by some Marxists, presumably in order to emphasize the differences between Marx's theory and Keynesian theory, since the latter is taken to have uncongenial implications of reformism. On these questions see, for example, Yaffe (1973), who manages, apparently unaware of any problem, to construct what he calls Marx's theory of the cycle without a decline in output at any point being explicitly shown.

37.   Purchase and sale are always separated in commodity production. The problem for Marx here is to show why an imbalance between them occurs.

38.   This probably explains why Marx calls the underconsumptionist argument of previous theorists a tautology (*Capital* II, 414—15). See below p. 217.

39.   In *TSV* Marx uses the term "cost price" in the sense in which he writes of "price of production" in *Capital*.

40.   In one place Marx also says that a decline in the rate of profit blunts the "stimulus to gain" (*Capital* I, 619).

41.   See above p. 121. Marx's argument on this point is not completely explicit. It is probably most reasonable to say that in pre-capitalist commodity production crises are not actualized as *recurrent periodic phenomena*. Logically, crises due to random shocks presumably do occur. Historically, however, they would not be serious, since commodity production only comes to *dominate* social production with the development of capitalism.

42.   Sweezy (1946, pp. 145—6) makes a very similar distinction in his discussion of Marx's theory of crisis.

43. Or, alternatively, that they react so as to produce these difficulties in other ways. See Marx's analysis of the "absolute overproduction of capital" (*Capital* III, 250).

44. Although not explicitly stated, this point seems to underlie the similar argument of Bronfenbrenner (1965).

45. This is not, of course, inconsistent with increasing real wage *rates*, since net output per man also rises with increasing levels of economic activity. There are, however, two possible escape routes from this objection. In the first place, it may be that capitalists *expect* a reduction in the profit share in net output as labour power reserves begin to dry up, and precipitate a realization crises by their reactions to this expectation. Secondly, a *sudden* increase in the wage share at the very top of the boom might not be caught in annual (or even perhaps in quarterly) data. It is worth noting that a "full employment ceiling" plays a prominent part in modern non-Marxian theories of the trade cycle (see Matthews, 1959).

46. For other similar statements see, for example, *Capital* III, 244, 250, 256—8, 484; *TSV* II, 492, 522, 525, 528, 535; *TSV* III, 56, 122.

47. "Disproportionality" can also lead to a boom in the converse situation (see below, p. 219).

48. The empirical evidence would tend to support Marx on this point of increasing economic interdependence; see Yan and Ames (1965) and Carter (1966).

49. This is the most appropriate assumption to make in discussing Marx's view of capitalist growth.

50. This does not mean that capitalism is "production for consumption". But it does mean that profit is a function of the level of consumption, so that accumulation is similarly related.

51. "Appropriate" or "desired", that is, in terms of what the capitalist class desire to maintain profitability. It is not, of course, a concept to which individual capitalists consciously relate (any more than is the "capital-output ratio" of modern growth theory). A tendency for the stock of constant capital to adjust to the level of consumption is a result of capitalists' competitive behaviour in aggregate via changes in the rate of profit.

52.   Marx believes that this growth path is most favourable to the working class, and is very likely to raise wages (*Capital* I, ch. xxv, sec. i.) This is not certain, however, assuming a constant organic composition of capital implies a constant rate of exploitation. Thus, in terms of equation [6.16a] above, although λ_v does not decrease, e does not rise either. Thus nothing in general can be said about the comparative effects on g_v of the two types of growth path.

53.   The revolutionary consequences of crises do, however, seem more important to Marx in the *Communist Manifesto* and the *Grundrisse*.

54.   Recent contributions to the literature on the issues discussed in this chapter are listed in the supplementary bibliography. Ganguli (1972) discusses Marx's debt to Quesnay. Dougherty (1974) analyses the effects of technical change in terms of a model similar to (though considerably more sophisticated than) that of Appendix 1, Section 6.8. Sowell (1972) is a detailed study of the development of Say's Law, a question also examined by Roberts and Stephenson (1973, ch. 6).

7

The geographical expansion of capitalism

7.1 Introduction

So far we have followed Marx in assuming a closed capitalist economy. The source of Marx's model here is Western Europe, and in particular England. This chapter deals with Marx's theory of the geographical expansion of capitalism into an *international* system[1].

However, due in part to the logical-historical method, Marx never systematically dealt with this issue in his main theoretical work. The planned books on international trade, world market and the state were never completed or, as far as is known, even set down in rough form. We have only hints of what might have come, and consequently we are forced to rely mainly on Marx's journalism, where his views are more clearly expressed, although still limited.

Sections 7.2, 7.3 and 7.4 are purely expository: 7.2 deals with the nature of capitalist expansion and integrates it into Marx's economic model as a whole; 7.3 and 7.4 deal with Marx's views on the effects of capitalist expansion on the capitalist economies themselves, and on certain non-capitalist economies. On this basis section 7.5 tries to uncover possible inconsistencies in Marx's analysis. Finally, 7.6 provides a general evaluation of Marx's work in this area.

7.2 The nature of capitalist expansion

Marx notes that many historical modes of production had tendencies to expand their geographical boundaries (see, for example, *Grundrisse* pp. 182, 490). However, capitalist expansion is unique because it is the "first historical mode of production that is carried by its own momentum toward embracing the whole world within its net of productive relations" (Avineri, 1969, p. 2).

In explaining why this is the case, Marx's reasoning at the most general level concerns the historically specific form of capitalist motivation, which he sees as the desire for *unlimited* accumulation of wealth and thus a strong tendency to accept no self-imposed constraints on action. This is associated with the historically unique extension of rational methods to achieve this end, thus accepting no traditionalist constraints on action (see above, pp. 15f). This can be seen in part 1 of the *Manifesto* (*SW* I, 108—19) and the *Grundrisse* (for example, pp. 408f). Marx also provides an enlightening example when discussing the British opium trade with China.

"While the semi-barbarian stood on the principle of morality, the civilized opposed to him the principle of self ... the representative of the antiquated world appears prompted by ethical motives, while the representative of overwhelming modern society fights for the privilege of buying in the cheapest and selling in the dearest markets" (*CM*, pp. 343—4).

There was no necessary reason why this expansionist force had to work itself out in terms of the free "exchange of equivalents" and capital export (as portrayed, for example, in neoclassical theory). This would have been a self-imposed limitation uncharacteristic of capitalism's historically specific nature. Thus imperialism involving direct plunder and political rule for profit, using whenever necessary the power of the national state, was in historical fact an important manifestation of capitalism's expansionary nature. Indeed, Marx's analysis of capitalist expansion is largely concerned with imperialism.

As a more specific cause of capitalist expansion Marx notes the importance of the desire for increasing markets: "The need of a constantly expanding market for its products chases the bourgeoisie over the whole surface of the globe. It must nestle everywhere, settle everywhere, establish connexions everywhere" (*SW* I, 112). This he traces back to recurrent deficiencies in aggregate demand in the home market (*SW* I, 114; *CM*, pp. 106—7), and further back to the main causes as he saw them, limited consuming power in the home market and the falling rate of profit (*Capital* III, 237—9; 244—5). The same causes underlie the export of capital (*Capital* III, 242, 256, 258—9; *CM*, p. 107).

7.3 The effect on capitalist economies

Marx's main concern is with the effect of capitalist expansion on the non-capitalist world. However, he does briefly at scattered points consider the effects on the capitalist economies themselves[2].

Interestingly enough Marx believed that up to the 1860s India was an overall burden on the British economy, though particular sections of the British capitalist class and sections of other property owners obviously benefited very substantially (*CM*, pp. 81–2, 122, 134). Sections of the working class also indirectly benefited (*PP*, pp. 101–2). But on a strict financial calculation for *all* economic groups Marx maintains that, despite the intense exploitation of India, benefits were less than costs. Since the costs were mainly financed through taxation, this means that the net financial benefits to the property owning classes as a whole must, in Marx's economic model, be negative[3]. It was because *particular* sections of the property owning classes had predominant political power, and their interests favoured colonization, that India was first colonized (*CM*, pp. 234–9, 330–5, 366–74, 456–66). However, Marx's analysis here concerns the period prior to any significant modernization of India, which he expected to take place when the industrial capitalists became powerful enough to dominate colonial policy. In this situation Marx may well have changed his view (but we are unaware of an explicit statement where he does).

Of more direct theoretical interest is Marx's recognition that colonization can directly reduce the domestic reserve army of unemployed through emigration (*Capital* I, 451). Further, Marx noted that significant balance of payments deficits were possible in non-capitalist economies (*CM*, p. 68). Thus export booms in capitalist economies could indirectly deplete the domestic reserve army of unemployed (*PP*, pp. 101–2). Foreign trade and the export of capital were seen as possible offsets to the falling rate of profit. Foreign trade cheapened both constant and variable capital and raised the rate of exploitation, thus also raising the average rate of profit. Capital export could raise the rate of profit by being invested in areas where the rate of profit was higher than in the domestic economy and by reducing the domestic rate of accumulation, thus slowing down the rise in the organic composition, which Marx conceived as a force bringing down the profit rate (*Capital* III, 237–40).

However, in none of these cases does Marx imply that the complications introduced are anything more than modifications to the analysis carried out on the assumption of a closed economy. The real significance of international trade, capital export and colonialism for the economic contradictions of capitalism appear to lie in Marx's belief that they can intensify crises of effective demand. For example, penetration into new foreign markets may lead to a large initial increase in demand, but, for various reasons, this may not be sustained. Also the instabilities inherent in the anarchic nature of the world market are transmitted to all open economies, and to an increasing degree as they become more dependent on international economic relations[4] (see Chapter 6 and *CM*, pp. 67–75).

It should also be noted that Marx points out the increased possibility of wars between the advanced countries themselves as well as with potential colonies (see, for example, *SW* I, 117; *CM*, pp. 59—63, 238—9).

7.4 The impact on the colonies

Marx's main concern was with the impact of imperialism on the colonies, although in fact India was the only case which he discussed in any detail. Nevertheless, since he tended to view India as a paradigm for Asia as a whole, Marx believed his analysis had wider scope.

Crucial to Marx's appreciation of the significance of imperialism was his analysis of pre-colonial society in India, which he termed "Asiatic society". This has only two significant component parts: at the bottom a multitude of small villages and at the top an authoritarian state. There are no independent intermediate forms of social organization. Marx argued that this form of society was *unchanging* in the sense that there were no internal forces working to change the structure over time; all movement was of processes operating *within* the structure. They posed no threat to the existence of the structure itself.

Marx believed that the villages were virtually self-sufficient, self-governing and regulated internally by the traditional institutions of caste. He argues that, "The simplicity of the organization for production in these self-sufficing communities ... supplies the key to the secret of the unchangeableness of Asiatic societies" (*Capital* I, 358). The key to the "simplicity" of the economic organization, in turn, Marx considered to be the union of primitive agriculture and industrial handicrafts within each village (see, for example, *Grundrisse*, p. 486; *CM*, pp. 88—95; *Capital* I, 357—8). Consequently there was near complete rural isolation and no dependence on urban manufacture. Thus there was negligible, if any, commodity production, a factor Marx considered a prerequisite for autonomous capitalist development (see above, p. 45). Each village was, therefore,

"autonomous, autarchic, inward looking, cut off from the outside world and hence capable of serving as the basis of conservatism, immobility and stagnation" (Avineri, 1969, pp. 8—9).

". . . they took no interest whatsoever in the affairs of state. It was no concern of theirs that monarchs lived or died, that kingdoms came into being or were destroyed. Each village was concerned only with its own boundaries" (Thorner, 1966, pp. 40—1).

Marx considered that the character of the oriental state arose primarily from the economic need for large-scale public works and in particular agricultural irrigation. To carry out this function, as well as to service its unproductive activities, it absorbed through taxation the surplus production of the villages.

The Ruler, although despotic, was not necessarily stable. There was a "constant dissolution and refounding of Asiatic states, and never ceasing changes of dynasty" (*Capital* I, 358). This, however, was not in Marx's terms *historical* change, for the "structure of the economic elements of society remains untouched by the storm clouds in the political sky" (*ibid*).

There existed, for Marx, no intermediate autonomous feudal or capitalist class. Any "aristocratic" element which could be said to exist had no position independent of the state; it

"owed its position to revokable state appointments and to stipends consisting of temporary grants or alienations of the public land revenue . . . and feudal forms could not disguise its original and continuing dependence on state power and its lack of all enduring freestanding rights of its own" (Stokes, 1973, pp. 137—8).

Similar factors account for the absence of an autonomous bourgeois class. The lack of commodity production in the villages prevented any significant development of urban manufacture. Any towns were no more than military camps, whose traders and manufacturers were predominantly concerned with servicing state requirements. Consequently, there was no real basis for the development of an independent bourgeois class as in the West.

Thus, Marx wrote that "Indian society has no history at all, at least no known history. What we call its history, is but the history of the successive intruders who founded their empires on the passive basis of that unresisting and unchanging society" (*CM*, p. 132). The key factor explaining this state of affairs was the unique mode of production (*CM*, p. 455).

It was on the basis of this view of Asiatic society that Marx assessed the historical significance of imperialism. Indian society (and in Marx's view Asiatic societies generally) was unchanging. There were no internal dialectical forces making for historical progress. Capitalism, which Marx considered to be a necessary basis for socialism, had thus to be created by *external* forces: "England has to fulfil a double mission in India: one destructive, the other regenerating — the annihilation of old Asiatic society, and the laying of the material foundations of Western society in Asia" (*CM*, pp. 132—3). Marx believed that English capitalism would in fact accomplish this dual historical function.

Most important of all, English commerce exerted a revolutionary influence on the Indian village; the "low prices of its goods served to destroy the spinning and weaving industries, which were an ancient integrating element of this unity of industrial and agricultural production" (*Capital* III, 334). Thus, the main factor preventing historical change was undermined by the same process which destroyed pre-capitalist commodity production in the West. Coupled with this was neglect by the imperialist powers of the public works on which traditional agriculture was based and in the absence of which it was ruined (*CM*, p. 90).

Marx believed that the process of destruction largely preceded the modernizing phase of development. Thus, he wrote in 1853 that "the historic pages of . . . [British] rule in India report hardly anything beyond destruction. The work of regeneration hardly transpires through a heap of ruins. Nevertheless it has begun" (*CM*, p. 133). He went on to list the evidence of this development. He noted the creation of political unity in India under a strong state which, as an instrument of its rule, created a modernized Indian army, thus ensuring henceforward that India will cease to be the "predestined prey of conquest". This was "the *sine qua non* of Indian self-emancipation". The introduction of a free press and Western education would create an Indian intelligentsia "endowed with the requirements for government and imbued with European science"; the creation of private property rights in land — "the great desideratum of Asiatic society" — would form the basis for capitalist development in agriculture (*ibid*, pp. 132—3).

Most important of all Marx expected capitalist industrial development to take place.

"Till [the middle of the nineteenth century] . . . *the interests of the moneyocracy which had converted India into landed estates, of the oligarchy who had conquered it by their armies, and the millocracy who had inundated it with their fabrics, had gone hand in hand. But the more the industrial interest became dependent on the Indian market, the more it felt the necessity of creating fresh productive powers in India, after having ruined her native industry. You cannot continue to inundate a country with your manufactures, unless you enable it to give you something in return"* (*CM*, p. 107).

To this end the "millocracy . . . intend now drawing a net of railways over India". This will lead to the introduction of all "those industrial processes necessary to meet the immediate and current wants of railway location, and out of which there must grow the application of machinery to those branches of industry not immediately connected with railways"[5]. These developments would further undermine village isolation and destroy its traditional organization (*ibid*, 133—7).

There is no doubt that Marx supported the destruction of Asiatic society and the modernizing effect of imperialism. For Marx, Asiatic

242

society did not change. Since capitalism is considered a necessary historical step towards human freedom, the external force of capitalist imperialism is supported for its progressive historical effects. The issue is not really about India being *forcibly conquered* by the British, as Marx states quite clearly:

"India, . . . could not escape the fate of being conquered, and the whole of her past history, if it be anything, is the history of the successive conquests she has undergone. . . . The question, therefore, is not whether the English had a right to conquer India, but whether we prefer India conquered by the Turk, by the Persian, by the Russian, to India conquered by the Briton" (CM, p. 132).

Marx is in no doubt which he prefers, for previous conquerors were "conquered themselves by the superior civilization of their subjects". The British, on the other hand, were "the first conquerors superior, and therefore, inaccessible to the Hindoo civilization" (CM, p. 133). They destroyed traditional Indian society, and in doing so caused "the only *social* revolution ever heard of in Asia" (*ibid*, p. 93)[6].

Marx has few, if any, regrets about the passing of Asiatic society. There was little, if anything, worth preserving:

"We must not forget that these idyllic village communities, inoffensive though they may appear, had always been the solid foundation of Oriental despotism. . . . We must not forget that these little communities were contaminated by distinctions of caste and by slavery, that they subjugated man to external circumstances instead of elevating man to be the sovereign of circumstances, that they transformed a self-developing social state into never changing natural destiny, and thus brought about a brutalizing worship of nature, exhibiting its degradation in the fact that man, the sovereign of nature, fell down on his knees in adoration of Hanuman, the monkey and Sabbala, the cow" (CM, p. 94).

These are harsh words indeed. But it would be a mistake to assume they are any softer for the British imperialists. Marx supports capitalist imperialism because of its progressive historical consequences. He does not support or condone its methods, the interests of its practitioners or the apologetics or its ideologists. Consequently he is not inhibited from repeatedly criticizing the sheer brutality, greed and hypocrisy of the "civilized" conquerors (see, for example, *ibid*, pp. 81–7, 89–90, 224–7, 280–4, 299–305, 320–4).

Marx's complex attitude on this is summarized clearly in the following.

"England, it is true, in causing a social revolution in Hindostan, was actuated only by the vilest interests, and was stupid in her manner of

enforcing them. But that is not the question. The question is, can mankind fulfil its destiny without a fundamental revolution in the social state of Asia? If not, whatever may have been the crimes of England she was the unconscious tool of history in bringing about the revolution" (CM, p. 94).

As we have seen at many points, Marx's theory of history is "that 'progress' necessarily assumes a catastrophic form: the ancient social order is violently disrupted, and capitalist industrialization unfolds in the midst of terrifying upheavals whose meaning is concealed from the participants" (Lichtheim, 1971, p. 122).

Thus, despite the brutality of imperialism Marx does not see any alternative course of historical development which would have the progressive consequence of bringing Asia into the modern world[7]. Indeed Marx seems to have had some worries as to whether even this was always sufficiently powerful to accomplish the requisite task. He seems to have no doubts in relation to India because of the direct control exercised by the British, but he is worried about the Chinese situation.

"[The] indirect and only sporadic nature of European control over the Chinese market gave Marx cause for doubt whether the obstinate unchanging Chinese society would not, after all, be able to withstand change. ...... The direct corollary of this would be that Marx would have to welcome European penetration in direct proportion to its intensity: the more direct the European control of any society in Asia, the greater the chances for the overhauling of its structure and its ultimate incorporation into bourgeois, and hence later into socialist, society" (Avineri, 1969, pp. 19—20; see also CM, pp. 393—9, 465; Capital III, 334).

7.5 The consistency of Marx's analysis

We now ask whether Marx's ideas on imperialist expansion are internally consistent and accord with other aspects of his theory. There is, firstly, a problem in the way in which Marx incorporates Asiatic society into his general materialist conception of history. Marx designates "the Asiatic, ancient, feudal and modern bourgeois modes of production" as so many "epochs marking progress in the economic development of society" (*Critique*, p. 21). This raises a problem if the stages are interpreted as consecutive and universally applicable. As we have just seen, Marx's analysis shows India jumping from the Asiatic form straight to the capitalist; and Asiatic society, as its name implies, never existed in the West. However, it is also inconceivable that Marx could have made such a simple error as this. The problem, therefore, probably arises from a misinterpretation of Marx's meaning in the above passage, as Hobsbawm (1964, p. 38) concludes from his analysis:

"The statement that the Asiatic, ancient, feudal and bourgeois formations are 'progressive' does not . . . imply any simple unilinear view of history. . . . It merely states that each of these systems is in crucial respects further removed from the primitive state of man".

Further, when Marx writes of the Asiatic mode of production in the passage we have just quoted, it is not clear to which societies it refers; it seems likely however that in this passage he gives it a more general meaning than when he refers to the historically specific Asiatic society as found in India. He is, in fact, referring to a particular type of economic relationship between producers, irrespective of any geographic location. In short, Marx took Indian society as a particular and surviving form of primitive communism; a condition he held to be universal at some stage in all development. Thus India (or more generally, Asia) provided Marx with an indication of the nature of the historical starting point in all societies, and the term "Asiatic mode of production" thus referred to this stage: a general stage whose characteristics, Marx believed, could be understood from the particular example of Asiatic society (*CM*, p. 466)[8].

However, if there really is no problem in the above, Marx definitely appears to be far from consistent in his analysis of the property system of Asiatic society. In 1853 he writes that "the basic form of all phenomena in the East . . . to be the *absence of private property* in land. This is the real key even to the Oriental heaven" (*CM*, p. 451). This is repeated in *Capital* (III, 791), where he states that at most there was "private possession" (see also *CM*, p. 450). Now not only does Marx fail to explain precisely how this alleged absence provides the "key" to analysis: in particular, how it relates to the self-sufficiency of the village in terms of the union of agriculture and industry; but at other places he states that "property in land does seem to have existed" in some villages in India (*CM*, p. 457). This is reaffirmed in *Capital* (I, 357), when he notes that there are various kinds of village community.

Instead of focusing on the diversity he generally concentrates on the "simplest form", in which land was owned and cultivated collectively. This might be explained by Marx's apparent belief that communal ownership was the "original form" of village organization (*Capital* III, 333; above, p. 35). However, this implies that there is historical development in Asiatic society. But this, as we have seen, Marx simultaneously denies.

This leads to a third problem of internal consistency. The problem here is that, despite his recognition of the extraction of the surplus by the state bureaucracy, the recognition of private property, inequality and even slavery in some villages, Marx at no time appears to conceive of Asiatic society as a *class* society. Wittfogel (1957), in particular, has criticized Marx on this score by arguing with some force that in terms of his own theory he should have done so[9].

The most likely explanation of why Marx took the position he did is his view that the existence of classes and the conflict which took place between them was a sufficient, if not a necessary, condition for historical change. In the absence of such change in Asiatic society, then, he had to accept that there were no genuine classes. This, in turn, was reaffirmed by his analysis of social strata in Asiatic society. The point here is that Marx's concept of class does not relate simply to statistical aggregates or social strata, but to groups who are in some degree united by a sense of common identity due to a similarity of interest based on a common economic position. But such a common economic position may *not* lead to any class consciousness and in this case the collectivity does not really form a class at all[10]. Thus, given the position of the Oriental bureaucracy, the introspective nature of the villagers and the traditionally ordered form of the village structure in Marx's outline of Asiatic society (above, pp. 239—43), Marx could substantiate his lack of designation in class terms.

Fourthly, and most important of all, there is a problem, the existence of which Marx never admits, concerning the generality of the materialist conception of history. The central idea of Marx's theory is that stages of historical development are dialectically related. Each stage grows out of the internal contradictions of the preceding stage and in a similar manner gives rise to new stages. But Asiatic society is not integrated into this scheme, for it has on Marx's own analysis no dialectical forces of internal change built into its structure. He does admit that his analysis of *particular historical processes* — for example, primitive accumulation — relates only to Western Europe (see above, p. 53). This qualification can be accepted as *not* undermining the materialist conception of history, for the European primitive accumulation is only a specific form that a particular pattern may take within the general scheme. The point we make here, however, is much more fundamental, for it implies that the conceptual framework of the scheme itself is applicable only to certain patterns of history: that is, to those of Western Europe. Marx's concept of Asiatic society "thus poses a serious challenge to the assumption that Marx developed a philosophy of history universal in its applicability" (Avineri, 1969, p. 13).

Lastly, we must consider two points which result from Marx's own intellectual development in the light of new historical evidence and study. Thorner (1966, p. 60—6) cogently argues that, in the late 1870s, Marx began to take the view that Asiatic society *did* experience historical change, which involved the emergence of private property systems. In this case the problems internal to Marx's theory, outlined above, need to be judged as less important than they would otherwise appear, for they no longer exist as part of a reasonably finished and definitive view.

In the same years, however, Marx's view of the prerequisites for socialism also began to change. After the publication of *Capital* I in 1867, Marx became increasingly interested in forms of primitive communism, and this led him into a detailed study of Russian social conditions (which he regarded as semi-Asiatic). The socialist potential of the village commune was a controversial subject in the Russian revolutionary movement. Marx's views leaned towards the narodniks, that is, those who argued that socialism could be developed on the basis of the existing village community and without its dissolution through capitalist development. He wrote in 1877 that

> *"if Russia continues to pursue the path she has followed since 1861, she will lose the finest chance ever offered by history to a people and undergo all the fatal vicissitudes of the capitalist regime"* (CM, p. 468).

In 1881 he states that the village community

> *is the* point d'appui *of social regeneration in Russia*

but adds that

> *"the pernicious influences which attack it from all sides . . . [must be eliminated so as] . . . to assure it of normal conditions for a spontaneous development"* (quoted in Lichtheim, 1963, p. 108)[11].

Again in 1882 he states,

> *"If the Russian Revolution becomes the signal for a proletarian revolution in the West, so that both complement each other, the present Russian common ownership of land may serve as the starting point for a communist development"* (SW I, 100—1).

As can be seen, Marx's judgment is conditional. In the first and third passage he maintains that the development towards communism is possible, without passing through an intermediate stage of capitalism, providing internal capitalist development in Russia can be eradicated. The fourth passage seems to require a simultaneous proletarian revolution in the advanced capitalist countries as an additional prerequisite. Thus, despite the brevity of these remarks and their conditional nature, they do show Marx as now believing that capitalist development may not be the only path of historical progress, or the most beneficial. This is a reversal of the position he previously held.

Further, there is no obvious reason why Marx's remarks on Russia might not apply to certain Asiatic societies. He may, therefore, have changed his position on Asiatic society and capitalist imperialism. We have no evidence that he did, but taken to their logical conclusion, Marx's views on Russia are inconsistent with this theoretical analysis of, and unconditional support for, imperialism in general.

Overall, therefore, Marx's views on Asiatic society and imperialism are not internally consistent or in accord with other aspects of his analysis. Although he can be defended in some cases, where apparent inconsistencies can be shown to disappear on further enquiry, in other cases he cannot. These latter problems by no means involve minor issues. As has been indicated they include questioning the generality of the materialist conception of history itself.

7.6 An assessment

An evaluation of the validity of Marx's view of the effects on the advanced capitalist economies themselves is rather difficult because, as we have seen (above, pp. 237–9), Marx makes no more than occasional isolated remarks on this problem. However, in the context of his economic theory he did rightly pin down the areas where capitalist expansion was important; in particular, as a result of and a counteracting influence to the reserve army, the falling rate of profit and limited consuming power in the home market. Nevertheless, we have already seen (above, pp. 199f) that the theory of the reserve army and falling rate of profit are open to serious question even within the framework of a closed capitalist economy. Detailed consideration of the impact of capitalist expansion on these aspects of Marx's theory, therefore, would not seem worth while.

Marx's theory of the limited consuming power of the home economy rests on firmer ground. It is not, however, true that capital exports have provided an outlet for surplus output:

"Property income from British overseas investment was in excess of the outflow of capital throughout most of the nineteenth century and up to 1914 ... [and in the period since 1945]. ... The income from overseas investment in underdeveloped lands both by the U.K. and U.S.A. has generally exceeded the outflow of private capital to these lands, but both have been declining in relative importance" (Barratt Brown, 1972, pp. 54–5)[12].

On the other hand Marx's remarks as to the probability of clashes between imperialist powers were highly perceptive. The uneven development of capitalism geographically and the consequential emergence of German and Japanese competition to the established colonial powers led to economic struggles with war employed as a principal instrument. Further, as we see from Marx's analysis of the financial net cost of India, there is no necessity within his theory to explain imperialist actions in terms of *national* or even overall *class* balance sheets. It is rather the distribution of power within the property owning classes which he sees, quite rightly, as crucial. Again, Marx's brief references to the destabilizing effect of the world market on effective demand were right on target. We now know it would be much easier to keep a *closed* capitalist economy on an even keel at a high level of aggregate demand.

We now turn to Marx's analysis of Asiatic society and the impact of capitalism upon it. This too is open to serious question on a number of grounds. Marx's generalization from India to Asia can easily be criticized; the successful industrialization of Japan, for example, indicates that the nature of Asian societies differed considerably[13]. But even in relation to India itself Marx's analysis faces great problems[14]. Thus, for example, modern historians of India have

"long since retreated from the notion of an unchanging East and the dogma of the absence of private property in land as the key to its history. . . . Oriental despotism, despite Wittfogel, is too wide and value-loaded a concept to survive as a working tool. . . . The political and social as well as the economic self-sufficiency of the traditional Indian village is recognized as a dubious half truth" (Stokes, 1973, p. 139—40)[15].

Moreover current opinion on the impact of the British in India has the tendency "to minimize change of any sort, whether destructive or constructive" (*ibid*, p. 142).

It is now obvious that Marx drastically overestimated the effect British imperialism was to have on industrializing India. This is not simply due to overoptimism concerning the modernizing influence of the railways, but is symptomatic of a more deeprooted error. In associating capitalist expansion with deficient aggregate consumption at home (*Capital* III, 237, 244—5) Marx linked imperialism to a force that was much less powerful than his macroeconomic theory suggested (see above, pp. 223—6). And in associating it with the falling rate of profit he linked it to a force that did not operate at all as he conceived it. Marx, therefore, was probably prone to overestimate the outward impetus which was actually inherent in western capitalism. This failure is therefore due, at least in part, to the excessively dramatic picture that he painted of the economic contradictions of capitalism itself[16]. Certainly he was correct in arguing that capitalism requires an ever increasing market. But his theory of the subsistence wage prevented him from seeing that it could be generated *internally* on a sufficient scale. The fact is that imperialist annexation of colonies by

Western capitalist powers (let alone the need to modernize them) reflected no economic forces which dictated the necessity of such a policy for the economic survival or prolongation of the system[17].

However, Marx's analysis here can be regarded as being broadly correct in qualitative terms, if not in quantitative terms. He correctly predicted the direction of change which imperialism would cause, even if he exaggerated its magnitude. Imperialism manifestly fails to modernize the third world directly, mainly because it has never involved large scale capital exports to build up industry there. But, equally clearly, it has created internal forces in those societies which now push towards modernization, forces which were either absent or extremely weak prior to the impact of Western capitalism. Warren (1973) provides a provocative argument to the effect that many third world countries have achieved considerable success towards achieving a capitalist industrialization.

The question remains as to what we can learn from Marx's analysis of imperialism today. The major lesson would seem to lie at the methodological level and involve the way orthodox theory conceptualizes capitalism. Despite all his errors Marx's statement of the forces lying behind capitalist expansion at the most general level (see above, p. 237) shows real insight into the nature of the system. It is an insight which neoclassical economic theory in particular ignores. The latter views the acquisitiveness and rationality inherent in capitalism as operating solely in terms of individual free exchange. Obviously imperialism and other coercive forms of economic action, whether or not they involve state power, will not fit into such a scheme of thought, for the action patterns are not those of free exchange, and are rarely individualistic. Thus neoclassical theorists, who often pride themselves on the generality of their theory, are in fact working in terms of a highly limited theoretical framework which focuses on a *special* case of rational economic action. Moreover it is a special case that lends itself most easily to apologetics. The assumption of individual free exchange when coupled with the other neoclassical assumptions of exogenous preferences and perfect certainty can be easily made to show a gain in utility to all parties involved in economic relations.

This point, which is suggested by Marx's theory of imperialism, is by no means confined to the area of international economic relationships. Other examples illustrating the point can easily be found. For instance Marx argues:

"As soon as . . . adverse circumstances prevent the creation of an industrial reserve army and with it the absolute dependence of the working class

upon the capitalist class, capital ... rebels against the 'sacred' law of supply and demand, and thus tries to check its inconvenient action by forcible means and State interferences" (Capital I, 640)[18].

This point would seem particularly relevant in understanding the current situation in a number of advanced capitalist economies[19].

These forms of rational economic action cannot be incorporated into a theoretical scheme which conceives the mechanics of rational action independently of their historically specific forms. It is also difficult to justify their exclusion. Thus, while Marx was an early pioneer whose substantive propositions are often open to a heavy battery of criticism today, he did provide a scheme of thought which contains considerable relevance for a modern analysis of imperialism and other forms of coercive economic action[20].

Notes

1. Consequently we do not deal with colonization in the context of primitive accumulation, but only with Marx's analysis of imperialism in the era when capitalism had become firmly established in the West.

2. Marxist theories after Marx tend to give this aspect much more emphasis.

3. When wages are at subsistence level the incidence of taxation must fall on the property owners.

4. This point does not necessarily contradict Marx's argument that domestic crises are also a force underlying capitalist expansion. Cumulative movements, with both aspects as parts, are quite conceivable.

5. It is not clear whether Marx expected the industrialization to be predominantly carried out by the English bourgeoisie, or whether elements in Indian society were expected to take the initiative.

6. When there was competition between imperialist powers for domination over some area Marx always supported that which he considered to be the most progressive.

7. Consequently Marx opposes traditionalist revolts and partial defensive modernizations (see, for example, Avineri, 1969, pp. 24–9).

8.   On this see Thorner (1966); also Lichtheim (1963), Shiozawa (1966), Kiernan (1967) and Hobsbawm (1964).

9.   However, Wittfogel's own explanation (1957, p. 387) of why he did not is rather naive.

10.   See, for example, *The Eighteenth Brumaire of Louis Bonaparte* (*SW* I, 394–487), where Marx makes the distinction between a "class in itself" and a "class for itself".

11.   Letter to Vera Zasulich, quoted in Lichtheim (1963, p. 108); a slightly different translation is given in *SC*, p. 340.

12.   In the light of this evidence Baran and Sweezy (1968, p. 113) write: "One can only conclude that foreign investment, far from being an outlet for domestically generated surplus, is a most efficient device for transferring surplus generated abroad to the investing country."

13.   Japan was largely an unknown quantity to the West until Marx's death.

14.   This is also true of most other mid-nineteenth century views which in important respects were very close to Marx, although obviously lacking his grand vision.

15.   See also Thorner (1966) and Kiernan (1967).

16.   As we have seen (above, p. 243) Marx had doubts on Western capitalism's ability to modernize China, but the limitations as he saw them stemmed from the nature of Chinese society, not that of Western capitalism.

17.   Marx, in fact, never seems to make an explicit statement to the contrary. Thus, while he undoubtedly saw imperialism as a *necessary consequence* of the development of capitalism, there is no clear-cut evidence that he took the view, later associated with Lenin (1916) and Luxemburg (1913), that imperialism was a *necessary condition* for the survival of the entire system. His discussion of foreign trade, capital export and imperialism in his major theoretical works is extremely brief. Further, this cannot be simply explained by the nature of Marx's method. It has been observed by Meek (1973, pp. viii–xi) that Marx's original plan of his work was not immutable, and was changed quite significantly from that

outlined in the *Grundrisse*. It seems fair to conclude, from all this, that he did not attribute to imperialism such great importance as many of his followers.

This, however, concerns Marx's *views*. These are not identical with the logical dictates of his model which *do imply* that imperialism was crucially important to the survival, or prolongation, of capitalism in the face of deficient aggregate consumption. (Other offsets to this, such as a large expansion of luxury demand or increases in the real wage, are precluded by his theory.) Consequently, while his analysis of the contradictions of capitalism may well have led him to overestimate the strength of the expansionist forces, as we suggest, it is because he fails to follow logic rigorously here that his *views* on the significance of imperialism cannot be identified with those of later Marxists.

18.   On this see also Dobb (1946, pp. 23f).

19.   It is, of course, open to the objection that such State policy is conducted in the "national" interest as an anti-inflation measure. However, the empirical evidence which we have as to the role of the modern capitalist state would suggest that Marx's analysis is not far amiss. See, for example, Miliband (1969), Domhoff (1967) and Mills (1956).

20.   The supplementary bibliography contains references to Emmanuel (1974) and McMichael, Petras and Rhodes (1974), who attack Warren's thesis on capitalist industrialization.

8

Conclusion

Having completed our exposition and critical review of Marx's political economy, we now attempt to answer three broad and related questions. What is Marx's place in the history of economic analysis? What applicability does his political economy have for contemporary economic theory? Which of Marx's propositions are relevant to a critique of modern capitalism?

Judged against his predecessors and contemporaries, Marx's achievements in substantive economic analysis were considerable. He exposed serious logical and empirical defects in classical political economy, and extended and refined the logic of classical value theory with unparalleled insight. He rightly emphasized the theoretical and empirical importance of production relations as opposed to the phenomena of market exchange. His analysis of the process of capitalist reproduction provided a coherent two-sector model of economic growth, in which the problems Marx sought to highlight were not recognized as such by orthodox theorists for fifty years after his death. This he linked with a fragmented but perceptive account of the endogenous causes of cyclical instability in unregulated capitalism. He was the first economist to build an analysis of economic development based on the pivotal importance of technical change. His account of the pressures leading to economic centralization and the growth of monopoly, and to the development of the international capitalist system and imperialist rivalries, were accurate and perceptive[1].

In these areas Marx had made such great progress it is difficult to appreciate just how backward the next two generations of orthodox economists were. In price theory, neoclassical economists retreated from the analysis of the relations of production into the sterile swamps of utility theory. The theory of income distribution became a sophisticated and often deliberate apologia for capitalist property relations, in which subjective "sacrifices" and the characteristics of "things" replaced the structure of social relationships in the explanation of property incomes. Harmony was substituted for conflict, equilibrium for disequilibrium analysis, static theory for dynamics. Unemployment was seen as an exogenously determined aberration, rather than as the result of endogenous forces created by the structure of capitalist reproduction. Indeed the very problems posed by Marx all but disappeared from the agenda.

This degeneration did not survive intact the traumatic experience of the 1920s and 1930s. In particular Keynes re-exposed the absurdity of Say's Law, and showed how aggregate demand might normally be insufficient to maintain full employment in an unregulated capitalist system. Macro-economics was reborn, and with it the theory of growth. In consequence more than one of the new generation of Keynesians developed an interest in Marx. Robinson (1942, p. 95), for example, completed her own survey of Marx with the view that "if there is any hope of progress in economics at all, it must be in using academic methods to solve the problems posed by Marx". Marxian economics thus threatened for a while to become academically respectable.

There are, however, three reasons why this respectability might no longer seem legitimate outside the narrow area of the history of economic analysis. Firstly, capitalism itself has changed in important ways. For example, since 1945 advanced capitalism has not been subject to major economic crises, while it has sustained a faster rate of growth than ever before. Associated with this has been a massive extension of state intervention in, and influence over, the economy. As we have seen, Marx concentrated his analysis on those factors disrupting stable capitalist development, and provided little systematic discussion of the economic role of the state. Centralization of capital has now taken place, and although Marx recognized this process very clearly he did not provide analysis of a developed system of monopoly capital. We must also note here Marx's failure to account for the growth in the *economic* power of trade unions. These factors also indicate that mechanisms, other than those to which Marx gave prominence, have increasingly been used to create and realise surplus value.

Thus many of the theoretical problems facing economists today are the *reverse* of those posed by Marx. For example: why have serious realization crises been absent over the last thirty years? What determines long-run differences in the rate of profit between monopolized sectors? How is it that the profit share in net output has not increased? What factors determine the relationship between an increase in money wages and a change in real wages?

These points indicate the historically specific nature of Marx's own substantive economic theory. This cannot be taken as a criticism of Marx, for there is no reason to suppose that his analysis is free from a historical relativity which affects all aspects of society and economy. Indeed, *on Marx's own argument* it would be wrong to expect that a theoretical structure developed in and relevant to one stage of capitalism could be applied, without drastic revision, to a later and different stage.

Secondly, much of Marx's substantive analysis is faulty, as we have seen in Chapters 5 to 7. In particular Marx's analysis of economic contradictions independent of deficiencies in aggregate demand must be judged the key failure, followed by the difficulties inherent in the quantitative aspects of the labour theory of value. Those who argue that Marx's substantive economic theory is largely valid face insurmountable problems if they also accept, as some seem not to, the standards of scientific proof; and Marx himself recognized no other standards.

Thirdly, there have been major changes in non-Marxian economic theory. Marx's designation of the economic theory of his time as "vulgar" was undoubtedly correct: it did concentrate on surface "appearances", it was certainly ahistorical, and it was often overtly apologetic. These criticisms are still valid in terms of much of modern (and especially neoclassical) economics. The concept of "consumer sovereignty" provides an especially blatant example: "The consumer is, so to speak, the King . . . each is a voter who uses his money as votes to get the things done that he wants done" (Samuelson, 1964, p. 56). As Robinson (1971, p. 144) rightly observes, neo-classical theory "(with whatever reservations and exceptions) represents the capitalist world as a kibbutz operated in a perfectly enlightened manner to maximize the welfare of all its members"[2].

It would be wrong, however, to take Marx's statements about vulgar economy uncritically, and to write off all modern theory indiscriminately. It is, for example, quite clear that we now possess more refined tools of analysis than those available to Marx. The subject has certainly become more rigorous, due in part to the extensive employment of mathematics. The truths contained in Marx's value and macro-economic theory have undoubtedly been improved upon by theorists to whom Marx's label of "vulgar" is not applicable.

We can readily admit that Marx anticipated many important developments in modern theory, and Samuelson's (1957, p. 911) description of Marx as a "minor post-Ricardian" is ludicrous. But it is not clear that this entitles Marx to anything more than respect as an important forerunner of such theorists as Keynes, Leontief and Sraffa.

The relevance of Marx's substantive political economy is thus somewhat limited. It is important, however, not to confuse this judgment with the assessment of Marx's sociological method, which is highly relevant for contemporary theory. At this level, indeed, it is the relevance of orthodox theory rather than that of Marx which must be questioned.

We have referred to this point at various places in the previous chapters. Neoclassical economists work from assumptions which, because they are ahistorical and thus lack specific social content, do not fit capitalist economies even as crude approximations. Despite this criticism, however, neoclassical theory might still be defended on grounds of practicality; that is, on the grounds that its propositions are useful as an aid to the solution of concrete economic problems. On this criterion, the criticism of its assumptions would become less relevant.

But this is not a strong line of defence. The most sophisticated version of neoclassical theory, the modern general equilibrium analysis of Arrow, Debreu and Hahn, is now recognized by its exponents to be useful primarily in showing what *cannot* be said about models based on neoclassical assumptions (see Hahn, 1973; also Harcourt, 1974). More generally, neoclassical theory is certainly of little use in explaining what we do know about the "laws of motion" of modern capitalism. The aggregate versions of neoclassical theory, which initially appeared to have some empirical applicability, were thoroughly discredited in the capital-reversal and reswitching debates of the 1960s (Harcourt, 1972). The neoclassical analysis of specific areas such as the theory of the firm, the operation of labour markets, and "economic welfare", is similarly barren (see, respectively, Andrews, 1964; Gordon, 1972; Graaf, 1957).

We have already stated (above pp. 55–8) our reasons for considering a sociologically based method to be most appropriate for economic analysis. This view also appears to be (implicitly or explicitly) a common strand in the various and diffuse attacks mounted on orthodox theory in recent years. It is increasingly recognized that economics is a *social* science, and that social relations and the distribution of class power are ignored by economists at their peril (see, for example, the eminently non-Marxist Galbraith, 1973).

This does not mean that Marx's own sociological method can itself be used today without modification. As we saw in Chapters 1 and 2, it interpenetrates very greatly with a substantive analysis which often proves to be faulty. Nevertheless, as Marx has been the only major economist to date who has systematically and comprehensively wrestled with the problems of employing a sociological method in abstract theoretical work, the study of his achievements and failures has an important potential for the development of alternative frameworks of economic analysis today.

It is unlikely that the basic principles of Marx's own method, however refined in the light of changes in capitalism and the defects of his own theory, will be generally accepted, since they are correctly seen as hostile to established privilege and entrenched ideologies. Marx intended his methodological principles to constitute precisely such a critical instrument for unmasking domination and mystification. It would prove difficult to eliminate this element in Marx's methodology in order to placate those who find it distasteful — and this includes the majority of academic economists in advanced industrial societies, both East and West.

This leads to the question of the contemporary relevance of Marx's critique of capitalism. Particularly in the light of the limitations of his substantive analysis, it obviously cannot be accepted uncritically. But it is important to note the essence of this critique. The crucial point here is that it is not one-dimensional, but a hierarchical series of related propositions, some of which may retain their validity even if others do not. At the most general level Marx's critique is stated in his theory of freedom and alienation; at a lower level it is stated in his theory of exploitation and class; at an even lower level it is expressed in his analysis of the specific "laws of motion" of the capitalist system.

The fact that Marx's account of the "laws of motion" is defective in certain important respects does not entail that the more general critique is no longer relevant. It is our view that Marx's theory of freedom and alienation, and his qualitative analysis of exploitation, remain substantively intact as a critique of capitalist society. Certainly we are unconvinced by the contrary views expressed in orthodox economic and political theory. In either case, however, Marx remains relevant for those who seek a reasoned political orientation, and particularly for those who reject the proposition that fate is inherent in the nature of history.

Notes

1. For a brief review of some alternative assessments see Dobb (1973, pp. 141–2), and Hunt and Schwartz (1972, pp. 24–30).

2. For a more general discussion of the apologetic nature of neoclassical theory see Blackburn (1969); Dobb (1940) and (1970); Harcourt (1972); Hunt and Schwartz (1972); Meek (1967) and (1973); Myrdal (1953); Robinson (1964) and (1971); Rothschild (1971). Sometimes ideology degenerates into farce: Robinson (1971), chapter I, suggests that the only type of society to which Walrasian general equilibrium theory might apply is a prisoner of war camp!

Bibliography

I. Works by Marx and Engels

Numerous editions exist of much of Marx's work. We have attempted to cite and quote from standard editions readily available in Britain, wherever possible using the Moscow (and the closely related Lawrence and Wishart) editions. Where frequent reference is made to a work, we have in the text used the abbreviations given below. Marx uses emphasis very heavily in his writing; unless otherwise stated, all emphases in quotations from Marx are found in the original.

KARL MARX and FRIEDRICH ENGELS

Selected Works, 3 vols, Moscow: Progress Publishers, 1969–70 (cited as *SW* I, II, III).

Selected Correspondence, Moscow: Progress Publishers, 1965 (cited as *SC*).

The Holy Family, Moscow: Foreign Languages Publishing House, 1956.

The German Ideology, ed. C. J. Arthur, London: Lawrence & Wishart, 1970 (cited as *GI*).

Karl Marx on Colonialism and Modernization, ed. S. Avineri, New York: Anchor Books, 1969 (cited as *CM*).

The Communist Manifesto (cited from *SW* I, pp. 98–137).

KARL MARX

Capital, 3 vols, Moscow: Foreign Languages Publishing House, vol. I, 1970; vol. II, 1967; vol. III, 1971 (cited as *Capital* I, II, III).

Theories of Surplus Value, 3 vols, London: Lawrence & Wishart, 1963, 1969, 1972 (cited as *TSV* I, II, III).

A Contribution to the Critique of Political Economy, ed. Maurice Dobb, London: Lawrence & Wishart, 1971 (cited as *Critique*).

Grundrisse, Harmondsworth: Penguin, 1973.

The Poverty of Philosophy, New York: International Publishers, 1971 (cited as *PP*).

Early Writings, ed. T. Bottomore, London: Watts, 1963.

Writings of the Young Marx on Philosophy and Society, ed. L. Easton and K. Guddat, New York: Anchor Books, 1967 (cited as *YM*).

Karl Marx: the Early Texts, ed. David McLellan, London: Macmillan, 1968 (cited as *Early Texts*).

Karl Marx: Selected Writings in Sociology and Social Philosophy, ed. T. Bottomore and M. Rubel, Harmondsworth: Penguin, 1963 (cited as *KM Phil*).

Wage Labour and Capital (cited from *SW* I, 142−74).

Wages, Price and Profit (cited from *SW* II, 31−76).

FRIEDRICH ENGELS

Socialism Scientific and Utopian (cited from *SW* III, 95−151).

Ludwig Feuerbach (cited from *SW* III, 335−76).

II. Other works

ANDREWS, P. W. S. (1964) *On Competition in Economic Theory*, Macmillan.

ARON, R. (1965) *Main Currents in Sociological Thought*, vol. 1, Weidenfeld & Nicolson.

AVINERI, S. (1968) *The Social and Political Thought of Karl Marx*, Cambridge University Press.

AVINERI, S. (1969) "Introduction", in S. Avineri, ed., *Karl Marx on Colonialism and Modernization*, Anchor Books, pp. 1−28.

260

BAJT, A. (1970) "A postmortem note on the 'transformation problem' ", *Soviet Studies*, 21(3), 371—4.

BAJT, A. (1971) "Labour as scarcity in Marx's value theory: an alternative explanation", *History of Political Economy*, 3(1), 152—69.

BARAN, P. and SWEEZY, P. (1968) *Monopoly Capital*, Penguin.

BARRATT BROWN, M. (1972) "A critique of Marxist theories of imperialism", in R. Owen and R. Sutcliffe, eds., *Studies in the Theory of Imperialism*, Longman, pp. 35—70.

BAUMOL, W. A. (1970) *Economic Dynamics: an introduction*, Macmillan.

BIENEFELD, M. A. (1972) *Working Hours in British Industry: an economic history*, London School of Economics and Weidenfeld & Nicolson.

BLACKBURN, R. (1969) "A brief guide to bourgeois ideology", in A. Cockburn and R. Blackburn, eds, *Student Power: problems, diagnosis, action*, Penguin, pp. 163—213.

BLAUG, M. (1960) "Technical change and Marxian economics", *Kyklos*, 13(4), 495—509.

BLAUG, M. (1968) *Economic Theory in Retrospect*, Heinemann.

BÖHM-BAWERK, E. von (1896) *Karl Marx and the Close of His System*, ed. P. Sweezy, Kelley, 1966.

BORTKIEWICZ, L. von (1907) "On the correction of Marx's fundamental theoretical construction in the third volume of 'Capital' ", in E. von Böhm-Bawerk, *Karl Marx and the Close of His System*, ed. P. Sweezy, Kelley, 1966, pp. 199—221.

BOSE, A. (1971) "Marx on value, capital and exploitation", *History of Political Economy*, 3(2), 298—334.

BOTTOMORE, T. and RUBEL, M. (1963) "Introduction", in *KM Phil.*, pp. 17—63.

BRONFENBRENNER, M. (1965) "Das Kapital for the modern man", *Science and Society*, 29(4), 419—38.

BRONFENBRENNER, M. (1967) "Marxian influences in bourgeois economics", *American Economic Review*, 57, Papers and Proceedings, May, 624—36.

BRONFENBRENNER, M. (1973) "Marx, Samuelson and their latest critics", *Journal of Economic Literature*, 11(1), 58—63.

BROWN, E. H. PHELPS, and BROWNE, M. (1968) *A Century of Pay*, Macmillan.

CARTER, A. (1966) "The economics of technical change", *Scientific American*, 214(4), 25—31.

CLOWER, R. W. (1965) "The Keynesian counter-revolution: a theoretical appraisal", in F. H. Hahn and F. Brechling, eds, *The Theory of Interest Rates*, Macmillan, pp. 103—25.

COGOY, M. (1973) "The fall of the rate of profit and the theory of accumulation: a reply to Paul Sweezy", *Bulletin of the Conference of Socialist Economists*, Winter, 52—67.

DOBB, M. H. (1940) *Political Economy and Capitalism: some essays in economic tradition*, Routledge & Kegan Paul.

DOBB, M. H. (1946) *Studies in the Development of Capitalism*, Routledge & Kegan Paul.

DOBB, M. H. (1967) "Marx's 'Capital' and its place in economic thought", *Science and Society*, 31(4), 527—40.

DOBB, M. H. (1970) *Welfare Economics and the Economics of Socialism*, Cambridge University Press.

DOBB, M. H. (1973) *Theories of Value and Distribution since Adam Smith: ideology and economic theory*, Cambridge University Press.

DOMHOFF, W. (1967) *Who Rules America?*, Prentice-Hall.

ERLICH, A. (1967) "Notes on Marxian model of capital accumulation", *American Economic Review*, 57, Papers and Proceedings, May, 599—616.

FAN-HUNG (1939) "Keynes and Marx on the theory of capital accumulation, money and interest", *Review of Economic Studies*, 7, 28—41.

FEINSTEIN, C. H. (1968) "Changes in the distribution of national income in the United Kingdom since 1860", in J. Marchal and B. Ducros, eds, *The Distribution of National Income*, Macmillan, pp. 115—38.

FURNISS, E. S. (1920) *The Position of the Laborer in a System of Nationalism: a study of the labor theories of the later English Mercantilists*, 2nd edn, Kelley, 1965.

262

GALBRAITH, J. K. (1973) "Power and the useful economist", *American Economic Review*, 63(1), 1—11.

GAREGNANI, P. (1970) "Heterogeneous capital, the production function and the theory of distribution", *Review of Economic Studies*, 38(3), 407—36.

GIDDENS, A. (1971) *Capitalism and Modern Social Theory*, Cambridge University Press.

GORDON, D. F. (1959) "What was the labour theory of value?", *American Economic Review*, 49, Papers and Proceedings, May, 462—72.

GORDON, D. M. (1972) *Theories of Poverty and Underemployment*, D. C. Heath.

GOUGH, I. (1972) "Marx's theory of productive and unproductive labour", *New Left Review*, 76, Nov.—Dec., 47—72.

GRAAF, J. de V. (1957) *Theoretical Welfare Economics*, Cambridge University Press.

GÜSTEN, R. (1965) "Bemerkungen zur Marxschen Theorie des Technischen Fortschrittes", *Jahrbücher für Nationalökonomie*, 178, 109—21.

HAHN, F. (1973) "The winter of our discontent", *Economica*, n.s., 40, 322—30.

HAHN, F., and MATTHEWS, R. C. O. (1964) "The theory of economic growth: a survey", *Economic Journal*, 75, December, 799—902.

HARCOURT, G. C. (1972) *Some Cambridge Controversies in the Theory of Capital*, Cambridge University Press.

HARCOURT, G. C. (1974) "The cambridge controversies: the afterglow" in M. Parkin and A. R. Nobay, eds., *Contemporary Issues in Economics*, Manchester University Press.

HARRIS, D. J. (1972) "On Marx's scheme of reproduction and accumulation', *Journal of Political Economy*, 80(3 : 1), 505—22.

HEERTJE, A. (1972) "Essay on Marxian economics", *Schweizerisches Zeitschrift für Volkswirtschaft und Statistik*, 108(1), 33—45.

HIMMELWEIT, S. (1974) "The continuing saga of the falling rate of profit: a reply to Mario Cogoy", *Bulletin of the Conference of Socialist Economists*, Autumn, 1—6.

HOBSBAWM, E. J. (1964) "Introduction", in Karl Marx, *Pre-Capitalist Economic Formations*, ed. E. J. Hobsbawm, Lawrence & Wishart.

HUNT, E. and SCHWARTZ, J. (1972) "Introduction", in Hunt and Schwartz, eds, *A Critique of Economic Theory*, Penguin, pp. 7—35.

JEVONS, W. S. (1871) *Theory of Political Economy* (cited from the 4th edn, London, 1931).

KALECKI, M. (1954) *Theory of Economic Dynamics*, Allen & Unwin.

KEAT, R. N. and URRY, J. R. (1974) *Science and Social Theory* (mimeo).

KIERNAN, V. (1967) "Marx and India", *Socialist Register*, pp. 159—89.

KLEIN, L. R. (1947) "Theories of effective demand and employment", *Journal of Political Economy*, **55**, April, 108—32.

KREGEL, J. A. (1971) *Rate of Profit, Distribution and Growth: two views*, Macmillan.

KRELLE, W. (1971) "Marx as a growth theorist", *German Economic Review*, 9(2), 122—33.

LAIBMAN, D. (1973—74) "Values and prices of production: the political economy of the transformation problem", *Science and Society*, 37(4), 404—36.

LENIN, V. I. (1916) *Imperialism: the highest stage of capitalism*, Moscow: Progress Publishers, 1968 edition.

LEONTIEF, W. W. (1938) "The significance of Marxian economics for present-day economic theory", *American Economic Review*, **28**, March, 1—9.

LICHTHEIM, G. (1963) "Marx and the 'Asiatic Mode of Production' ", *St. Anthony's Papers*, **14**, 86—112.

LICHTHEIM, G. (1971) *Imperialism*, Allen Lane.

LOWE, A. F. (1954) "The classical theory of economic growth", *Social Research*, 21(2), 127—58.

LUXEMBURG, ROSA (1913) *The Accumulation of Capital*, ed. Joan Robinson, Routledge & Kegan Paul, 1951.

MacINTYRE, A. C. (1969) "Recent political thought", in D. Thomson, ed., *Political Ideas*, Penguin.

264

MacINTYRE, A. C. (1971) *Marxism and Christianity*, Penguin.

MARSHALL, A. (1890) *Principles of Economics*, 8th edn, Macmillan, 1962.

MATTHEWS, R. C. O. (1959) *The Trade Cycle*, Cambridge University Press.

McLELLAN, D. (1971) *The Thought of Karl Marx: an introduction*, Macmillan.

MEDIO, A. (1972) "Profits and surplus-value: appearance and reality in capitalist production", in E. Hunt and J. Schwartz, eds, *A Critique of Economic Theory*, Penguin, pp. 312—46.

MEEK, R. L. (1967) *Economics and Ideology and Other Essays: studies in the development of economic thought*, Chapman & Hall.

MEEK, R. L. (1968) "Discussion of Sweezy's paper", in R. V. Eagly, ed., *Events, Ideology and Economic Theory*, Wayne State University Press, pp. 120—3.

MEEK, R. L. (1972) "Marginalism and Marxism", *History of Political Economy*, 4(2), 499—511.

MEEK, R. L. (1973) *Studies in the Labour Theory of Value*, Lawrence & Wishart (first published 1956, reprinted with new introduction 1973).

MILIBAND, R. (1969) *The State in Capitalist Society*, Weidenfeld & Nicolson.

MILL, J. S. (1848) *Principles of Political Economy* (reprinted Penguin, 1970).

MILLS, C. WRIGHT (1956) *The Power Elite*, Oxford University Press.

MOORE, S. (1966) "Ricardo and the state of nature", *Scottish Journal of Political Economy*, 13, November, 317—31.

MORISHIMA, M. (1973) *Marx's Economics: a dual theory of value and growth*, Cambridge University Press.

MORISHIMA, M., and SETON, F. (1961) "Aggregation in Leontief matrices and the labour theory of value", *Econometrica*, 29, April, 203—20.

MYRDAL, G. (1953) *The Political Element in the Development of Economic Theory*, Routledge & Kegan Paul.

NAQVI, K. A. (1960) "Schematic presentation of accumulation in Marx", *Indian Economic Review*, 5, February, 13—22.

NELL, E. (1967) "Theories of growth and theories of value", *Economic Development and Cultural Change*, 16, October, 15—26.

NELL, E. (1972) "Economics: the revival of political economy", in R. Blackburn, ed., *Ideology in Social Science: readings in critical social theory*, Fontana, pp. 76—95.

NICOLAUS, M. (1973) "Foreword", in Karl Marx, *Grundrisse*, pp. 7—66.

OKISHIO, N. (1961) "Technical changes and the rate of profit", *Kobe University Economic Review*, 7, 85—99.

OKISHIO, N. (1963) "A mathematical note on Marxian theorems", *Weltwirtschaftliches Archiv*, 91(2), 287—98.

OLLMAN, B. (1971) *Alienation: Marx's conception of man in capitalist society*, Cambridge University Press.

PARSONS, T. (1968) *The Structure of Social Action*, Collier-Macmillan.

PASINETTI, L. L. (1960) "A mathematical formulation of the Ricardian system", *Review of Economic Studies*, 27, February, 78—98.

PASINETTI, L. L. (1969), "Switches of technique and 'rate of return' in capital theory", *Economic Journal*, 79, September, 508—31.

POPPER, K. (1961) *The Poverty of Historicism*, Routledge & Kegan Paul.

RICARDO, D. (1821) *On the Principles of Political Economy and Taxation*, vol. I of *The Works and Correspondence of David Ricardo*, ed. P. Sraffa, Cambridge University Press, 1951.

RICARDO, D. (1815—23) *Pamphlets and Papers 1815—1823*, vol. IV of *ibid*, 1951.

RICARDO, D. (1816—18) *Letters 1816—1818*, vol. VII of *ibid*, 1952.

RICARDO, D. (1819—21) *Letters 1819—1821*, vol. VIII of *ibid*, 1952.

RICHARDSON, G. B. (1959) "Equilibrium, expectations and information", *Economic Journal*, 69, June, 223—37.

ROBBINS, L. (1946) *The Nature and Significance of Economic Science*, Macmillan.

ROBBINS, L. (1958) *Robert Torrens and the Evolution of Classical Economics*, Macmillan.

ROBINSON, JOAN (1942) *An Essay on Marxian Economics*, Macmillan (cited from 2nd edn, with new introduction, 1966).

266

ROBINSON, JOAN (1960) *Collected Economic Papers*, Vol. II, Blackwell.

ROBINSON, JOAN (1964) *Economic Philosophy*, Penguin.

ROBINSON, JOAN (1965) "A reconsideration of the theory of value", in *Collected Economic Papers*, Vol. III, Blackwell.

ROBINSON, JOAN (1971) *Economic Heresies*, Macmillan.

ROBINSON, JOAN, and EATWELL, JOHN (1973) *An Introduction to Modern Economics*, McGraw-Hill.

ROLL, E. (1961) *A History of Economic Thought*, 2nd edn, Faber.

ROSDOLSKY, R. (1956) "Zur neueren Kritik des Marxschen Gesetzes der fallenden Profitrate", *Kyklos*, 9(2), 208–26.

ROSDOLSKY, R. (1957–58) "Der esoterische und der exoterische Marx: zur kritischen Würdigung der Marxschen Lohntheorie", *Arbeit und Wirtschaft*, 11, 348–51 and 388–91; 12, 20–4.

ROTHSCHILD, K. W. (1971), ed., *Power in Economics*, Penguin.

RYAN, A. (1970) *The Philosophy of the Social Sciences*, Random House.

SAMUELSON, P. A. (1939) "Interactions between the multiplier analysis and the principle of acceleration", *Review of Economics and Statistics*, 21, May, 75–8.

SAMUELSON, P. A. (1957) "Wages and interest: a modern dissection of Marxian economic models", *American Economic Review*, 47, December, 884–912.

SAMUELSON, P. A. (1959a) "A modern treatment of the Ricardian economy: I: the pricing of goods and of labor and land services", *Quarterly Journal of Economics*, 73(1), 1–35.

SAMUELSON, P. A. (1959b) "II: Capital and interest aspects of the pricing process", *Quarterly Journal of Economics*, 73(2), 217–31.

SAMUELSON, P. A. (1960) "Wages and interest: a modern dissection of Marxian economic models: reply", *American Economic Review*, 50, September, 719–21.

SAMUELSON, P. A. (1964) *Economics*, 4th edn, McGraw-Hill.

SAMUELSON, P. A. (1967) "Marxian economics as economics", *American Economic Review*, 57, Papers and Proceedings, May, 616–23.

SAMUELSON, P. A. (1970) "The 'transformation' from Marxian 'values' to competitive 'prices': a process of rejection and replacement", *Proceedings of the National Academy of Sciences*, 67(1), 423–5.

SAMUELSON, P. A. (1971) "Understanding the Marxian notion of exploitation: a summary of the so-called transformation problem between Marxian values and competitive prices", *Journal of Economic Literature*, 9(2), 399–431.

SAMUELSON, P. A. (1972) "The economics of Marx: an ecumenical reply", *Journal of Economic Literature*, 10(1), 50–1.

SAMUELSON, P. A. (1973) "Samuelson's reply on Marxian matters", *Journal of Economic Literature*, 11(1), 64–8.

SCHUMPETER, J. A. (1954) *A History of Economic Analysis*, Allen & Unwin.

SETON, F. (1957) "The 'transformation problem' ", *Review of Economic Studies*, 24(3), 149–60.

SHERMAN, H. (1967) "Marx and the business cycle", *Science and Society*, 31, 486–504.

SHERMAN, H. (1971) "Marxist models of cyclical growth", *History of Political Economy*, 3(1), 28–55.

SHIOZAWA, K. (1966) "Marx's view of asiatic society and his 'asiatic mode of production' ", *The Developing Economics*, 4, September, 299–315.

SHOUL, B. (1957) "Karl Marx and Say's law", *Quarterly Journal of Economics*, 71, November, 611–29.

SHOUL, B. (1967) "Karl Marx's solutions to some theoretical problems of classical economics", *Science and Society*, 31(4), 448–60.

SMITH, A. (1776) *The Wealth of Nations* (cited from Volume I of the sixth edition, London: Methuen).

SOLOW, R. M. (1963) *Capital Theory and the Rate of Return*, North-Holland.

SOMERVILLE, H. (1933) "Marx's theory of money", *Economic Journal*, 43, June, 334–7.

SOWELL, T. (1960) "Marx's 'increasing misery' doctrine", *American Economic Review*, 50, March, 111–20.

SOWELL, T. (1963) "Marxian value reconsidered", *Economica*, n.s., 30, August, 297–308.

SOWELL, T. (1967) "Marx's 'Capital' after one hundred years", *Canadian Journal of Economics*, 33(1), 50–74.

SRAFFA, P. (1926) "The laws of returns under competitive conditions", *Economic Journal*, 36(4), 535—50.

SRAFFA, P. (1951) "Introduction", *The Works and Correspondence of David Ricardo*, vol. I, Cambridge University Press.

SRAFFA, P. (1960) *The Production of Commodities by Means of Commodities: prelude to a critique of economic theory*, Cambridge University Press.

STEEDMAN, I. (1971) "Marx on the falling rate of profit", *Australian Economic Papers*, 10, June, 61—6.

STEINDL, J. (1952) *Maturity and Stagnation in American Capitalism*, Blackwell.

STIGLER, G. J. (1958) "Ricardo and the 93 per cent labour theory of value", *American Economic Review*, 48, June, 357—67.

STOKES, E. (1973) "The first century of British colonial rule in India: social revolution or social stagnation?", *Past and Present*, 58, 136—60.

SWEEZY, P. M. (1946) *The Theory of Capitalist Development: principles of Marxian political economy*, Dobson.

SWEEZY, P. M. (1968) "Karl Marx and the industrial revolution", in R. V. Eagly, ed., *Events, Ideology and Economic Theory*, Wayne State University Press, pp. 107—19.

THORNER, D. (1966) "Marx on India and the Asiatic mode of production", *Contributions to Indian Sociology*, 9, 33—66.

THWEATT, O. W. (1962) "A growth equation analysis of the Ricardian and Marxian theories of growth", *Pakistan Economic Journal*, 12(2), 65—74.

TSURU, S. (1952) "Business cycle and capitalism: Schumpeter vs. Marx", *Annals of the Hitotsubashi Academy*, 2, April, 134—47.

TSURU, S. (1953) "Marx's 'Tableau économique' and 'underconsumption' theory", *Indian Economic Review*, 1(3), 1—13.

TSURU, S. (1954) "Keynes versus Marx: the methodology of aggregates", in K. Kurihara, ed., *Post-Keynesian Economics*, Rutgers University Press.

VENABLE, V. (1966) *Human Nature, the Marxian view*, Meridian Books.

WALKER, A. (1971) "Karl Marx, the declining rate of profit, and British political economy", *Economica*, n.s., 38, November, 362—77.

WARREN, B. (1973) "Imperialism and capitalist industrialisation", *New Left Review*, 81, Sept.—Oct., 3—44.

WICKSTEED, P. H. (1884) "The Marxian theory of value", in *Common-sense of Political Economy* (cited from the 2nd edn, vol. II, Routledge and Kegan Paul, 1933, pp. 705—24).

WILENSKY, H. (1961) "The uneven distribution of leisure: the impact of economic growth on "free time'," *Social Problems*, 9(1), 32—56.

WINTERNITZ, J. (1948) "Values and prices: a solution of the so-called transformation problem", *Economic Journal*, 58, June, 276—80.

WITTFOGEL, K. (1957) *Oriental Despotism*, Yale University Press.

WOLFSON, M. (1966) *A Reappraisal of Marxian Economics*, Columbia University Press.

YAN, C. and AMES, E. (1965) "Economic interrelatedness", *Review of Economic Studies*, 32, October, 299—310.

YAFFE, D. S. (1973) "The Marxian theory of crisis, capital and the state", *Economy and Society*, 2(2), 186—232.

●

SUPPLEMENTARY BIBLIOGRAPHY

BAUMOL, W. J. (1974) "The transformation of values: what Marx 'really' meant (an interpretation)", *Journal of Economic Literature*, 12(1), 51—62.

DOUGHERTY, C. R. S. (1974) "On the secular macro-economic consequences of technical progress", *Economic Journal*, 84(335), 543—65.

EATWELL, J. (1974) "Controversies in the theory of surplus value: old and new", *Science and Society*, 38(3), 281—303.

EMMANUEL, A. (1974) "Myths of development vs. myths of under-development", *New Left Review*, 85, May—June, 61—82.

GANGULI, B. N. (1972) "Karl Marx on Quesnay", *Indian Economic Review*, 7(2), 129—69.

HARE, P. G. (1974) "Skilled labour in the Marxist system: a comment", *Bulletin of the Conference of Socialist Economists*, 9, Autumn, 1—3.

LEBOWITZ, M. A. (1973—4) "The current crisis of economic theory", *Science and Society*, 37(4), 385—403.

McMICHAEL, P., PETRAS, J., and RHODES, R. (1974) "Imperialism and the contradictions of development", New Left Review, 85, May–June, 83–104.

MORISHIMA, M. (1974) "The fundamental Marxian theorem: a reply to Samuelson", Journal of Economic Literature, 12(1), 71–4.

MORRIS, J. and LEWIN, H. (1973–4) "The skilled labour reduction problem", Science and Society, 37(4), 454–72.

ROBERTS, P. C. and STEPHENSON, M. A. (1973) Marx's Theory of Exchange, Alienation and Crisis, Stanford University Press.

RONCAGLIA, A. (1974) "The reduction of complex labour to simple labour", Bulletin of the Conference of Socialist Economists, 9, Autumn, 1–12.

ROWTHORN, R. (1974a) "Skilled labour in the Marxist system", Bulletin of the Conference of Socialist Economists, 8, Spring, 25–45.

ROWTHORN, R. (1974b) "Neo-Ricardianism or Marxism?", New Left Review, 86, July–Aug., 63–87.

SAMUELSON, P. A. (1974a) "Insight and detour in the theory of exploitation: a reply to Baumol", Journal of Economic Literature, 12(1), 62–70.

SAMUELSON, P. A. (1974b) "Rejoinder: Merlin unclothed, a final word", Journal of Economic Literature, 12(1), 75–7.

SAMUELSON, P. A. (1974c) "Karl Marx as a mathematical economist", in G. Horwich and P. A. Samuelson, eds., Trade, Stability and Macroeconomics: essays in honor of Lloyd Metzler, Academic Press.

SOWELL, T. (1972) Say's Law: an historical analysis, Princeton University Press.

Index

276

Variable Capital, *see under* Capital
Vulgar political economy, 44, 60, 62, 225

Wage curve, 208, 227—8, 232
Wage frontier, 208
Wage goods, 89, 138
Wage Labour, *see* Capitalism, Labour-power, Proletariat
Wages, differentials in, 130—2; *see also* Exploitation, Labour power,

Industrial reserve army,
Malthusian population principle
Walras's Law, 126—7
War, 239, 248
Western Europe, 28, 235, 245
Western society, 240
Working class, *see* Proletariat
Working day, 103
World market, *see* Cyclical fluctuations, Imperialism

NAME INDEX

278